ICFA Continuing Education
The CAPM Controversy: Policy and Strategy Implications for Investment Management

March 9–10, 1993
New York, New York

Robert D. Arnott
Robert J. Bernstein
Marshall E. Blume
William L. Fouse, CFA
Russell J. Fuller, CFA
Vilas Gadkari
Bruce I. Jacobs
William E. Jacques, CFA
Denis S. Karnosky

Mark P. Kritzman, CFA
Josef Lakonishok
Kenneth N. Levy, CFA
Jonathan A. Reiss, CFA
Stephen A. Ross
Ian G. Sims
Donald L. Tuttle, CFA, *Moderator*
David A. Tyson, CFA
Richard A. Weiss

Edited by Diana R. Harrington and Robert A. Korajczyk

AIMR Education Steering Committee 1993–94

Ian R. O'Reilly, CFA, *Co-Chairman*
  Toronto, Ontario, Canada

Eliot P. Williams, CFA, *Co-Chairman*
  Windsor, Connecticut

Abby Joseph Cohen, CFA
  New York, New York

Lea B. Hansen, CFA
  Toronto, Ontario, Canada

Charles F. O'Connell, CFA
  Chicago, Illinois

Frank K. Reilly, CFA
  Notre Dame, Indiana

Donald L. Tuttle, CFA
  Charlottesville, Virginia

To obtain an AIMR Publications Catalog or to order additional copies of this publication, turn to page 127 or contact:

AIMR Publications Sales Department
P.O. Box 7947
Charlottesville, Va. 22906
U.S.A.
Telephone: 804/980-3647
Fax: 804/977-0350

The Association for Investment Management and Research comprises the Institute of Chartered Financial Analysts and the Financial Analysts Federation.

© 1993, Association for Investment Management and Research

All rights reserved. No part of this publication may be reproduced, stored in a retrieval system, or transmitted, in any form or by any means, electronic, mechanical, photocopying, recording, or otherwise, without the prior written permission of the copyright holder.

This publication is designed to provide accurate and authoritative information in regard to the subject matter covered. It is sold with the understanding that the publisher is not engaged in rendering legal, accounting, or other professional service. If legal advice or other expert assistance is required, the services of a competent professional should be sought.

From a Declaration of Principles jointly adopted by a Committee of the American Bar Association and a Committee of Publishers.

ISBN 1-879087-28-6

Printed in the United States of America

10/15/93

Table of Contents

Foreword vi
    Katrina F. Sherrerd, CFA

Biographies of Speakers vii

The CAPM Controversy: An Overview 1
    Diana R. Harrington and Robert A. Korajczyk

The Capital Asset Pricing Model and the CAPM Literature 5
    Marshall E. Blume

Is Beta Useful? 11
    Stephen A. Ross

The CAPM and Equity Management, Asset Allocation, and Performance Measurement 16
    Robert D. Arnott

The Small-Firm Anomaly, Liquidity Premiums, and Time-Varying Returns to Size 25
    Russell J. Fuller, CFA

Low-P/E Investing: Why It Works and How to Capture the Returns 33
    William E. Jacques, CFA

Is Beta Dead or Alive? 38
    Josef Lakonishok

A Long-plus-Short Market-Neutral Strategy 42
    Bruce I. Jacobs and Kenneth N. Levy, CFA

Global Investment in a CAPM Framework 56
    Denis S. Karnosky

International Capital Market Integration and Global Asset Allocation 62
    Richard A. Weiss

Currency Anomalies: Strategy Opportunities and Hedging Implications 67
    Mark P. Kritzman, CFA

International Fixed-Income and Currency Strategies 75
    Vilas Gadkari

(continued on next page)

Prospective Real Yields and Active Global Bond Management 85
    Robert J. Bernstein and Ian G. Sims

The CAPM and Fixed-Income Markets 95
    David A. Tyson, CFA

Strategies to Exploit Term Structure and Credit-Spread Anomalies 102
    Jonathan A. Reiss, CFA

What Have We Learned? What Does It Mean? And What Does the Future Hold? 110
    William L. Fouse, CFA

Bibliography 118

Self-Evaluation Examination
    Questions 124
    Answers 126

Order Form 127

Selected AIMR Publications 128

ICFA Board of Trustees, 1993–94

Eliot P. Williams, CFA, *Chairman*
Boston, Massachusetts

Brian F. Wruble, CFA, *Vice Chairman*
Philadelphia, Pennsylvania

Charles D. Ellis, CFA, *AIMR Chairman*
Greenwich, Connecticut

John L. Maginn, CFA, *AIMR Vice Chairman*
Omaha, Nebraska

Abby Joseph Cohen, CFA
New York, New York

Thomas L. Hansberger, CFA
Ft. Lauderdale, Florida

Frederick L. Muller, CFA
Atlanta, Georgia

Ian R. O'Reilly, CFA
Toronto, Ontario, Canada

Norton H. Reamer, CFA
Boston, Massachusetts

Frank K. Reilly, CFA
Notre Dame, Indiana

Guy G. Rutherfurd, Jr., CFA
New York, New York

AIMR Council on Education and Research

Ian R. O'Reilly, CFA, *Chairman*
Toronto, Ontario, Canada

Keith P. Ambachtsheer
Toronto, Ontario, Canada

Gary P. Brinson, CFA
Chicago, Illinois

Charles D. Ellis, CFA
Greenwich, Connecticut

H. Russell Fogler
Gainesville, Florida

W. Van Harlow III, CFA
Boston, Massachusetts

Lawrence E. Harris
Los Angeles, California

Martin L. Leibowitz
New York, New York

Roger F. Murray
Wolfeboro, New Hampshire

John W. Peavy III, CFA
Dallas, Texas

André F. Perold
Boston, Massachusetts

Frank K. Reilly, CFA
Notre Dame, Indiana

Stephen A. Ross
New Haven, Connecticut

Eugene C. Sit, CFA
Minneapolis, Minnesota

Bruno Solnik
Jouy-en-Josas Cedex, France

James R. Vertin, CFA
Menlo Park, California

Staff Officers

Thomas A. Bowman, CFA
Executive Vice President

Michael S. Caccese
Senior Vice President and General Counsel

Katrina F. Sherrerd, CFA
Senior Vice President

Donald L. Tuttle, CFA
Senior Vice President

Randall S. Billingsley, CFA
Vice President

Karin B. Bonding, CFA
Vice President

Raymond J. DeAngelo
Vice President

Julia S. Hammond, CFA
Vice President

Robert M. Luck, CFA, CPA
Vice President

Roger L. Blatty
Assistant Vice President

Moira C. Bourgeois
Assistant Vice President

N. Joy Hilton
Assistant Vice President

Dorothy C. Kelly
Assistant Vice President

Jane P. Birckhead, CPA
Treasurer and Controller

Foreword

The capital asset pricing model has been widely accepted for decades as a framework for explaining the trade-off between risk and expected return in securities markets. That acceptance is not universal, however. The results of empirical tests showing deficiencies in the CAPM and criticism that it is too simplistic have caused some people to pronounce the CAPM dead.

In the CAPM, optimal portfolios are constructed by holding combinations of the risky market portfolio and a riskless asset. The proportions of each are determined by the investor's risk tolerance. The CAPM can also be used to determine the appropriate risk premium for an individual security or asset. The CAPM assumes that, in assessing the riskiness of an individual asset, investors are concerned only with the asset's systematic risk—that is, the portion of the risk associated with moves in the market, as measured by beta. Unsystematic risk—that is, company-specific risk—can be eliminated through diversification and, therefore, is not priced.

As Harrington and Korajczyk note in their overview, the popularity of beta as a means of measuring the risk of a portfolio spread rapidly through the investment community, but researchers soon began to find some troubling discrepancies when they tested the model empirically. For one thing, the relationship between expected returns and betas was flatter than expected. For another thing, some researchers found evidence of the existence of so-called anomalies, inconsistencies between the market's behavior and the efficient market hypothesis. These anomalies are hard to rationalize within the context of the CAPM. Finally, some researchers criticize the CAPM for its apparent failure to produce reliable forecasts of near-term market conditions. In short, the critics conclude, as Ross says, "The CAPM is a wonderful theory. It is also useless in a practical way."

On the other side of the issue, some researchers and practitioners defend the CAPM for what it is and what it can do. Karnosky, for example, reminds us that the CAPM, like all theories of behavior, attempts to explain relationships among variables rather than to forecast the pattern of a variable over time. It provides the foundation for developing models that generate expected future asset prices and returns. Lakonishok considers the CAPM the only widely accepted risk measure, without which life would be miserable. According to the defenders, the CAPM may not be valid as theory, but it is useful.

The validity and utility of the CAPM will continue to be discussed by the financial community, and *The CAPM Controversy* makes no vain attempt to bring closure to the discussion. The volume does, however, highlight certain key dimensions of the controversy: CAPM anomalies, using the CAPM to implement investment strategies, international issues, and applying the CAPM in the context of fixed-income investments.

AIMR wishes to thank the speakers at the CAPM seminar for sharing their research and practical experience and for assisting in the preparation of this volume. Special thanks are extended to Diana Harrington and Robert Korajczyk, who contributed the overview and self-examination for this publication, and to AIMR's Donald L. Tuttle, CFA, the very able moderator of the seminar.

The speakers contributing to the seminar were: Robert D. Arnott, First Quadrant Corporation; Robert J. Bernstein, Delaware Investment Advisers; Marshall E. Blume, the Wharton School of the University of Pennsylvania; William L. Fouse, CFA, Mellon Capital Management Corporation; Russell J. Fuller, CFA, RJF Asset Management; Vilas Gadkari, Salomon Brothers Asset Management, Ltd.; Bruce I. Jacobs, Jacobs Levy Equity Management; William E. Jacques, CFA, Martingale Asset Management; Denis S. Karnosky, Brinson Partners; Mark P. Kritzman, CFA, Windham Capital Management; Josef Lakonishok, the University of Illinois; Kenneth N. Levy, CFA, Jacobs Levy Equity Management; Jonathan A. Reiss, CFA, Sanford C. Bernstein & Company, Inc.; Stephen A. Ross, Yale University; Ian G. Sims, Delaware International Advisers, Ltd.; Donald L. Tuttle, CFA, AIMR; David A. Tyson, CFA, The Travelers Insurance Company; and Richard A. Weiss, Vantage Global Advisors.

Katrina F. Sherrerd, CFA
Senior Vice President
Publications and Research

Biographies of Speakers

Robert D. Arnott serves as president and chief investment officer of First Quadrant Corporation. He was formerly president and chief investment officer of TSA Capital Management and vice president and strategist with Salomon Brothers. The author of numerous articles, Mr. Arnott is a four-time recipient of the Financial Analyst Federation's Graham and Dodd Scroll Award for his research on asset allocation, equity market duration, and the relationship between the business cycle and security selection. Mr. Arnott is a co-editor with Frank Fabozzi of Asset Allocation and Active Asset Allocation (Chicago: Probus, 1988 and 1992). He is a member of the editorial board of The Journal of Portfolio Management and the Journal of Investing, and he serves on advisory boards for the Chicago Mercantile Exchange, Chicago Board Options Exchange, and Toronto Stock and Futures Exchanges. Mr. Arnott graduated from the University of California with degrees in economics, applied mathematics, and computer science.

Robert J. Bernstein is senior vice president, director of Institutional Fixed Income, and a member of the Fixed Income Policies Committee at Delaware Investment Advisers. Mr. Bernstein is also a director of Delaware International Advisers, Ltd. Previously, Mr. Bernstein was associated with IBM Corporation and was a senior partner of an independent oil company. He is a member of the Institute for Quantitative Research and on the advisory board of the Salomon Center (Stern School of Business) at New York University. Mr. Bernstein is a graduate of the Wharton School of the University of Pennsylvania.

Marshall E. Blume is Howard Butcher III Professor of Finance and director of the Rodney L. White Center for Financial Research at the Wharton School of the University of Pennsylvania, as well as a principal in the investment advisory firm of Prudent Management Associates. Dr. Blume has conducted extensive research into investments, the financial markets, and investor behavior. He is a director of the Pennsylvania Economy League and a trustee of Rosemont School. Dr. Blume served on the U.S. Government Accounting Office advisory committee investigating the October 1987 market crash and was a commissioner on the Knoll/Shaffer Bi-Partisan Commission on Pennsylvania Pension Fund Investments. He received his M.B.A and Ph.D. from the University of Chicago.

William L. Fouse, CFA, is chairman and chief executive officer of Mellon Capital Management Corporation. He previously served as senior vice president, chief investment officer, and deputy manager of Wells Fargo Investment Advisors and as vice president and manager of the Trust Operations Research Division at Mellon Bank. Mr. Fouse received the Financial Analyst Federation's Graham and Dodd Award for articles on risk and liquidity in the *Financial Analysts Journal*. He is currently an associate editor of the *Financial Analysts Journal* and a board member of the Institute for Quantitative Research in Finance. Mr. Fouse received his M.B.A. from the University of Kentucky.

Russell J. Fuller, CFA, serves as president of RJF Asset Management. Previously, Dr. Fuller held positions as security analyst for First Mid America, as general partner and portfolio manager for Capital Investment Group, Ltd., as vice president and director of research for Connors Investor Services, and as vice president and manager of strategy development at Concord Capital Management. He has also served as professor of finance and chairman of the Finance Department at Washington State University, and as a visiting professor of finance at the University of British Columbia and the University of Auckland, New Zealand. Dr. Fuller is the author of numerous articles and co-author with James Farrell of *Modern Investments and Security Analysis* (New York, N.Y.: McGraw-Hill, 1987). He serves on the editorial board of *The Journal of Portfolio Management*. Dr. Fuller received his B.A., M.B.A., and Ph.D. degrees from the University of Nebraska.

Vilas Gadkari is director of Salomon Brothers Asset Management, Ltd., and formerly served as chief investment officer, director in the Research Department, and head of the International Relative Values Group, at Salomon Brothers International, Ltd. (London). Mr. Gadkari has published numerous articles on the topic of international fixed-income investment strategies, with particular emphasis on risk management for multicurrency portfolios. He received his B.Tech. in chemical engineering from the Indian Institute of Technology and his M.S. in operations research from Rutgers University, and has been a doctoral student at Columbia University's Graduate School of Business.

Bruce I. Jacobs is principal and co-founder of Jacobs Levy Equity Management. Dr. Jacobs formerly served as first vice president of the Prudential Insurance Company of America and senior managing director of a quantitative equity management affiliate of the Prudential Asset Management Company. Previously, he was on the finance faculty of the Wharton School of the University of Pennsylvania. Dr. Jacobs has written a series of articles on equity management that have appeared in the Financial Analysts Journal, The Journal of Portfolio Management, and The Japanese Security Analysts Journal. He is on the advisory board of The Journal of Portfolio Management. Dr. Jacobs is a past recipient of the Financial Analysts Federation's Graham and Dodd Award. He received his B.A. from Columbia College, an M.S. in operations research and computer science from Columbia University's School of Engineering and Applied Science, an M.S.I.A. from Carnegie-Mellon University's Graduate School of Industrial Administration, and an M.A. in applied economics and a Ph.D. in finance from the Wharton School of the University of Pennsylvania.

William E. Jacques, CFA, is a partner, executive vice president, and chief investment officer of Martingale Asset Management, where he is responsible for the development of valuation and trading strategies. Mr. Jacques formerly served as a trustee and vice president of Batterymarch Financial Management and as a vice president of J.P. Morgan Investment Management, where he began his career as a research analyst. He earned a bachelor's degree in mathematics and economics from Lafayette College and an M.B.A. in finance from the Wharton School of the University of Pennsylvania.

Denis S. Karnosky, managing partner of the Asset Allocation Group of Brinson Partners, is responsible for the development and management of asset allocation policy and strategy, performance measurement, and the development of new products and systems. Dr. Karnosky also serves as chairman of the firm's Asset Allocation Committee and as a member of the firm's senior management team for developing and coordinating overall business and investment strategy. Previously, Dr. Karnosky held the positions of deputy to the undersecretary for monetary affairs and director of the Office of Monetary Policy Analysis in the U.S. Treasury Department. He also served as an economic advisor to the National Bank of Austria and the General Confederation of Italian Industry. Dr. Karnosky earned a B.A. from Blackburn College, an M.A. from the University of Missouri, and a Ph.D. from Duke University.

Mark P. Kritzman, CFA, is a founding partner of the investment advisory firm, Windham Capital Management. Previously, he was a vice president of Bankers Trust Company and has held various positions at AT&T and The Equitable Life Assurance Society. Mr. Kritzman is a past president of the Society of Quantitative Analysts, a member of the editorial boards of the Financial Analysts Journal and The Journal of Financial Engineering, and a member of the review board of the Research Foundation of the Institute of Chartered Financial Analysts. He is the author of Asset Allocation for Institutional Portfolios (Homewood, Ill.: Dow Jones-Irwin, 1987) and co-editor and co-author with S.J. Brown of *Quantitative Methods for Financial Analysis* (Charlottesville, Va.: Research Foundation of the ICFA, 1987). He also writes a column for the *Financial Analysts Journal* entitled "What Practitioners Need to Know." Mr. Kritzman holds a B.S. degree in economics from St. John's University and an M.B.A. from New York University.

Josef Lakonishok is Karnes Professor of Finance at the University of Illinois. He previously taught at the University of North Carolina, the University of British Columbia, Cornell University, and Tel Aviv University. Dr. Lakonishok is the author of numerous articles and is co-author with Robert Haugen of *The Incredible January Effect* (Homewood, Ill.: Dow Jones-Irwin, 1987). A recent paper by R. Vishny, A. Schleifer, and Dr. Lakonishok on the money management industry, published in *Brookings Papers on Economic Activity, Microeconomics*, has been the subject of many articles in the financial press. Dr. Lakonishok holds B.A. and M.B.A. degrees from Tel Aviv University and a Ph.D. degree from Cornell University.

Kenneth N. Levy, CFA, is principal and co-founder of Jacobs Levy Equity Management. He was formerly managing director of a quantitative equity management affiliate of the Prudential Asset Management Company. Mr. Levy has written a series of articles on equity management for the *Financial Analysts Journal, The Journal of Portfolio Management*, and *The Japanese Security Analysts Journal*. He is a past recipient of the Financial Analyst Federation's Graham and Dodd Award. He holds a B.A. in economics from Cornell University and an M.B.A. and M.A. in applied economics from the Wharton School of the University of Pennsylvania.

Jonathan A. Reiss, CFA, is the director of fixed-income research and a shareholder at Sanford C. Bernstein & Company, Inc. He is a member of Sanford Bernstein's Fixed-Income Investment Policy Committee and oversees the development of the models that underlie the firm's fixed-income investments. Mr. Reiss has taught as an adjunct assistant professor at Columbia University's School of Business. He received a B.S. in civil engineering from the Massachusetts Institute of Technology.

Stephen A. Ross holds the Sterling Professorship of Economics and Finance at Yale University and is a principal of Roll and Ross Asset Management Corporation, which specializes in the application of the Arbitrage Pricing Theory formulated by Mr. Ross and developed with Richard Roll of the University of California at Los Angeles. Prior to his current position, Dr. Ross was professor of economics and finance at the Wharton School of the University of Pennsylvania. He has authored many articles in finance and recently co-authored an introductory textbook in finance. Dr. Ross is the recipient of numerous prizes and awards, including the Financial Analyst Federation's Graham and Dodd Award for financial writing, the Pomerance Prize for excellence in the area of options research, and the University of Chicago's Leo Malamed Prize for the best research by a business school professor. He received a B.S. in physics from the California Institute of Technology and a Ph.D. in economics from Harvard University.

Ian G. Sims serves as senior portfolio manager and director of Delaware International Advisers, Ltd., where he is responsible for global fixed-income and currency products. Previously, he was associated with the Standard Life Assurance Company and with the Royal Bank of Canada, where he held positions in global bond research and fund management. He has also served as a senior fixed-income and currency portfolio manager with Hill Samuel Investment Advisers, Ltd. Mr. Sims is a graduate of the University of Leicester and holds a postgraduate degree in statistics from the University of Newcastle-upon-Tyne.

Donald L. Tuttle, CFA, is senior vice president of the Association for Investment Management and Research, where he is responsible for educational programs. Previously, he taught at Indiana University, where he chaired the Finance Department from 1970 to 1980. He also was professor of finance at the University of North Carolina. Dr. Tuttle is the author of many articles in leading finance journals and of five books on security analysis and portfolio management, including the second edition of *Managing Investment Portfolios: A Dynamic Process* (with J.L. Maginn, Boston, Mass.: Warren Gorham & Lamont, 1990) He is a former president, vice president, and executive director of the Financial Management Association and a former associate editor of *The Journal of Finance* and *Financial Management*. Dr. Tuttle received B.S., B.A., and M.B.A. degrees from the University of Florida and a Ph.D. from the University of North Carolina at Chapel Hill.

David A. Tyson, CFA, is vice president of The Travelers Insurance Company, where his responsibilities include portfolio management and management of Travelers' surplus accounts and convertible portfolio. He also manages the quantitative investment group. Dr. Tyson was previously responsible for quantitative equity research and product development at the Equitable Investment Management Corporation. Dr. Tyson received a B.A. in finance and political science from the Wharton School of the University of Pennsylvania and an M.B.A. in finance and Ph.D. in economics from New York University's Stern School of Business.

Richard A. Weiss is senior vice president of Vantage Global Advisors. Formerly, he was a senior vice president of MPT Associates and managing director and senior investment strategist at TSA Capital Management. Earlier in his career, Mr. Weiss was an investment strategist for PaineWebber and a vice president and head of the quantitative analysis and systems area at Mellon Bank. He received a B.S. in finance and statistics from the Wharton School of the University of Pennsylvania and an M.B.A. in finance from the University of Chicago.

The CAPM Controversy: An Overview

Diana R. Harrington
Babson Distinguished Professor of Finance
Babson College

Robert A. Korajczyk
Associate Professor of Finance
J.L. Kellogg Graduate School of Management
Northwestern University

The capital asset pricing model of Sharpe (1964), Lintner (1965), Mossin (1966), and Treynor (1961) is one of the fundamental contributions of modern financial theory. The CAPM, together with modern portfolio theory (Markowitz 1959), dramatically changed the way we think about investment management. The goal of the CAPM is to explain the trade-off between risk and expected return in securities markets. One expects investors to purchase risky securities only if those securities promise sufficiently higher compensation than safe securities. Many potential measures of risk exist, however. The CAPM uses investors' optimal portfolio choices to determine a natural measure of risk.

In the CAPM, investors' optimal portfolios are well diversified and are constructed by holding the risky market portfolio (the portfolio of all risky securities held in proportions that match their relative market values) and lending or borrowing at a riskless rate of interest. The insight offered by the CAPM provided theoretical impetus to the popularity of index funds. In assessing the riskiness of an individual asset, investors are concerned only with how the asset contributes to the risk of their optimal portfolios. Even though an asset has a large amount of uncertainty associated with its return, only the component of that uncertainty that is correlated with the market portfolio, or systematic risk, adds risk to an optimally chosen portfolio. The other component of uncertainty, unsystematic or unique risk, can be eliminated through diversification. The measure of an asset's risk that cannot be diversified is termed beta and is defined as the covariance between the asset's return and the market portfolio's return divided by the variance of the market portfolio's return.

The CAPM predicts that the expected return on any asset will be given by the pure time value of money (the return on a riskless asset) plus a risk premium. The risk premium is equal to the expected market risk premium (the expected return on the market portfolio in excess of the riskless return) scaled by the asset's particular level of risk (its beta). Thus, the only statistic that should allow analysts to predict differences in returns among assets is the differences in their betas.

During the past 30 years, the CAPM has been subjected to an enormous amount of theoretical and empirical scrutiny. On the theoretical front, the model has been generalized in various ways: The financial community has learned more about the assumptions concerning tastes and investment opportunities that are consistent with the model, and discussion has been ongoing about what it means to apply the CAPM with surrogates for the true (but unobserved) market portfolio and riskless asset. Empirical tests of whether the model makes realistic predictions (that is, whether beta, and only beta, explains average returns across assets) have uncovered apparent inconsistencies or anomalies. In this proceedings, for instance, Blume, Arnott, Fuller, and Jacques discuss anomalies in equity markets in which variables other than differences in betas, such as market capitalization, ratios of book value to market equity, price-to-earnings ratios, and dividend yields, explain cross-sectional differences in returns. Many researchers have even had difficulty obtaining a significant relationship between returns and betas.

The empirical research on the CAPM continues with increasingly refined statistical techniques and more extensive data. The unresolved issues in all of these tests form the basis of the CAPM controversy and the seminar that produced this proceedings.

Using Market Portfolio Surrogates

The CAPM controversy has several dimensions. The first is whether researchers can hope actually to test the CAPM with current market surrogates, such as the S&P 500 portfolio. Given that researchers may be using an incomplete proxy for the market portfolio, how should they interpret the observed anomalies? One possibility is that the anomalies arise merely because the market portfolio is incorrect. In his presentation, Ross shows that a surrogate market portfolio may be very close to being a mean–variance-optimal portfolio, although no relationship exists between expected returns and betas with respect to the market surrogate. This may be true even though an exact linear relationship exists between betas and expected returns if the portfolio is mean–variance optimal (see Roll 1977, Roll and Ross 1993, Amihud, Christensen, and Mendelson 1992, and Kandel and Stambaugh 1993). Thus, the CAPM might actually be true, and the observed anomalies result from not using the correct market portfolio (see Jagannathan and Wang 1993).

Alternative Models and Market Inefficiencies

A second dimension of the controversy is the possibility that the CAPM is, in fact, not the correct model for determining expected returns; either some other rational model of market equilibrium explains the determinants of expected returns, or some enduring inefficiencies are at work in the markets. Much work has been carried out on testing alternative models of asset pricing. Within the frictionless-markets setting, variants of Ross's (1976, 1977) arbitrage pricing theory (APT) and Merton's (1973) intertemporal capital asset pricing model seem to have had the most success in applications. Ross, Blume, and Arnott discuss the APT as an alternative to the CAPM. Although these alternative models seem to perform better empirically than the CAPM, anomalies remain.[1] Models that incorporate frictions, such as transactions costs, liquidity, and asymmetric information, may be needed for an accurate model of expected returns.

If another rational pricing model is the appropriate pricing paradigm, then the observed anomalies relative to the CAPM are merely compensation for factors researchers have not been able to measure. On the other hand, the anomalies might be viewed as market inefficiencies to be exploited. This viewpoint would imply that portfolios should be managed actively to take advantage of the pricing anomalies and is advocated by most active managers. Active management in light of the observed anomalies is discussed by many seminar participants, including Arnott, Jacques, Kritzman, Bernstein and Sims, Gadkari, and Reiss.

---

[1] Anomalies are discussed in Jacobs and Levy (1988); the empirical evidence on multifactor asset pricing models versus the CAPM is summarized in Connor and Korajczyk (Forthcoming 1994).

Data Mining

A third dimension of the controversy is concern on the part of researchers and practitioners about whether past statistically significant anomalies will be evident in the data in the future. As Benjamin Disraeli once remarked, "There are three kinds of lies: lies, damned lies, and statistics." Research in financial markets does not have the luxury of controlled experiments. Researchers cannot go back to 1926 and start the economy over with different initial conditions. Therefore, we need to work with a relatively static set of data. In this proceedings, Arnott considers the situation in which the financial community collectively tests 1,000 different independent trading strategies, all of which have no real added value. He points out that, if the time-honored 5 percent significance level is used, 50 strategies that are spuriously statistically significant can be expected.

Throughout the proceedings, the presentations and the follow-up questions reveal a keen interest in determining the likelihood of true, rather than spurious, significance. This healthy skepticism about statistical significance is no doubt a result of most of us seeing significant back-tests turn into subsequent insignificant portfolio performance. Arnott cites an important example—the small-capitalization anomaly, in which small firms tend to earn more than predicted by the CAPM (Banz 1981). In the decade after the discovery of the small-capitalization anomaly, investors attempting to take advantage of the anomaly did not fare well. The small-cap effect may be back for the 1990s, or it may not be. In any event, Arnott's presentation makes us aware that any apparent anomaly may have been unearthed by data snooping or data mining.

Additional Problems with Statistical Tests

A fourth dimension of the controversy is the issue of whether statistical tests of the CAPM (or any other asset pricing model) are implemented or interpreted correctly. Both Arnott and Fuller bring up the issue of beta misestimation. Variables such as market capitalization may be correlated with errors in the estimated risk measures (see Handa, Kothari, and Wasley 1989 and Kothari, Shanken, and Sloan 1992). The effects of return mismeasurement, often the result of bid–ask spreads and differential order flow across time, may also lead to spurious anomalies. Fuller argues that a large component of the small-cap anomaly comes from such return mismeasurement. In addition, the data often used by researchers can be contaminated by various selection biases, some of which can be quite subtle (see Banz and Breen 1986 and Kothari, Shanken, and Sloan 1992). Thus, apparent anomalies might be the result of poor implementation of the models.

The issue of how statistical tests are interpreted also comes into play in the CAPM controversy. One of the empirical results researchers find perplexing is that they often find the estimated premium for beta risk to be not significantly different from zero. An estimate can turn out to be insignificantly different from zero because it is close to zero, because it is not estimated very precisely, or for both reasons. Lakonishok points out that, although the estimated premium for beta risk is often not significantly different from zero, it is also not significantly different from 6 percent. Thus, researchers may be confusing statistical significance with economic significance (see McCloskey 1985). Many of the same issues have arisen in the literature devoted to portfolio performance evaluation.

CAPM Anomalies

The implications of the CAPM anomalies are, obviously, as controversial as the CAPM itself. If the anomalies are artifacts of data mining or improper statistical methodology, then the best thing to do is ignore them. If they come from sources of risk that are not properly accounted for by the CAPM, then we need to determine what those sources of risk are and whether they are properly priced. For example, the profitability of portfolio strategies based on book-to-market ratios has been ascribed to risk associated with financial distress (Fama and French 1992, 1993). If that source of risk appears to be mispriced (an issue that is discussed in Lakonishok's question and answer session) then profitable portfolio strategies can result. The same would be true if the anomalies arose from true market inefficiencies that are expected to persist.

If the anomalies are caused by market frictions not accounted for by the standard asset pricing models, such as the CAPM and APT, then some profitable strategies might exist for managers who are less affected by the frictions than other managers. For example, if the small-cap anomaly is a liquidity premium, managers who have the ability to run low-turnover portfolios may be able to benefit from the liquidity premium. Jacobs and Levy discuss implementing portfolio strategies based on anomalies and advocate long-and-short strategies that seek to take advantage of overpricing as well as underpricing.

Market Surrogates Revisited

Most empirical research on the CAPM, and consequently, most discoveries of anomalies, have used only data on equities traded in the United States. For example, the market portfolio surrogate is usually an equity portfolio similar to the S&P 500 Index. Clearly, this portfolio is far from consisting of all investable assets. Domestic fixed-income markets are excluded, as are non-U.S. markets in assets and currencies. Given the size of these markets in relation to U.S. equity markets, a logical next step is to use broader sets of assets to investigate the CAPM and its anomalies. As Karnosky points out, while investors in U.S. equities can easily move their investments to U.S. bonds, movement of funds across national boundaries has not always been easily accomplished. Therefore, in the international arena, segmentation of markets has been common. In the past decade, however, a dramatic decrease in barriers to capital movements has increased the integrity of financial markets. Karnosky discusses the pricing and portfolio implications of totally or partially segmented markets and the implications of moving from segmented to integrated markets. Weiss discusses the effects of moving from segmented to integrated markets on the appropriate mode of analysis for asset valuation.

Currency positions play an integral part in international portfolios, either as a mechanism to hedge currency risk or as a separate asset class. As in equity markets, research into currencies has documented anomalies. Kritzman describes the evidence of the predictability of returns on currency forward positions. This anomaly was first documented at the same time as the small-cap anomaly (Bilson 1981), but the forward currency anomaly seems to have been more consistent through time than the small-cap anomaly. Some, but not all, of the forward currency predictability is explicable with standard models (see Giovannini and Jorian 1989 and Korajczyk and Viallet 1992). Kritzman describes optimal dynamic currency-hedging policies that take into account the forecastability of the forward currency returns.

Gadkari also discusses currency hedging and active bond-portfolio management. He finds that high-yielding bond markets provide attractive investment opportunities. This finding is closely linked to the findings of Bernstein and Sims regarding the use of prospective real yield (nominal yield minus an inflation forecast) to implement an active global bond portfolio.

Tyson investigates risk premiums in domestic bond markets. He finds evidence of a time-varying risk premium that is related to business cycles. This finding is consistent with some evidence in equity markets linking equity risk premiums to business cycles. Reiss also finds time-varying risk premiums in fixed-income markets. The evidence indicates that variability in forward–spot spreads is caused more by variability in risk premiums than by variability in expected changes in interest rates. The same behavior is found in forward currency markets (see Kritzman's presentation). That is, variations in forward–spot currency spreads are the result more of variation in the currency risk premium than variation in the expected appreciation or depreciation of the currency.

The CAPM in the Past and Future

Fouse evaluates the past record of the CAPM, the small-capitalization anomaly, and the pricing of liquidity. He argues that periods of history in which prices of beta risk and of liquidity change correspond to those periods in which beta does not do well in terms of explaining *ex post* returns. Looking forward, he anticipates a positive premium for small-cap stocks, but not of the magnitude earned before the early 1980s.

The CAPM controversy will continue to be discussed in the financial community. The debate about the existence, causes, and consequences of pricing anomalies will remain important building blocks of financial theory and practice. This volume highlights the dimensions of the CAPM controversy and provides a foundation for future analysis. If we revisit the controversy in a future AIMR seminar, presentations will undoubtedly stress:

- the persistence, or lack thereof, of extant anomalies as a check against data mining;
- validation of anomalous results on new data sources (e.g., using data on emerging markets);
- analyses designed to eliminate (or at least adjust for) selection biases in standard data sources;
- technological advances in statistical methods designed to make our tests more informative;
- more explicit modeling of the asset pricing process that incorporates market frictions; and
- the inevitable documentation of new anomalies.

The Capital Asset Pricing Model and the CAPM Literature

Marshall E. Blume
Howard Butcher III Professor of Finance
The Wharton School, University of Pennsylvania

> A notable accomplishment of the capital asset pricing model is that it turned the focus of investing from single assets to whole portfolios. Although its assumptions are unrealistic and many empirical anomalies have come to light, theoretical work continues to generalize the CAPM to relax some assumptions, to add price-explanatory factors, and to broaden the measurement of risk.

The controversy over the CAPM has many ingredients. Although dissecting a controversy and examining its parts always involves some degree of simplification, this presentation separates the controversy into three ingredients: the asset-allocation model, expected return relationships, and volatility models. First, I will define the CAPM and describe some of the empirical contradictions to the efficient market hypothesis, and then I will comment on where beta stands in this controversy.

Origins of the CAPM

The literature on asset pricing is substantial. Jeremy Siegel and I recently reviewed this body of literature beginning with Graham and Dodd's (1934) *Security Analysis*. Implicit in Graham and Dodd's original theory was the idea that a stock has an intrinsic value. If an investor purchased an asset or stock at a price below its intrinsic value, the asset over time would move up to its intrinsic value without risk. Graham and Dodd recognized that people hold different expectations of the future, but they had little to say about diversification. The basic idea was that, if every stock bought was below its intrinsic value, the overall portfolio would be a good one and would make money as the values of the component stocks rose to their intrinsic values.

The legal profession translated this intellectual idea into the Prudent Man rule for investing personal trusts. According to this rule, a trust manager must invest in each asset on its own merit. If each asset is safe, then the total portfolio will be safe. For example, futures cannot be used under the Prudent Man rule because they are inherently risky—even though investment managers now know that when futures are combined with other assets, they can reduce portfolio risk.

Markowitz (1959) then developed mathematics for the efficient set. He postulated that any portfolio could be evaluated in terms of two parameters: the expected return on the portfolio and the volatility (or uncertainty) of getting that expected return; volatility was measured by the variance, or standard deviation, of portfolio return. He developed a parametric quadratic programming algorithm. At each level of expected return, this algorithm minimized the variance; at each level of risk, it maximized the expected return. This concept of looking at an entire portfolio changed the way investors think about investing.

Markowitz focused on the portfolio as a whole, not explicitly on the individual assets in the portfolio, which was clearly at odds with the Prudent Man rule for personal trusts. In fact, until the Employee Retirement Income Security Act passed in the mid-1970s, investing in derivatives to reduce the risk of a portfolio was, for the most part, legally imprudent.

The optimality conditions for the efficient set depend on certain variables. The expected risk premium on an individual asset is defined as the difference between the expected return of the asset as perceived by the investor and the risk-free rate of return, which is typically the T-bill rate (a taxable investor would use after-tax returns). As a condition for opti-

Note: This presentation is based on Blume and Siegel (1992).

mality, the expected risk premium on each asset must be proportional to the expected risk premium on the efficient portfolio; the constant of proportionality is the beta coefficient. (Markowitz assumed no transaction costs and no impediments to short sales.) The beta coefficient, then, is defined relative to an efficient portfolio, which can differ from one investor to another, and different efficient portfolios will imply different beta coefficients. The beta coefficient for a particular security measures the contribution of that security to the overall risk of the efficient portfolio. If an asset's beta is greater than 1 and more of that asset is added to the portfolio, the volatility of the portfolio will initially increase. If beta is less than 1 and the proportion of that asset increases, volatility is initially reduced.

With the Markowitz model, each asset will have a different beta depending on the efficient portfolio implied by an investor's judgment about future expected returns and risks of individual assets. Mathematically, the result looks like a CAPM, but it is not one; it is an optimality condition for an efficient portfolio.

People with different views will have different optimality conditions. The model is consistent, for example, with investors having different tax rates. Suppose the short-term interest rate is 6 percent. A tax-free investor would plug 6 percent into the algorithm; an investor who pays taxes at 50 percent would plug 3 percent into the algorithm. Thus, efficient sets will differ from one individual to another. Individuals can even have different views of before-tax expected returns and risk characteristics of individual assets.

The most important assumption in Markowitz's efficient-set algorithm is that a portfolio can be evaluated by two parameters: the expected return of the portfolio and the standard deviation of the portfolio. The algorithm has no assumption that the market got the prices right, so security analysts have a role: If one analyst has better judgment than others, that analyst will do better in the long run. Markowitz said nothing about market efficiency.

Markowitz's theory is not a model of equilibrium in the capital markets. It is a way of combining judgments to pick a good portfolio. Different investors could have different portfolios, and a portfolio that is efficient to one investor may be inefficient to another. The expected risk premium of every asset in a portfolio will be proportional to the expected risk premium of the portfolio as judged by the investor in that portfolio. One investor may construct a portfolio and say the expected risk premium is 6 percent; another may look at the same portfolio and say it is only 5 percent.

Sharpe (1964) described the nature of portfolio selection under the assumption that all investors attribute the same expected returns and risk characteristics to all assets (see also Mossin 1966 and Lintner 1965). Sharpe demonstrated that, under this condition of homogeneous expectations, the best portfolio of risky assets to hold is a totally diversified one in which each security is held in proportion to its value in the market. In an efficient market, the risk premium on each stock is proportional to the risk premium on the entire stock market (the expected return on the market minus the risk-free rate), where the constant of proportionality (called the beta coefficient of the stock) is related to the covariance of the individual stock and market returns. Sharpe developed these ideas into a formal model to explain the differences in risk premiums of individual stocks, which came to be known as the capital asset pricing model.

According to the CAPM, every investor holds the market portfolio of risky assets in conjunction with a long or short position in the safe asset. If investors want more risk than the market portfolio, they short (borrow) at the risk-free rate; if they want less risk, they put some of their money into the market portfolio and put the rest in very safe assets. Therefore, the market portfolio of risky assets is efficient and Markowitz's optimality conditions apply. The expected risk premium on every asset is proportional to the expected risk premium on the market, and its constant proportionality is the beta. With the CAPM, beta coefficients are unique because the efficient risky portfolio for each investor is the same portfolio, namely, the market portfolio, with respect to which betas are measured.

The CAPM is based on several simplifying assumptions. Some of the critical assumptions include the homogeneous beliefs of investors, no taxes, complete liquidity, and no transaction costs. The model assumes that people look at a portfolio in terms of only two parameters—the expected return and the variance of the return. Taxes are not included because taxes would cause expected returns to differ. All assets must be completely liquid so as to be readily marketable.

Given these assumptions, investors will hold the same market portfolio and the CAPM will follow Markowitz's mathematics. These assumptions do not describe the real world, but that does not mean that the economic model is wrong. The question is whether the model captures enough reality to be useful.

Empirical Contradictions to the CAPM

The popularity of beta as a means of measuring the risk of a portfolio spread rapidly through the investment community, but researchers soon began to find some troubling discrepancies between the predictions of an efficient market and the empirical data. The early tests of the CAPM found that the relationship between expected returns and betas measured relative to a market portfolio was flatter than expected. Low-beta assets had higher expected returns than predicted, and high-beta assets had lower returns. All of these relationships were extremely weak and varied from period to period. Sometimes for periods of 10 or 20 years, the relationship would be wrong; then, something would happen and it would be right for a while. This phenomenon was not overly disturbing; perhaps the beta was slightly mismeasured. Basically, the relationship between expected returns and betas was positive.

As Roll (1977) strongly maintained, any empirical test of the CAPM would encounter theoretical difficulties. In theory, the market portfolio in the CAPM consists of all risky assets, including real estate, bonds, and other nonequities. In practice, the empirical tests of the CAPM measured the return on the market portfolio of only a subset of risky assets—often proxying this market portfolio by a stock index such as the S&P 500. Roll showed that the use of an incomplete measure of the market portfolio resulted in mismeasuring the beta coefficients of individual assets, and he then argued that this mismeasurement made tests of the CAPM meaningless.

Despite these problems, by the end of the 1970s, the CAPM was the most sophisticated pricing mechanism available to portfolio managers. It was widely used in investment analysis.

Anomaly Literature

A large body of evidence supported the early version of the efficient market hypothesis, but a growing number of studies raised questions about its validity. Many of these studies identified so-called anomalies, inconsistencies, in the efficient market hypothesis. These anomalies are hard to rationalize with any reasonable theory of equilibrium in the context of the CAPM, although people have tried.

■ *Value Line tests.* The first anomaly was reported by Black in an article in the *Financial Analysts Journal* in 1973. He found some predictability in the recommendations of the *Value Line* rankings; that is, the stocks ranked number one tend to do better than stocks ranked number five. That finding did not disturb too many people, because many of the companies ranked number one in *Value Line* were small. Investors could not put a lot of money into them. Some, but not many, people at the margin could make some money.

■ *Closed-end investment companies.* Another anomaly is the discount on closed-end investment companies. Some people have tried to rationalize this discount as the value of the management fee option the managers have. These discounts are large, however, and it is hard to believe managers could waste that much money.

■ *Size and calendar anomalies.* Several researchers have found a difference between the returns on large- and small-capitalization stocks. Liquidity effects might account for some difference among stocks, but the problem is that, in some tests, large-capitalization stocks did better than small-capitalization stocks in some periods. Then, researchers found that most of that size effect occurred in the first three days of January.

Another calendar-related anomaly is the dividend-yield effect. This effect refers to the U-shaped relationship between expected returns and dividend yields. Zero-dividend stocks have very high expected returns; then the return drops, and it goes up again for high-dividend-yield stocks. Virtually all of this pattern is attributable to returns in January.

These anomalies are at odds with the CAPM predictions. In recent years, however, some of them may have diminished or disappeared. Whether this change is the result of investors acting on the results of these studies or is just a statistical happenstance has yet to be determined.

Volatility Tests

A further setback to the efficient market hypothesis consists of the growing body of research on the volatility of financial markets. Although markets may often seem to the casual observer to be extremely volatile, proponents of the efficient market hypothesis claim that rapid price movements are just a consequence of new information being rapidly incorporated into the valuation of securities.

The value of any asset is the present value of the future cash flows that it spins off. Shiller (1989), however, found statistical evidence that financial markets, and particularly the stock market, are too volatile to be explained by the behavior of these cash flows. This finding has spawned considerable debate, and the outcome is not yet settled.

Returns Predictability

An issue related to the excess volatility of the market was evidence that the returns to stock prices display "mean reversion"—that is, periods of high returns followed by periods of low returns and vice versa. If stock prices follow a random walk, stock returns would not tend to revert to some statistical mean. Several studies have demonstrated a tendency, however, for stock returns to revert to some average value over long periods. Early evidence of mean reversion led to tests of the predictability of future returns based on past returns.

Recent studies have found that stock returns are far more predictable over long horizons than originally thought. Supplementing the evidence of positive short-run correlations of returns, this research showed that long periods of high returns are followed by periods of low returns and vice versa. This negative long-run correlation applies to individual stocks as well as the market. Not only do past returns influence future returns, but recent research has confirmed that both the price-to-earnings ratio and the dividend yield have strong explanatory power in long-run statistical tests.

These findings focused the debate on whether return predictability represents movements of the market away from fundamental intrinsic value or whether it is related to long-term changes in expected returns, perhaps associated with changes in real economic conditions. The fact that these long-term market movements appear correlated across assets and economies does little to resolve the debate. Clearly, more sophisticated models of asset pricing than the CAPM are needed to identify the determinants of the expected returns on financial assets.

Further Developments in Asset Pricing

In an attempt to explain the empirical anomalies found in security prices, theoretical work has continued to generalize the CAPM. Extensions include restrictions on short selling, an economy that does not possess a risk-free asset, the effects of taxes, and the effects of transaction costs. Although these refinements have led to somewhat different allocations among assets, they have not changed the substantive results of the CAPM.

The empirical inadequacies of the traditional CAPM and, later, the difficulty of identifying the market portfolio led Ross (1976) to offer an alternative theory of asset pricing. Ross proposed that a limited number of unspecified economic and financial factors, which could include production, interest rates, and inflation, drive asset returns. He showed that, unless the expected returns of individual assets bore a specific relationship to these factors, arbitrage possibilities would exist. This approach is called arbitrage pricing theory (APT).

APT generates a variance model focused on volatility—how to measure volatility in a portfolio and how to price volatility factors. It can be shown to be equivalent to the CAPM under certain assumptions. The underlying theory is that the factors against which investors wish to hedge are far too complicated to be summarized by some ill-defined market portfolio. Although empirical tests of APT multifactor models have been promising, the theory does not rest on as strong a theoretical foundation as the CAPM.

Where Beta Stands

If an investor is concerned about the variance of portfolio returns, the betas of individual assets provide useful information, because betas have a role in measuring a portfolio's volatility. Betas measure the contribution of an asset to the overall volatility. Using betas to measure volatility does not imply or rely on the validity of the CAPM, so betas can be used to measure volatility without having a valid CAPM. In fact, if expected returns and betas are not related and if a portfolio is to be evaluated solely in terms of expected returns and variances, the investor would invest in low-beta stocks and have much less volatility and the same expected return as with a portfolio with a lot of volatility.

Explaining expected returns requires variables in addition to beta. Beta is a measure of volatility, but other factors relate to pricing an asset: tax status, liquidity, and the ability to hedge against changes in the consumer price index. If, for example, unanticipated inflation occurs, what will happen to the price of a long-term bond? One would like an asset to go up in value in a time of unanticipated inflation. The behavior of the assets under inflation will thus be a factor influencing expected returns on assets.

Conclusion

The controversy over the CAPM has many ingredients; some may be palatable, and some not. The CAPM is like a menu: You do not have to like everything in order to have a good meal.

Question and Answer Session

Marshall E. Blume

Question: Why do you use the term "expected return" when referring to historical realized returns?

Blume: I am not doing that. If I want to run Markowitz's efficient set or a tactical asset-allocation model, I want to put in my best judgment about the future values of the parameters. One way of getting those future values is by looking at historical data; ultimately, however, what values go into the model is a judgment call, not a simple extrapolation of historical numbers. In fact, 20 or 30 years of data provide little insight into expected returns of a volatile asset. I would much rather use a dividend discount model to assess an expected return on equities. With T-bills, at least, I can get an expected return. These models must use subjective judgments tempered by the historical past.

Question: To what extent does increased use of derivatives in equity and fixed-income portfolios impair the usefulness of the CAPM for portfolio construction and return analysis?

Blume: The inclusion of derivatives does not impair the usefulness of these models. In fact, it probably increases their usefulness, because one of the implicit assumptions in CAPM-based models is zero transaction costs, and the derivatives reduce the cost of constructing portfolios. For example, if I wanted a portfolio to have half the volatility of the S&P 500, I could meet this goal traditionally by placing 50 percent of my money in the S&P and 50 percent in safe, risk-free, assets. Alternatively, if all my funds were in the S&P 500, I could sell a sufficient number of futures contracts on the S&P 500 to reduce the volatility. Mathematically, that move is the same as investing in the risk-free asset. If I have a manager who is good at the S&P risk and adds 1 percent of alpha, then I could swap out of the S&P Index into the risk-free asset and pick up the entire alpha. Using the other technique, I get only half the alpha. Derivatives dramatically expand the horizon.

Question: Do you believe in time diversification? How does it enter into the risk-measurement and beta controversies?

Blume: In time diversification, the geometric or annual compound rates of return will converge over time into a fixed number. One must blow that up to see what actually happens to wealth. Even though the compound annual rates of return contain small errors, when these errors are compounded over long periods, they result in great differences in final wealth. The more subtle case for time diversification is that the returns have negative autocorrelation: If you lose today, you can make it up tomorrow.

Question: You commented on the empirical finding that the CAPM line is too flat. Could the reason be that we are assuming too low a rate on the risk-free asset?

Blume: That possibility is certainly one rationalization people have used. In the CAPM, the risk-free rate is clearly related to the revision horizon of the portfolio manager. If a portfolio manager revises a portfolio every quarter, then a quarterly risk-free rate must be used. Even using certificates of deposit instead of T-bills does not produce enough of a bang to explain the flatness.

Question: Is semivariance a more useful risk measure than a two-sided statistic?

Blume: If a portfolio does much better than expected, calling that excess return "risk" does not seem normal, but that information should not be excluded from a risk analysis. Investors can gain information about the downside potential of an investment from the upside, even though the upside is pleasant. Whenever a manager has a realized return much better than normal, the chances are good that the same money manager in another market could have a return much less than expected. Because semivariance throws out some very valuable data, I almost always prefer to use the variance rather than a semivariance estimate.

Question: Options and futures may reduce transaction costs, but they also create opportunities for abnormal distribution rather than a straight mean–variance distribution. Please comment.

Blume: This issue goes to the heart of the use of Markowitz's efficient-set calculations. Markowitz assumed that the only two parameters of a distribution that matter are the expected return and the variance of that return. To obtain that result theoretically, returns must be normally distributed. If they are, the mean and variance are all that count. In real investments, other things may count. For example, the Pennsylvania State Lottery is a hard investment to justify on the basis of a mean–variance model. The expected return is about –100 percent. It could be justified in a mean–variance skewness model, however, because a small probability of a very high payoff exists, in which case the mean–variance viewpoint is inadequate. In many situations, a simple mean–variance model is inadequate and other parameters of the return distribution must be reviewed. Derivatives are a cheap way to obtain different return distributions, which might be related to parameters other than the S&P Index and so forth.

Question: Did you say APT has no economic underpinning?

Blume: APT is primarily a theory of volatility; the CAPM is based on a utility framework. APT assumes that returns are distributed by a model with a limited number of common factors. It is silent as to which factors, but given those factors, the model then shows that the elimination of arbitrage between different portfolios of assets requires certain relationships between the expected returns on the assets and the response coefficients to the common factors of the individual securities. That is what I consider APT.

The interesting question about APT and the CAPM is this: What are the measures of volatility? The description of these common factors is not really part of APT. How returns are generated and what factors are important in explaining rates and return requires a separate theory. With those factors, APT places strong restrictions on how expected returns are related to the response coefficients.

Question: Taxes on investment returns are a function of cash flow, holding period, and asset class. Taxes are applied differently to the price and income return components of total return. Why apply tax rates to total returns prior to optimization rather than after? Should it be done in a multiperiod planning framework?

Blume: The original Markowitz model exists in a one-period world, so a blended tax rate could be applied to any particular asset. If more of the income came from capital gains, assumed to be realized at the end of the period, then the model would use a different tax rate from that applied to an ordinary bond, on which almost all of the return would be ordinary income.

A current major development on Wall Street with personal investing is to determine the optimal times to realize capital gains and losses. To do so requires a dynamic programming approach. Some of the large New York firms are already developing such products for their private clients. Particularly if our tax rates increase, the difference between capital gains and ordinary income could make these dynamic models much more important than they now are.

The CAPM is a rarefied model that assumes certain behavior. Using a utility-based framework to maximize expected utility while minimizing the impact of taxes is nevertheless a valid approach, even if the CAPM does not work. Beta would still matter in that framework, because the investor is worried about volatility.

Is Beta Useful?

Stephen A. Ross
Sterling Professor of Finance and Economics
Yale University School of Organization and Management

> Most empirical tests have failed to find a systematic relationship between beta and expected return. Nevertheless, beta is a useful variable because it provides information about relative risk among portfolios

The controversy over the CAPM is not new. In a recent *Economist* article, Richard Roll and I reviewed what is being discussed about the CAPM in the press and in academic literature (Ross and Roll 1993). The article was triggered by the recent Fama and French article (1992), which concludes that the beta of any particular stock does not appear to have a very strong relationship to the return of that stock. What Fama and French found was not new—many researchers have observed the same thing—but they did it in such a forceful and comprehensive fashion that the world took note. For all the discussions implying caution about beta, the empirical truth is that no systematic relationship can be discerned between expected return and beta.

The Beta/Expected Return Relationship

The theoretical relationship between beta and expected return is well known. The theory says the capital market line should rise at a rate equal to the slope of the excess return of the market portfolio over and above the risk-free rate. Most empirical studies, however, have not supported this relationship.

My first acquaintance with the conflict between theory and reality happened years ago when a company asked me to help with a cost-of-capital issue. It seemed natural to look at an empirical estimation of the relationship between beta and expected return. We believed that, if this theory had merit, on average, over time, the stocks with betas in the bottom 10 percent would have the lowest return and those in the highest beta class would have the highest return; an upward-sloping line would connect them. What we got was a flat line, which means that having a low, middle, or high beta does not matter; the expected return is the same. This result is very depressing.

Over the years, a steady stream of papers has examined this phenomenon. These papers have certain common elements. One is that most people do not find a relationship between the expected return on a stock and its beta. About a third of the papers do find such a relationship, because it can be tickled out of the data if you work at it enough. A Turkish friend of mine has a wonderful phrase: "If you torture the data long enough, it will confess to any crime." These findings are an example of torturing to get the desired result. The papers also tend to agree on the following observation: Almost anything else you add to the equation to explain the return on stocks seems to do better than beta by itself.

Beta is not very useful for determining the expected return on a stock, and it actually has nothing to say about the CAPM. For many years, we have been under the illusion that the CAPM is the same as finding that beta and expected returns are related to each other. That is true as a theoretical and philosophical tautology, but pragmatically, they are miles apart.

The CAPM says the market portfolio is a mean–variance-efficient portfolio. No other portfolio can be constructed with the same long-run average return and lower risk. Furthermore, the statement that the market portfolio is mean–variance efficient is equivalent to the CAPM. Everything we know about the CAPM is contained in that sentence. If the market is really mean–variance efficient, then it should explain cross-sectionally expected returns. In particular, expected returns should be linearly related to betas on the market portfolio. We do not find that to be the case.

Several explanations have been offered for why empirical tests of the CAPM are so poor. One is that the indexes used for the efficient market portfolio are not good proxies of the market. The S&P 500 does not represent the whole market. The market includes real estate, government bonds, corporate bonds, human capital, educational capital, and so forth, but the S&P 500 covers only large-capitalization stocks.

A second possibility is that the theory is not true and the market is not efficient. An efficient market would be very useful in its own right. If we knew that the market portfolio is efficient and that the CAPM is true, that knowledge would be a powerful guide to investment management. Investors could buy the index knowing that it is an efficient portfolio: You cannot construct a portfolio with lower risk and the same return.

So, either these tests of the CAPM are not using the right proxies (or they are so plagued by measurement error one cannot tell), or the theory is not true.

Is the Market Portfolio Efficient?

The empirical question is: Does the expected return on a stock have a linear relationship, so that the portfolio of stocks with higher betas has a higher expected return? Our results suggest the answer is no. In this framework, γ_0 is the risk-free rate—maybe T-bills—and γ_1 is the risk premium, or the expected return on the market minus the risk-free rate. Assuming an average yearly return of about 14 percent for the market and a risk-free rate of about 3, the risk premium would be 11 percent. Instead, we find $\gamma_1 = 0$, and we do not find any relationship between the expected return and the beta.

The second question is: How far inside the efficient frontier must a portfolio be to get a relationship of zero? Our results suggest not very far. We discovered another curve, which is about 22 basis points inside the efficient frontier. At every combination of return and standard deviation inside that curve, one can find a portfolio with a zero relationship between expected return and its beta. Being on the efficient frontier requires a straightforward, positive relationship between expected return and beta. If the index is inefficient, that relationship may not exist.

What is somewhat remarkable is that one can be very close to the efficient frontier and still find no relationship. This result is depressing, because measuring to the precision of 20–30 basis points is difficult. In fact, 10,000 years would be needed to determine whether the theory is correct or whether the S&P 500 Index is within 20 basis points of the efficient frontier (assuming a standard deviation of about 20 percent a year and no change in the market). If the portfolio is not within 20 basis points of the efficient frontier, the exact results we found are entirely possible.

The current state of financial researchers' knowledge comes largely from testing whether betas are related to expected returns. Theory is almost silent on whether the portfolio being used as a benchmark is efficient. This current testing and all the noise have nothing to do with whether one should be buying the market portfolio or managing to a market portfolio benchmark, or with whether the market portfolio will be a long-run efficient portfolio. The simple truth is we do not know. We have done some direct tests, but they are weak and cannot tell the difference between being efficient and being between 3 percent and 4 percent away from being efficient. Can we reject the hypothesis that the market is efficient? No, but we cannot reject the hypothesis that it is not efficient either. Statistics may not be a good guide in this case.

The first thing Roll and I discovered in our recent analysis is that distinguishing between being efficient and inefficient is difficult. In particular, a portfolio with no ability to explain expected returns may be very close to an efficient portfolio. This troublesome fact circumscribes the kinds of interpretations we are used to. It says that we are not testing the CAPM but testing whether we can find a portfolio that explains expected return. This search relates to the cost-of-capital problem. From a corporation's perspective, as opposed to that of an investment manager, the expected return on the firm's stock is the cost of the capital stock the corporation issues. Corporations like to use portfolios of like stocks as a guide to help them assess the actual cost of issuing stock. The CAPM, if it worked, would provide a nice way to do that. If I wanted to determine the expected return on a new project, for example, all I would need to do is determine the beta of that project. But this method does not work empirically.

Is the CAPM Useful?

The CAPM is an elegant way to encapsulate our understanding about return and risk issues and how they relate to each other. The problem is that the theory cannot be tested in any practical sense. It cannot be proved or disproved. The theory discusses real-world factors, but there is no way to determine whether it is a truth teller or falsehood teller. It is irrelevant to what is happening in the world. Nonetheless, the CAPM is an elegant theory. It says that if everyone thought about means and variances and added them up in all the right ways, if no one had any constraints, and if everyone were rational, then the market portfolio would be a mean–variance-efficient portfolio.

People have argued with us about these results. One question they ask is: If the CAPM is wrong, what should we do? One possibility is to use the arbitrage pricing theory (APT). What if the analyst does not want to go through all that trouble? An analyst is better off saying, "If you want my return forecast on your stock, you will get the same as the market." If the theory cannot tell the difference between two stocks on the basis of their betas, then the analyst cannot either. If the analyst wants a rough bottom line of what the market thinks will occur to a particular stock, that line is what the analyst thinks will happen to the market. That is the best an analyst can do.

The CAPM does have one practical use. We are pretty good at measuring beta, and all other things being equal, on average, a stock with a higher beta will increase more when the market goes up and it will fall more when the market goes down than stocks with lower betas. The long-run average return on the stock, however, will not be higher or lower simply because it has a higher or lower beta. If the market goes up relevant to its long-run expectation, then stocks with higher betas will fare better on average and stocks with lower betas will suffer on average.

Unfortunately, the relationship of beta with stock ups and downs does not always hold. During the 1987 crash, for example, when the market dropped 20 percent, MCI Communications Corporation dropped about 12 percent. MCI went into the market with a beta of 1.4, according to our best measurements, but it fell like it had a beta of 0.6. Which was right, 0.6 or 1.4? I did not know, so I averaged the two, which is where I would have been if I had simply started out thinking the beta was 1.0. Because empirical research shows that the slope of the line is zero, and if the CAPM is the only theory you use, then you are in the position of believing that all stocks have the same expected return.

Methodological Issues

Many people have complained about the methodologies used to test the CAPM. They believe these studies do not use the best statistics in econometrics: If something is done in the simplest way, no result is found, and the researchers try something fancy and find a result, they are falling into my Turkish friend's regime. They must wonder if the fancy methodology, rather than the actual facts, is responsible for the finding.

A simple sorting modification can improve the results achieved from the standard methodology. Some stocks have a lot of imprecision in the relationship between beta and expected returns; others are very precise. Mixing them together willy-nilly does not do the theory justice. The analyst should measure how precise each relationship is, stock by stock, and correct for imprecision. That process is sometimes called a heteroscedasticity correction, or generalized least squares regression (GLS).

Using the GLS technique, I got the same results from our research, but with a different effect. Using the old statistical methods, for any index anywhere inside the efficient frontier, I could find a portfolio that has no relationship with expected return. Using the fancy technique, the line starts at the lowest risk (with a minimum-variance portfolio) and goes straight across horizontally: Indexes above the line demonstrate a positive relationship between expected returns and beta, and vice versa. This result means that finding a positive or negative relationship has nothing to do with whether the theory is true or not. This pattern indicates only whether the benchmark being used has more return than the lowest risk portfolio that can be constructed. Anything used as a benchmark with a higher return than the lowest risk portfolio automatically produces a positive in these tests. Because systematic errors are associated with every stock, however, simply observing that something will produce a positive slope tells the analyst nothing about whether it will be a good predictor of the expected returns of the stock.

Conclusion

The CAPM is a wonderful theory. It is also useless in a practical way. It is not useful for telling people about the cost of capital or expected return, but it does have other uses. For example, beta alone is a useful variable. It tells us something about the relative risk of two portfolios, but not about their long-run returns. I am interested in both the expected return on a stock and in the stock's beta. What I have lost is the CAPM's notion that the two are related.

When managing a large portfolio, I am interested in its beta because that is a good measure of how risky the portfolio is. Beta provides some indication of the portfolio's tracking error relative to some benchmark. I cannot state with confidence, however, that because the portfolio has a higher beta, it will produce a higher expected return in the long run.

Question and Answer Session
Stephen A. Ross

Question: You stated that the risk premium could be zero if the market is 22 basis points from the frontier. Is this always the case?

Ross: Yes. The exact number will vary, but not the order of magnitude over any period using any of the measurements we have. Within a 25- or 30-basis-point distance from the efficient frontier is a portfolio that has a zero relationship between expected returns and beta.

Question: Can the market portfolio ever be efficient *ex post*?

Ross: The market portfolio is not efficient *ex post*. That still leaves the question of whether it is efficient *ex ante*. In any finite time period, you will always discover some stock that beat the S&P 500. Throughout 20 years of our history, owning Xerox Corporation was far more efficient than owning the S&P 500. Microsoft Corporation is another example of a stock that was better to own *ex post* than owning a market portfolio.

Ex ante, however, we are still in a quandary. The measurement error is so great that we cannot tell whether the market is efficient or not. Not being able to tell does not put us in the comfortable position of saying we will assume the market is efficient, because other portfolios may exist that are computable and discoverable that will do better than a market portfolio.

Question: Does the CAPM have validity when used in a discounted cash flow valuation because the purpose is to find a required rate of return rather than an expected rate of return?

Ross: There is no real distinction between a required rate of return and an expected rate of return in a well-functioning, liquid, efficient market. Maybe such a distinction exists in the actual market, but we cannot measure the difference because the stock markets are pretty efficient.

Figuring out what the discount rate should be in a discounted cash flow model is the challenge. I would recommend that you try the one suggested by the theory and also try the one suggested by the falsity of the theory. The only comfortable place to be is to remember that, no matter what sensible discount rate you use, you want to buy or sell the stock. If that decision overlaps the choice of a sensible rate—for a low-enough rate, it is a buy, and for a high-enough rate, it is a sell—then I am unsure about whether you would want to buy or sell that stock.

Question: If you create index portfolios that are enhanced, whether for low volatility or for excess return, are you approaching a more efficient portfolio or are you doing something beyond an efficient portfolio?

Ross: You are not doing anything beyond an efficient portfolio, because by definition, you cannot. If you have succeeded in enhancing the index, then you have succeeded in moving from the index toward the efficient frontier. Because whether the index is on the efficient frontier is difficult to tell, you should look hard at how you are improving it. I have heard of many different ways to enhance a particular benchmark—some legitimate and some not.

Question: What is your view on mean-reverting characteristics relative to the CAPM and efficient markets?

Ross: I have the same negative view as to whether the CAPM is useful. I have looked at many studies that purport to determine what will happen to the market return over long periods. The arguments are always the same. We cannot tell what will happen to the market next month, but we are good at telling what will happen during the next four or five years. The marketplace has long-run trends. If the P/E is too high now, we know the market will decline; if the P/E is too low, it will rise. All the various theories about what the market will do make some sense.

When the first CAPM studies came out, researchers went through a complicated statistical analysis to verify that, although they could not predict what the return would be next month, they could predict what would happen three to four years from now. So, we took the 800 months of market data that all these studies used and created artificial history (bootstrapping). We looked back over the 800 months from about 1920 to the present and picked a month at random from 1922, 1936, 1984, and so forth.

There was no predictability at all. We could not tell the next three years from the past three years. Then, we ran the same numbers other people had and got the same results they did. We proved we could, given the past four years in our artificial history, predict four years from now. Yet, I know I could not predict; I made the numbers up.

What does that say about the studies that claim to be predicting? It says they are fundamentally in error. They severely underestimated the potential significant errors, so they overestimated the significance of their results.

Nothing is scientifically documented yet on the predictability in long-run stock returns. There is no strong documentation, even from volatility tests, that a long-run predictability inhabits these returns. Indeed, because they do not seem to be working, people are now doing few such tests.

Question: If you must come up with a viable cost of capital for a corporation, what approach do you use?

Ross: I use APT.

Question: Where do your comments leave us with respect to APT?

Ross: APT does not say some mean–variance-efficient portfolio exists. The market portfolio has no special role in an arbitrage pricing context. When I do an APT analysis, I am looking for "pure play." I am looking for several stocks with returns I can measure, which I then form into a portfolio similar to the company for which I am trying to figure out the cost of capital.

Suppose I have a company with eight divisions. One division might be purely a food company, one might be purely an electronics company, and so forth. I form a portfolio of food companies, electronic companies, and so forth that mimics my company. By looking at the long-run return of that portfolio, I obtain an estimate of the long-run return or expected return for my particular stock. That is the germ of a superior way to make capital budgeting decisions within firms as opposed to determining expected rates of return and discount rates. We are so comfortable discounting cash flows, however, we like to think in those terms.

The CAPM and Equity Management, Asset Allocation, and Performance Measurement

Robert D. Arnott
President and Chief Investment Officer
First Quadrant Corporation

> Empirical research on risk-premium relationships casts doubt on the efficiency of markets in the CAPM sense. A number of factors appear to affect differential market returns, although the influence of these factors may or may not persist. Nevertheless, returns do appear to be related to beta, but less so than the CAPM suggests.

This presentation will explore the differences between what theory says about the way the capital markets should behave and what practitioners observe in practice. I will examine theory—past, present, and future—and the empirical evidence for the CAPM. I will also consider the implications of data mining, which is of increasing concern in a world where data are easy to collect and to process.

Theory

The basic premise of the CAPM is that expected returns and, eventually, actual returns are linearly related only to nondiversifiable risk. The empirical evidence on this premise is mixed. The reward to beta is persistently less than that predicted by the CAPM; rewards to other factors such as volatility, size, and book-to-price ratios are usually greater than the CAPM would support. Purists argue that we cannot reject the CAPM merely because its estimated rewards for beta are not equal to actual rewards for beta; they maintain that we cannot reject the idea of a relationship between beta and return. Researchers are plagued with the problem of dealing with noisy markets; centuries of data are needed to prove or disprove the theory conclusively.

Arbitrage pricing theory (APT), which was developed after the CAPM, suggests that asset returns are a function of various common risk factors. The APT model is silent on pricing and expected returns. In effect, it is a risk model, and the empirical findings support this view. Several factors seem to be priced, and many of these priced factors are not compatible with market efficiency. Hawawini and Keim (1992) examine the global evidence of APT.

Investors can be broken into two principal camps: those who believe markets are efficient and those who believe markets are inefficient. Proponents of efficient markets believe in equilibrium models (theoretical structures explaining why markets behave the way they do, in the context of efficient pricing) and favor passive management; they focus on risk control first, with return a secondary objective. The inefficient markets camp believes that the theoretical foundation for market inefficiency is found in behavioral finance; they seek anomalies and alphas first, with risk control secondary.

Market Inefficiency Research

To me, the evidence is persuasive that markets are not perfectly efficient anywhere in the world. This section presents, as an example of such evidence, the results of some research on this inefficiency that Henriksson and I (1989) have been conducting. The research tests the relationship between objective measures of the prospective return difference between any two asset classes and the subsequent realized return differences over a one-month horizon. Regression coefficients demonstrate the link between relative yields and subsequent relative performance.

Table 1 presents evidence of the link between stock earnings yield, bond yield, and cash yield, and the corresponding subsequent return differences. The difference between stock earnings yield and bond yield is sometimes called the equity risk premium. In the United States, if the earnings yield rises 100 basis points relative to bond yields, the stock market out-

Table 1. Relative-Return Coefficients: Stock Earnings Yield Minus Bond Yield, Stock Earnings Yield Minus Cash Yield, and Bond Yield Minus Cash Yield

Country	Stock Earnings Yield – Bond Yield	Stock Earnings Yield – Cash Yield	Bond Yield – Cash Yield
Australia	–0.23	–0.32	0.03
Austria	1.09	0.42	0.36**
Belgium	0.24	0.18*	0.12**
Canada	0.33	0.22	0.28*
Denmark	0.05	0.01	0.26*
France	0.16	0.95**	0.34**
Germany	0.46	0.35*	0.22**
Italy	0.04	0.32	0.24**
Japan	1.39*	1.64*	–0.09
Netherlands	1.64**	0.61**	0.27
Spain	2.90**	0.72	0.14
Sweden	0.79	0.24	0.01
Switzerland	0.86*	0.28	0.16**
United Kingdom	1.36**	0.14	0.06
United States	0.36	0.37**	0.30*
Average	0.76**	0.41**	0.17**

Source: Arnott and Henriksson (1989).

* Significant at the 5 percent level.
** Significant at the 1 percent level.

Table 2. Relative-Return Coefficients: 24-Month Trend in Stock Earnings Yield Minus Bond Yield

Country	Stock – Bond
Australia	–0.48
Austria	0.11
Belgium	0.36
Canada	0.44
Denmark	0.08
France	1.18*
Germany	0.66
Italy	0.14
Japan	4.16*
Netherlands	1.32**
Spain	2.58**
Sweden	1.00
Switzerland	0.96*
United Kingdom	1.22*
United States	0.49
Average	0.95**

Source: Arnott and Henriksson (1989).

* Significant at the 5 percent level.
** Significant at the 1 percent level.

performs bonds by an average of 36 basis points per month until the markets return to equilibrium.

This research was first carried out in the United States. So, one might surmise that the relationship would not export well if the markets are efficient. But we found the world average relationship to be more than twice as powerful as the U.S. relationship.

Similar results are found for other risk-premium relationships. Stock earnings yield minus cash yield is a powerful predictor of stock-versus-cash relative returns both in the United States and worldwide. All countries except Australia have positive relationships.

The bond-yield-versus-cash-yield relationship is simply a measure of the slope of the yield curve. When the yield curve is steep, bonds subsequently offer a larger-than-normal excess return relative to Treasury bills (or to each country's equivalent of T-bills). In the United States, for example, a 100-basis-point change in the slope of the yield curve translates into 30 basis points of excess returns of bonds over cash until equilibrium is restored. This relationship also exports well; it is a powerful relationship worldwide.

Table 2 presents 24-month trends in stock earnings yields minus bond yields. Some argue that this relationship shows not so much how far markets have strayed from a long-term equilibrium as how far they have strayed from a recent equilibrium. The research reported in this analysis recognizes that the equilibrium itself can move. Table 2 reveals a more powerful relationship than the simple risk-premium relationship. In the United States, a 100-basis-point rise in the risk premium of stocks over bonds translates into a 49-basis-point monthly excess return of stocks over bonds. The average worldwide relationship is roughly twice as powerful. For those who say the Japanese market behaves in an irrational fashion, this evidence suggests the contrary.

We have also found evidence of macroeconomic relationships. Table 3 relates the bond–cash return differential to changes in producer price index (PPI) inflation in every country that has a PPI measure. This evidence suggests that, even if the markets are efficient in factoring inflation in the consumer price

Table 3. Relative-Return Coefficients: Bond Yield Minus Cash Yield per 1 Percent Increase in PPI

Country	Bond – Cash
Australia	–0.06
Belgium	–0.12*
Canada	–0.91
Denmark	–0.47
France	–0.20**
Germany	–0.92**
Italy	–0.73**
Japan	–0.01
Netherlands	–0.25
Sweden	–0.46
Switzerland	–0.35**
United Kingdom	–0.78
United States	–0.90**
Average	–0.47**

Source: Arnott and Henriksson (1989).

* Significant at the 5 percent level.
** Significant at the 1 percent level.

index (CPI) into their pricing, they are not efficient in factoring in PPI inflation (which ultimately leads to CPI inflation). A rise in PPI inflation is generally followed by a rise in bond yields and, hence, underperformance of bonds. This relationship is not only concurrent but also leading.

As shown in **Table 4**, in virtually every market, stocks and bonds show degraded excess returns in

Table 4. Relative-Return Coefficients: 1 Percent Increase Change in Unit Labor Costs

Country	Stock – Cash	Bond – Cash
Belgium	–0.51	–0.11
Canada	–0.06	0.02
Denmark	–0.30	–0.67
France	–2.03*	–0.84
Germany	–0.30	0.01
Italy	–0.40	–0.17*
Netherlands	–1.16*	–0.70
Sweden	–0.04	–0.13
United Kingdom	–0.02	–0.54
United States	–0.44	–0.50
Average	–0.53**	–0.36**

Source: Arnott and Henriksson (1989).

* Significant at the 5 percent level.
** Significant at the 1 percent level.

the face of rising unit labor costs. With more money flowing to workers, less money is flowing to investors. The results for unemployment, as shown in **Table 5**, also support this view. If unemployment increases, stocks and bonds do well. This relationship was first identified in the United States, but the global evidence indicates that the inefficiencies identified in U.S. markets exist also in overseas markets.

Style Management Research

Research into style management also suggests cer-

Table 5. Relative-Return Coefficients: 1 Percent Increase in Unemployment

Country	Stock – Cash	Bond – Cash
Australia	0.40	0.80
Belgium	–0.16	0.08**
Canada	0.23**	–0.13
Denmark	–0.24	0.36
France	–0.07	0.49*
Germany	0.96*	0.12*
Japan	0.39**	0.02
Netherlands	0.21	0.09
Switzerland	2.09	0.16
United Kingdom	0.23	0.22
United States	0.69**	0.35
Average	0.40	0.23**

Source: Arnott and Henriksson (1989).

* Significant at the 5 percent level.
** Significant at the 1 percent level.

tain inefficiencies in the capital markets. **Table 6** presents the mean monthly factor returns and their standard deviations for the 13 BARRA factors, earnings revision, and residual reversal. The returns for these factors are sensitive to capital market variables, economic variables, and calendar effects.

Table 6. Common Factor Returns, Monthly, January 1973–December 1990

Factors	Mean	Standard Deviation	t-statistic
BARRA factors			
Variability in markets	–0.10%	1.43%	–1.0
Success	0.24	1.16	3.0
Size	–0.13	0.82	–2.3
Trading activity	–0.08	0.76	–1.5
Growth exposure	0.06	1.14	0.8
Earnings/price	0.29	0.76	5.6
Book/price	0.25	0.73	5.0
Earnings variation	–0.01	0.67	–0.2
Financial leverage	–0.04	0.48	–1.2
Foreign income	–0.03	0.36	–1.2
Labor intensity	0.03	0.59	0.7
Dividend yield	0.06	0.82	1.1
LOCAP	–0.19	1.91	–1.5
Other factors			
Earnings revision	0.50	0.60	9.9
Residual reversal	–0.52	0.90	–6.9

Source: Arnott, Dorian, and Macedo (1992).

Table 7 provides fairly compelling evidence of market inefficiencies. These factors are all cases in which publicly available information is predictive of subsequent performance of one class of assets relative to another. For example, the equity risk premium (defined as the earnings yield on the S&P 500 Index minus T-bill yields) is correlated with the subsequent performance of several BARRA factors of return. The "variability in markets" factor (which is not unlike beta), for example, is strongly correlated with the equity risk premium. When the equity risk premium is high and investors are frightened, investors are rewarded for investing in risky stocks, high-beta stocks, and small stocks. Investors are rewarded for investing in growth stocks at such times because of the long duration on those assets. They are also rewarded for investing in leveraged stocks.

Stock market variability is also linked to factor returns. Stock market turbulence rewards those stocks with the riskier attributes. The high-beta stocks do well after the market has been turbulent. Leveraged stocks, stocks with high earnings variability, growth stocks, and the highly liquid stocks (those that show high trading activity) are the types of stocks that do well when markets have recently been

Table 7. Sensitivity of Factor Returns to Market Variables

	Equity Risk Premium		Stock Market Variability		Cash-Yield Change	
Factor	Correlation	t-statistic	Correlation	t-statistic	Correlation	t-statistic
Variability in markets	0.29	4.5	0.19	2.8	–0.14	–2.0
Success	–0.15	–2.2	–0.20	–2.9		
Size	–0.14	–2.0	–0.14	–2.0	0.15	2.2
Trading activity	0.16	2.3	0.14	2.0		
Growth exposure	0.18	2.6	0.17	2.5	–0.16	–2.3
Earnings variation			0.16	2.3	–0.13	–1.9
Financial leverage	0.13	1.9	0.20	2.9	–0.15	–2.2
Foreign exposure					–0.18	–2.6
Dividend yield					–0.16	–2.3

Source: Arnott, Dorian, and Macedo (1992).

turbulent. This link would be consistent with behavioral finance: When markets are turbulent, investors are frightened; when investors are frightened, they are rewarded for bearing risk. Conversely, when markets are stable, investors are complacent and are not rewarded for bearing risk.

Table 7 also provides evidence of a link between the factors and cash-yield change. When T-bill yields rise, the rewards for the highest yielding stocks are usually poor because those stocks are under pressure from income-oriented investors to deliver higher yields also. This is not a concurrent relationship; it relates last month's change in T-bill yields to next month's performance for the various styles of stocks. The evidence also suggests that investors are not rewarded for long duration (as shown in the correlation for growth exposure) when T-bill yields are rising. Neither do such times reward high-dividend-yield and high-beta (or high "variability in markets") stocks.

The BARRA factors are also linked to economic variables. For example, **Table 8** shows the relationships to a percentage change in the PPI. There is a powerful negative correlation with stocks dependent on foreign income. The reason is that accelerating PPI inflation tends to push up bond yields. A rise in bond yields attracts foreign investment capital, which boosts the value of the dollar and damages the prospects of companies that are dependent on foreign income. If leading indicators have gone up in the past year, heavily leveraged companies and labor-intensive companies are likely to do better than other companies. During the preceding recession, most labor-intensive companies will have already cut costs; they enter the new economic cycle lean and well positioned for an economic recovery. When leading indicators have been up year after year, growth stocks have already made their move; accordingly, the high-E/P (earnings-to-price ratio) stocks also usually perform well. This analysis thus provides additional compelling evidence of inefficiencies, or predictive relationships.

Finally, the BARRA factors also show sensitivity to calendar effects. **Table 9** shows all of the statistically significant calendar effects identified in the BARRA time series. Note the lack of a significant relationship between firm size and the January effect. This relationship was identified and studied extensively, but the link seems to have disappeared. Was this anomaly "studied to death"?

Some other relationships, such as between success and the January effect, are significant. Companies that have done badly are often bludgeoned in year-end window dressing and year-end tax-motivated selling, which results in a snap-back effect in January. Stocks that have done exceptionally well tend to soften in January. The year-end book-to-price (B/P) effect is also strong.

Table 8. Sensitivity of Factor Returns to Economic Variables

	1 Percent Change in PPI		1 Percent Change in Leading Indicators	
Factor	Correlation	t-statistic	Correlation	t-statistic
E/P			0.22	3.2
Financial leverage			0.16	2.3
Labor intensity			0.16	2.3
Foreign income	–0.31	–4.6		
Yield	–0.23	–3.4		
Size	0.15	2.2		

Source: Arnott, Dorian, and Macedo (1992).

Table 9. Sensitivity of Factor Returns to Calendar Effects

	Significant January Effect		Other Significant Calendar Effects	
Factor	Correlation	t-statistic	Correlation	t-statistic
Success	−0.34	−3.0	NS	NS
Size	NS	NS	October 0.22	3.1
Trading activity	−0.20	−2.1	NS	NS
Book/price	0.38	3.0	October −0.23	−3.4
Earnings variation	0.27	2.5	NS	NS
Dividend yield	0.24	2.4	NS	NS

Source: Arnott, Dorian, and Macedo (1992).

NS = not significant.

The "other significant calendar effects" column indicates two October relationships that mirror the January relationships. These also may be largely a function of window dressing. The large stocks usually perform particularly well in October when investors lighten up on unknown stocks and seek to put name-brand stocks into their portfolios for year-end portfolio holdings. This pattern would be particularly true in the mutual fund business and true to a lesser extent in pension asset management.

Is the Market Efficient?

Based on the empirical evidence, the market does not appear to be efficient. Enough statistically significant relationships link risk premiums with subsequent rewards to suggest that certain style attributes are predictable. Similarly, links are found between the economy and capital market returns, calendar effects, and the well-known value-oriented effects relating to E/Ps and B/Ps.

If the market is not efficient, when theory suggests that rational investors should price the markets efficiently, the answer must be that investors are not entirely rational. This thesis forms the basis for behavioral finance. Investors tend to shun perceived risk, but perceived risk need not be identical to the diversifiable risk identified in the CAPM. The roots to risk perception are found in emotion. We are social creatures, seeking the solace of agreement. Failing conventionally is often less painful than risking unconventional failure.

If the market is inefficient, why is there only one Warren Buffett? There are three reasons. First, market inefficiencies change. The inefficiencies described in the preceding tables may not exist in the coming decades if too many investors seek to exploit them. Second, equilibrium relationships change. This phenomenon can confound any investment process based on "regression to the mean" or predicated on markets returning to long-term historical equilibrium relationships. Third, risk tolerance is usually lower than expected. Investors look at the historical evidence for a particular investment discipline, see a solid history of success with interspersed periods of disappointment, and say, "I could bear that disappointment." Living through that experience is very different, however, from looking at it on paper.

Inefficiencies can also disappear. Any active management process is inherently predicated on the idea that markets are in some fashion inefficient. Any market inefficiency is inherently an arbitrage opportunity. If widely exploited, it will eventually be arbitraged away. Good investment ideas are not eternal.

Nevertheless, contrarian strategies often persist, because they are inherently uncomfortable for the average investor. Contrary to most inefficiencies, price-to-earnings ratio has shown a good deal of longevity; it was described first in the 1920s as a possible means for choosing stocks.

Equilibrium models are not static. **Figure 1** provides evidence of changing equilibria drawn from our research on asset allocation. The graph represents the difference between stock earnings yields and T-bill yields. The squares mark important market peaks, and the circles show market bottoms. Following the 1973–74 market debacle, investors were so shaken that, for years afterward, they priced equities to reflect a demand for heightened reward. The market top in 1976 occurred at an equity risk premium higher than the 1970 market bottom. This factor led the only extant tactical asset allocation model in the late 1970s (the Wells Fargo model) to be bullish throughout the late 1970s, in spite of the bear market from late 1976 to early 1978. The tactical model missed the bear market because the equilibrium relationships themselves are not static.

One reason for persistent inefficiencies is the difference between corporate culture and investment culture. The successful corporate culture is one that aggressively rewards success and ruthlessly punishes failure. The successful investor frequently follows a pattern of paring back recent winners and favoring recent disappointing markets. Those who

Figure 1. Changing Equilibria

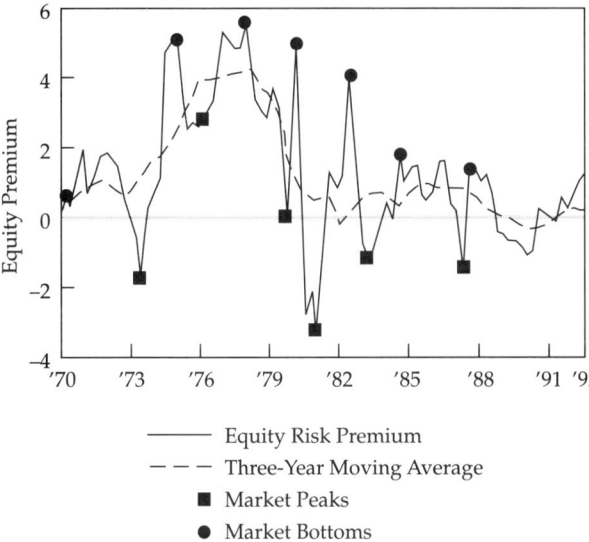

Source: First Quadrant Corp.

bail out after an extended period of disappointment usually live to regret that decision.

Poor investment decisions can often be traced to a hierarchy of pressures. The portfolio manager is pressured by the chief investment officer or chief executive officer of the investment management firm, who is pressured by the pension officer, who is pressured by the chief financial officer and treasurer, who are pressured by the pension committee of the board of directors. Each step increases the likelihood of cutting back on recent disappointing investments and favoring recent successes.

Bernstein put it another way when he suggested that the committed contrarian rejoices when markets fall and tends to rue rising markets. This counterintuitive behavior stems from the fact that a newly fallen market offers new contributions and income reinvestments at improved prospective returns. In effect, we should not be pleased with stocks and bonds trading at all-time highs; we should dread the reduced prospective returns!

Data Mining

Data mining is a serious concern for researchers and investors. Black (forthcoming) observed that there are two paths to expected returns: theory and data. He suggested that both are flawed. Theory overlooks the possibility of lingering true inefficiencies. Theory also does not precisely define what factors are priced. For example, what is the market portfolio? We know that the S&P 500 Index is not the market, but all attempts to identify what "market portfolio" should define have fallen flat.

The flip side is that empiricism leads to a false sense of security. Looking at historical relationships showing t-statistics of 3 or 4, we think we have found the Holy Grail, but countless others in our industry are typically finding it at the same time. The inefficiency can disappear quickly after being identified. Finding out that the market has been inefficient in the past does not necessarily indicate what the inefficiency will be in the future. Ross notes also that sometimes empiricism seems to contradict theory, although a little digging or a little thought could dispense with the conflicts.[1]

Many researchers have identified what they erroneously claim to be market inefficiencies. Schiller's (1981, 1990) work, for example, suggests that markets are not efficient because they are too volatile. This suggestion overlooks a fundamental fact, however, the Achilles heel of his analysis: A modest 0.5 percent change in the discount rate for real returns that investors price into the stock market will move the market 15 percent. That 15 percent is the normal annual volatility. It is easy to surmise that market risk tolerance moves with a standard deviation of 0.5 percent, measured in terms of the real rate investors price into the market. That alone easily accounts for all of the stock market volatility observed.

Others have cited the example of closed-end funds that always trade at a discount. Why should this be an inefficient market? The answer is that the net present value of the expense ratio, the fee, is taken out of the fund. If 1 percent a year is taken out to run the fund, the net present value of that amount translates into a 10 percent or 20 percent discount, which is what is observed in the real world.

The problems of data mining are several and subtle. One might be characterized as "the big lie": Say something loudly enough and often enough, and soon the flocks will believe. The big lie has characterized much of the investigation of the CAPM. Studies based on CRSP data from 1926 to 1960 suggest that the CAPM market line is a little too flat; studies ending in 1970 and those ending in 1980 also suggest the CAPM is a little too flat. The problem is that the same study is being repeated on essentially the same data! The studies are perceived to offer mounting evidence that the CAPM does not work, but we are hearing the same claims based on the same data. This evidence is mere data mining.

One can also be dissuaded from the truth by looking at the wrong null hypothesis. Are we trying to prove that the CAPM has a slope different from zero or that it has a slope different from the theoretical slope? Consider the example of Evelyn Adams, a woman who won a state lottery twice. Statisticians

---
[1] See Mr. Ross's presentation, pp. 11–13.

have determined that she could not have won twice by chance because the probability that a person could win a state lottery twice is 1 in 17 billion, so it must have been skill. What they overlook is the problem of the wrong null hypothesis: One should not ask what is the likelihood that a particular individual will win the lottery twice; one should ask what is the likelihood that someone among the millions who play in lotteries might conceivably win the lottery twice. Then, the odds come tumbling back down into more rational territory.

The phenomenon of disappearing inefficiencies also plagues us. The small-capitalization-stock effect was widely touted in the early 1980s. Within one or two years, however, small-cap stocks had begun their long and disastrous tumble, which ultimately lasted seven years—a seven-year bear market in small stocks versus large stocks.

In effect, data mining exists, in part, because 1 out of 20 randomly selected relationships is significant at the 5 percent level. If we examine 1,000 different relationships and find 50 statistically significant relationships, we should not be elated at finding the 50 "inefficiencies." We should question whether we are data mining—which leads us to a more current risk: As computer power and data become cheaper and more readily available, we run the risk of "empiricism overkill." With current computer technology, we can actually strip mine the data.

Relationship proxies are also an issue. The "market" factor can appear in many guises. If we take account of the fact that small stocks have a much higher beta than large stocks, the small-stock effect may be proxying for beta, particularly if we measure beta to include lead-and-lag relationships or measure a long-horizon beta. Daily betas for small stocks are close to 1.0, weekly betas are 1.1 or 1.2, and monthly betas are 1.4 or 1.5. To some extent, the small-stock effect may simply be a proxy for the CAPM.

Implications for Asset Management

Some real inefficiencies exist, and they are relatively easy to identify. The question is: How many of these relationships will work going forward?

The debate over the validity of the CAPM has several implications for asset managers. Suppose the CAPM is dead and the market line is flat. The implication is that investment managers should sell bonds and buy low-beta stocks. The returns will be improved without incremental risk. Corporate managers should emphasize the low-beta product lines in businesses and leverage their companies to the hilt. Long ago, Black (1980) pointed out some tax advantages in this strategy as well. As for beta, Haugen and Baker (1991) suggested that an efficient portfolio can be constructed by minimizing beta subject to certain constraints. Historical tests show that a low-beta/low-variability-in-markets strategy has worked well in the past. A flat CAPM market line means that this strategy adds value.

The validity of the CAPM also affects performance measurement. Kothari and Shanken (1992) for example, conclude that only risk-adjusted returns merit measurement, because measuring the performance of a stock manager and comparing it with T-bills or inflation is using the wrong benchmark. The question is simple: In looking at risk-adjusted returns, what risk do we adjust for? Do we adjust for beta, using a CAPM approach? If so, how do we account for the fact that we do not know the true beta of a stock or portfolio? Do we adjust for tracking error? Many consultants are moving in this direction. Or do we adjust for a customized benchmark as advocated by BARRA and several others in the consulting business? Looking at risk-adjusted measurements of return, our clients remind us that they cannot spend risk-adjusted returns. Ultimately, the whole quest of the investments game is one of earning real dollars.

Conclusion

Beta is a proven, legitimate risk measure. Its relationship with time-period-specific returns is proven: During a down market, high-beta stocks will almost certainly fall more than low-beta stocks; during an up market, high-beta stocks will almost certainly rise faster than low-beta stocks. The relationship with expectational returns or with long-term actual realized returns has been neither proved nor disproved. We will probably not live long enough to see the matter finally resolved. We are dealing with noisy markets; we will never see conclusive proof or disproof for the CAPM market-line relationship between beta and return. On this level, the whole controversy is much ado about nothing, because we can never ultimately know.

Asset management and performance measurement, however, require a view with regard to whether the CAPM is a suitable risk model. My personal view is that returns are related to beta, but less so than the CAPM suggests. Returns are related to other factors also, as evidenced by global studies. The capital markets do exhibit genuine inefficiencies, but inefficiencies change. Many are arbitraged away once they are widely known, widely explored, and widely used.

Question and Answer Session
Robert D. Arnott

Question: Over what period were your relative-return coefficients computed? Were these generally, excluding inflation, concurrent comparisons?

Arnott: The relationships reviewed in the global data were mostly for the 1972–87 period. They have been brought up to date, and the data have changed very little. None of these studies used concurrent relationships. As an investment manager, I am more interested in predictive relationships. For example, these studies addressed the equity risk premium today as compared with next month's relative performance.

Question: Why were certain countries and markets omitted from the labor-cost and unemployment charts?

Arnott: Data on unit labor costs and unemployment are either soft or nonexistent in some small markets. We did not exclude any market where we found data. In some instances, the relationship was perverse, but we did not omit any countries just because they did not conform.

Question: Have you captured shifts in timing of calendar effects as investors try to get ahead of one another? How do you statistically capture shifts in these anomalies?

Arnott: Statistics are a weak tool for capturing shifts in market anomalies. Statistics identify changes in market inefficiencies or market anomalies only long after those changes have occurred. We use certain anomalies, but we try to use them aggressively, before we think others might. For example, for the January effect, we use the entire month of December to position ourselves and use the entire month of January, after just two or three days into the month, to unwind those positions.

Question: You had a couple of October effects, one being book-to-price ratio. Do you think those October effects could simply be the result of chance?

Arnott: The October effects are powerful enough that I think they are not a result of chance, although that risk obviously exists. If you look at 12 BARRA factors for 12 months, you have 144 observations. If markets are random, you would expect to find statistical significance in at least seven of them. In January and October, there are far too many relationships for chance alone to explain. When in doubt, we try to err in favor of discarding relationships that may be flukes. For example, we found a powerful link between P/E return in June. I cannot see any rationale for that; so even with a t-statistic of 3.2, we tossed it out as probably the result of data mining.

The October effects have at least some concrete rationale. Law requires mutual funds to close their books for capital gains and other purposes by October 31. That requirement may be contributing to the October effects. October is also the start of the last quarter; it begins the time when those who might be tempted to engage in window dressing will do so. Window dressing is discussed a great deal in our business. It might be dismissed as something that no more than one out of ten money managers will bother to do, but even a few managers can have an impact on the market. The markets are moved at the margin by those who are buying and selling at the time. If even a small minority of managers are engaging in window dressing, that can actually move markets.

Question: Some of the inefficiencies you cite appear to require taking systematic risk to get excess returns. Please comment.

Arnott: Investing is a continuum of risk. We cannot choose between totally risk-free arbitrage on the one hand and taking a risky position on the other. Probably, no purely risk-free arbitrages exist, but some arbitrages present almost no risk, some arbitrages or hedges involve moderate risk, and so forth on out the risk spectrum. Most of the tables presented here identified inefficiencies that would involve taking some investment risk. They are not arbitrages. When I said that inefficiencies are arbitraged away, that was a fairly liberal use of the word "arbitrage."

Question: Do you think the use of neural networks and other similar techniques are equivalent to strip mining?

Arnott: They carry seeds of that risk. Neural networks find links that are not necessarily governed by any rational prior hypothesis. Neural network technology carries the risk of engaging in true, unadulterated data mining. We have looked at neural networks and found them not particularly fruitful. That might be because we were looking in the wrong direction or because the networks actually are not particularly fruitful.

We have looked at other forms of artificial intelligence and found some intriguing results suggesting that some forms of artificial intelligence may be powerful tools in investment management. Beware, however, because with the ability of artificial intelligence to comb through massive data and find subtle relationships comes a definite crossover from mere data mining into data strip mining.

Nothing is wrong with data mining so long as you know that is what you are doing and you rule out acting on data mining alone. The ability of artificial intelligence to comb through mountains of data in subtle ways makes it both a powerful and a dangerous tool.

Question: If markets have inefficiencies and active managers can produce excess returns, why do two-thirds of active managers underperform? Does it have to do with the degree of efficiency?

Arnott: It has nothing to do with the degree of efficiency. For all intents and purposes, institutional asset managers are the market. As a class, institutional asset managers cannot beat the market. In fact, they match the market minus their trading costs and their fees. Therefore, in aggregate, they will match the market minus a hurdle that might be as much as 1 percent. That says nothing about whether markets are efficient or whether managers have skill.

We did a study of the dispersion in SEI Corporation quartiles, from top quartile to bottom quartile for individual years, two-year spans, three-year spans, and so forth. If there is no skill in asset management, then the breadth of the quartile ranges should converge roughly with the square root of time. So, the breadth of the ranges for ten-year results should be less than one-third as large as for a one-year result. In fact, the ranges do converge, but more slowly than that.

We then hypothesized a world in which investors are split into two classes: those who have skill and those who do not. We hypothesized that those who have skill earn an alpha of X and those who do not have skill earn an alpha of $-X$. Both have an annual risk of Y, so a good manager can have a bad year, and vice versa. The X indicated by the slow convergence of the SEI quartile ranges is about 2 percent. If we assume that all investors are either good or not, then those who are good beat those who are not by about 4 percent a year. That 4 percent gap would lead to convergence of the quartile ranges that would almost exactly match what we have observed in practice.

The fact that managers, in aggregate, underperform is a truism, but it says nothing about market efficiency or inefficiency. Persuasive evidence exists that managers exhibit skill (or lack of skill). To identify which ones succeeded through skill and which through luck is still not easy.

Question: Do you believe that past alpha is a basis for expecting future alpha from equity managers? If not alpha, what are the predictive factors for managers who will outperform?

Arnott: Past alpha is related to future alpha, but because the relationship is so very weak, it should be close to the bottom of the list of factors used in selecting managers. What is important to study has sometimes been called the seven P's of asset management: people, process, philosophy, price, performance, product, and progress. When choosing among active managers, study their processes and philosophies and find out whether they have a rigorous discipline that should work. This qualitative analysis will serve you better than looking at reams of data and choosing a manager who happens to be at the top of the spectrum on five-year results.

The Small-Firm Anomaly, Liquidity Premiums, and Time-Varying Returns to Size

Russell J. Fuller, CFA
Vice President and Manager of Strategy Development
Concord Capital Management

> The small-firm anomaly does not appear to be significant, nor does it appear to be associated with a liquidity premium. The time-varying return to size is important, but it may be related to such factors as bid–ask bias, tax-loss selling, and portfolio rebalancing. Other factors, correlated with size, should also be examined before trying to forecast time-varying return to size.

Researchers have identified what appears to be a small-firm anomaly that is inconsistent with the capital asset pricing model. This presentation describes research conducted to explain the time-varying return to size using a liquidity-premium model. The material represents several years of work and considers the following questions:
- Have small-firm stocks generated an alpha in the past?
- If a small-firm alpha exists, is it a liquidity premium?
- Is the time-varying return to size important?
- Can the time-varying return to size be explained?
- Can the time-varying return to size be forecast?

The Small-Firm Anomaly

The small-firm anomaly is the abnormal return realized by small firms relative to large firms. I will begin by defining alpha and the differential return, or the time-varying return to size.

Alpha

Using the *ex ante* CAPM, the expected excess return (the return in excess of the risk-free rate) on a small-capitalization portfolio (subscripted s for any particular time period t) should be proportional to its beta times the expected excess return on the market (subscripted m):

$$E(R_{s,t} - R_{f,t}) = \beta_s E(R_{m,t} - R_{f,t}).$$

The *ex post* realization of a CAPM is

$$(R_{s,t} - R_{f,t}) = \alpha_s + \beta_s (R_{m,t} - R_{f,t}) + e_{s,t}.$$

The intercept is a measure of abnormal return and is sometimes referred to as Jensen's alpha. Thus, one estimate of alpha is simply the intercept from a regression of excess returns for the portfolio against excess returns for the market.

Time-Varying Return to Size

The simple differential return (DR), or time-varying return to size, can be defined as

$$DR_{s,t} = R_{s,t} - R_{m,t}.$$

That is, the differential return is the difference in the returns between a small-cap and a large-cap index. In this case, we use, respectively, the Ibbotson small-cap series and the S&P 500. The Ibbotson small-cap series comprises the smallest sized 20 percent of NYSE firms from 1926 to 1982; beyond 1983, it represents the actual return on the Dimensional Fund Advisors Index for small stocks. The time-varying return to size appears to be quite important. The *ex post* CAPM predicts that $\beta_s(R_{m,t} - R_{f,t})$ is the excess return for the small-cap portfolio and that alpha is zero. Also, by construction, the average of the error terms is zero. Thus, the risk-adjusted differential

---

Note: Mr. Fuller is currently president of RJF Asset Management. This presentation is based on research conducted by Russell J. Fuller, CFA; John L. Kling; and Michael J. Levinson.

return for any particular time period, $RADR_{s,t}$, is the difference between the actual portfolio excess return and the predicted excess return, which is the same as alpha plus the residual error term for each time period. That is,

$$RADR_{s,t} = (R_{s,t} - R_{f,t}) - \beta_s (R_{m,t} - R_{f,t}) = \alpha_s + e_{s,t}.$$

Finally, because the average residual is equal to zero, the average risk-adjusted return to size $RADR_s$ is equal to alpha.

Risk-adjusted differential returns from 1926 through 1992 are shown in **Figure 1**. In 1933, for example, on a risk-adjusted basis, the small-stock index exceeded the return on the S&P 500 by about 70 percent. (On a non-risk-adjusted basis, the differ-

Figure 1. Risk-Adjusted Differential Returns: S&P 500 versus Ibbotson Small-Cap Series, Year-Ends 1926–92

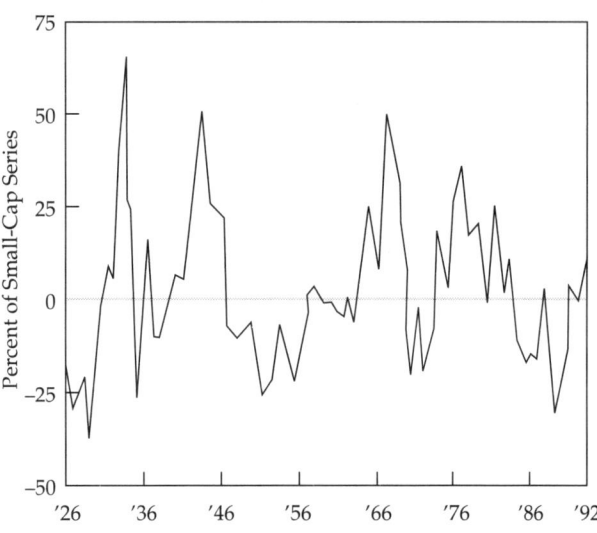

Source: Russell J. Fuller, using data from Ibbotson Associates.

Notes: Mean RADR = 1.9 percent. Mean absolute value RADR = 15.2 percent.

ential return was 90 percent.) This number appears to be overly large, and in fact, researchers should treat it as an outlier rather than a "normal" return. Over this period, the mean RADR, which is an estimate of alpha, was 1.9 percent—small relative to the year-to-year variations in returns. The mean of the absolute value of these numbers is 15.2 percent. Thus, on a risk-adjusted basis, in any one year, the small-cap index differed from the S&P 500 by about 15 percent.

Focusing on more recent history, **Figure 2** shows the RADRs of the S&P 500 versus the Ibbotson small-cap index for the 20-year period from 1973 through 1992. The alpha for small stocks during this period

Figure 2. Risk-Adjusted Differential Return: S&P 500 versus Ibbotson Small-Cap Series, 1973–92

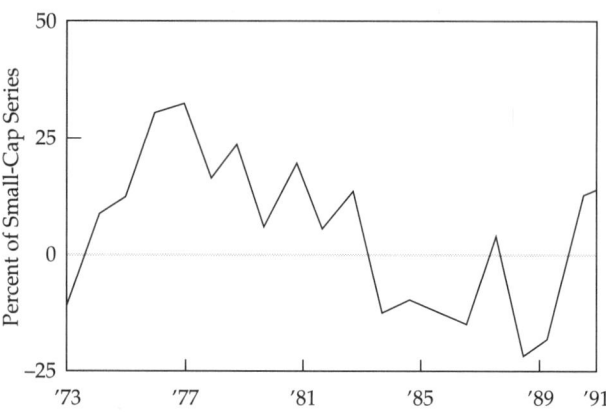

Source: Russell J. Fuller, using data from Ibbotson Associates.

Notes: Mean RADR = 5.3 percent. Mean absolute value RADR = 15.2 percent.

averaged 5.3 percent. The mean absolute value of the RADR was 15.2 percent, which is virtually the same as the value for the longer period.

To test whether the small-firm effect is caused by industry factors, we constructed an index of RADRs from industry-diversified size deciles. To reduce the problem of bid–ask spreads associated with year-end calendar data, we used February-to-January years. **Figure 3** shows the RADRs for the ninth decile. (The tenth decile contains the smallest capitalization firms. I prefer using the ninth decile rather than the tenth decile because any data errors will appear in the two extreme deciles.) The average market value for this ninth decile is larger than for the Ibbotson small-cap series. The mean RADR, or alpha, is 3.8 percent, and the mean absolute value is 10.3 percent. Even the ninth decile small-cap index controlled for industry diversification shows big differences between the return on a small-cap index and the return on the market. Thus, the time-varying return to size (RADR) is quite important.

Sources of Alpha

Where might the small-cap alpha come from? Two primary sources of alpha are unique information and bias. Unique information is information the rest of the market does not have. Someone with unique information should be able to earn an abnormal return using this information. The best evidence of this principle is insider trading.

Another primary source of alpha is investor bias. Some investors have a bias that causes them to price securities irrationally, although the bias might be perfectly rational in terms of their personal utility func-

Figure 3. Risk-Adjusted Differential Return: S&P 500 versus Industry-Diversified, Ninth Decile Small-Cap Index: February-to-January Holding-Period Returns, 1973–92

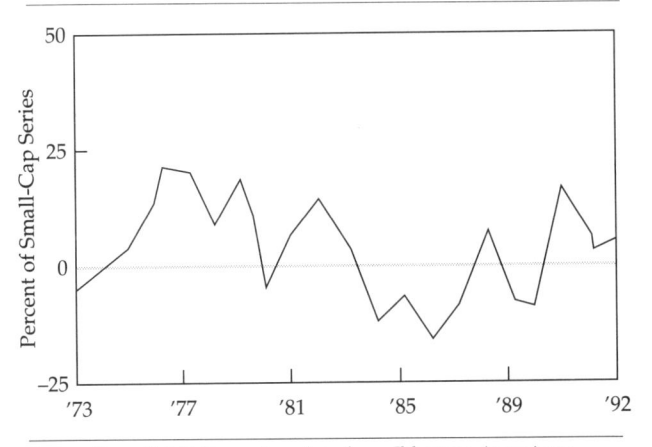

Source: Russell J. Fuller, using data from Ibbotson Associates.

Notes: Mean RADR = 3.6 percent. Mean absolute value RADR = 10.3 percent.

tions. Other investors can exploit this type of bias.

These sources of alpha do not, however, help explain the size anomaly. The small-firm effect is not caused by unique information: Everyone knows the size of a particular company. As for bias, a behavioral bias for small firms that would cause them to be irrationally priced is hard to determine.

Two other sources of alpha are misspecification of the model for normal returns and spurious results. Academics have focused on the idea that the model for normal returns may be misspecified. If the model is misspecified with respect to small size, however, it must not include a liquidity premium. Other academics claim that the small-firm anomaly is the result of spurious results. I believe many results related to the small-firm effect are, in fact, spurious. If so, the apparent alpha is not a true alpha.

Small-Firm Research

It is said that the value of a theory is whether we learn anything by trying to reject it. The CAPM passes this test with flying colors. Small-firm research is only one of many sets of tests of the CAPM from which we have learned a great deal about asset pricing.

Small-firm research can be classified into four primary subcategories: economic determinants of the return to size, original small-firm studies, methodological issues, and seasonality (the January effect, turn-of-the-year effects, etc.).

Economic Determinants

In my opinion, the most interesting area of research is on the economic determinants of the return to size, partly because the return to size is so large relative to the alpha. Probably the most interesting studies are Chan and Chen (1991), Chang and Pinegar (1989), and Fama and French (1992c).

Chan and Chen investigated the return to size as a function of degree of financial distress. They pointed out that small firms on the NYSE have different characteristics from OTC small firms (NYSE small firms tend to be the more financially distressed, when distress is measured as dividend cuts or high financial leverage); that NYSE small firms display different return patterns from those of OTC small firms; and that after controlling for marginal-firm risk, firm size does not appear to help explain returns.

Chang and Pinegar showed that the return to size may be related to industrial production. Thus, Chan and Chen's marginal firms may be reflecting sensitivity to changes in industrial production. Firms in financial distress are very sensitive to changes in industrial production; an upturn in the economy bails out a lot of marginal firms, which may be part of the economic link driving returns to size. Also, an upward blip in industrial production typically occurs around the turn of the year.

Fama and French investigated the return to size as a function of earnings. Their findings were inconclusive, and they were disappointed with that result. Their paper may be more interesting on the price-to-book-value issue, because they found a strong link between changes in earnings and abnormal returns for low price-to-book companies.

Original Studies

The original small-firm studies were by Banz (1981) and Reinganum (1981). They found alphas of 10–30 percent for small firms. Obviously, both academics and investment professionals were interested in that sort of alpha. People have become more sophisticated in the way they analyze the problem, however, and the typical small-cap study now shows an alpha of about 2 percent. Part of the reason for the lowered alphas has been the identification of spurious relationships, and part has to do with methodological issues.

Methodological Issues

Methodological issues are important for people who plan to do research in this area. The two key issues are risk measurement and return measurement. Risk measurement involves problems with nonsynchronous trading; the return-measurement problem is associated with buy-and-hold versus rebalancing strategies. Nonsynchronous trading is a problem because small-cap stocks do not trade every period and, therefore, appear to exhibit less volatility than larger cap stocks. Researchers who use normal ordinary least squares regressions to measure beta will severely understate the beta estimate. If the risk is understated, the alpha will be overstated.

An example of the return-measurement problem is that researchers using average daily returns are, in effect, assuming daily rebalancing of the portfolio, which is not realistic. Blume and Stambaugh (1983) and Roll (1983a) address this problem. A buy-and-hold strategy radically reduces the return on small-cap stocks compared with large-cap stocks.

Small-firm alphas are substantially reduced by adjusting betas for nonsynchronous trading and using buy-and-hold portfolios rather than rebalancing every period. These methodological changes do not, however, eliminate the small-firm effect.

Seasonality

Studies have determined that most of the small-firm effect occurs on the last trading day of December and the first four to five days of January. Several explanations have been offered for this observation, including tax-loss selling, portfolio rebalancing, and bid–ask bias.

The issue of tax-loss selling attracted a number of researchers and widespread debate until Jones, Lee, and Apenbrink (1991) established, in my opinion, that tax-loss selling does account for part of the turn-of-the-year effect. That result may seem to be simply common sense, but several serious papers have argued that tax-loss selling is not involved.

Several researchers have identified portfolio-rebalancing activities that affect returns at the turn of the year. Ritter (1988) found that small investors disproportionately sell small stocks in early December and buy small stocks in late December and early January. Dyl and Maberly (1992) found that odd-lot sales follow a similar pattern as found by Ritter, and the pattern is not entirely attributable to tax considerations.

Bid–ask bias has also been found to contribute to the seasonality effect. Keim (1989) documented that a disproportionate number of small-cap stocks trade at the bid toward the end of December and at the ask on December 31 and the first several days of January. Bhardwaj and Brooks (1992) showed that the turn-of-the-year effect and the bid–ask bias are primarily associated with low-priced stocks, which are not necessarily the same as small-cap stocks. These studies suggest that the seasonality effects are spurious, or at least not exploitable.

Spurious versus Real Effects

Research has shown that the size effect is correlated with marginal (distressed) firms, tax-loss selling, and portfolio rebalancing; but those are not true size effects. To the extent that these factors are causing returns to vary, size is only proxying for the real underlying factors. The real effects are risk premiums attached to marginal firms, to tax-loss-selling rebound, and to irrational portfolio rebalancing.

Our research shows that the size effect, or time-varying return to size, is also correlated with industry effects. In the first quarter of 1991, for example, bank stocks took off like rockets. (Bank stocks are disproportionately represented in the ninth and tenth deciles, because there are so many small banks.) I personally forecast a strong small-size effect in 1991, but my forecast had nothing to do with changes in federal policy, interest rates, or bank stocks. To claim that my forecast was a good one is a real stretch, because what was driving the positive small-firm effect in the first quarter of 1991 were bank stocks, and my forecast had nothing to do with bank stocks.

The goal is to sort out spurious results from real effects. The results of the study of bid–ask bias results suggest that much of the small-firm results are spurious and not exploitable. Any remaining small-firm effect may simply be a rationally determined premium for holding small, illiquid securities. Presumably, small stocks deserve a liquidity premium because they are very difficult to trade.

A Liquidity-Premium Asset Pricing Model

In two studies, Kling and I (1991, 1992) attempted to establish a relationship between liquidity and the size effect. We were able to develop a model using annual data that fit nicely—in fact, we were able to get the January effect to become nonsignificant—but the model did not perform well when monthly data were used for the non-January months. We found a positive liquidity premium for the year as a whole and for January but a *negative* liquidity premium for December. There is no rational reason why liquidity would ever be negatively priced.

In an effort to determine what causes the documented relationships in December and January, Kling, Levinson, and I recently investigated bid–ask bias as well as industry effects. **Table 1** illustrates how a bid–ask bias could develop. Suppose a stock is trading at about $10.00. The bid is $10.00 in November, December, January, and February, and the ask is $11.00 in each of those months. Thus, the closing price is what drives the monthly returns. Suppose the closing price is $10.50 in November, and because of tax-loss selling, rebalancing, or whatever, the closing price drops to $10.00 in December, causing a negative return in December. Then, because of

Table 1. Bid–Ask Bias: A Hypothetical Example

	November	December	January	February
Bid	$10.00	$10.00	$10.00	$10.00
Ask	11.00	11.00	11.00	11.00
Close	10.50	10.00	11.00	10.50
Return	NA	–4.76%	10.0%	–4.54%

Notes: NA = not applicable; arithmetic mean of December, January, and February returns = 0.56 percent; geometric mean of December, January, and February returns = zero percent.

the rebound from tax-loss selling or portfolio rebalancing, the closing price hits the ask in January and the return in January is 10 percent. Then, in February, the price comes back to $10.50. The closing price went from $10.50 in November to $10.50 in February with no change in the bid–ask spread. The monthly returns were negative in December and February, however, and very positive in January. Because of this behavior, results based on year-end returns will be biased. Therefore, we chose to use February–January years, because the seasonality bias in December and January cancels itself out.

Our methodology involved sorting stocks into size deciles at each annual portfolio date, either December 31 for calendar years or January 31 for the February–January years. Stocks were equal weighted within a size decile at the portfolio formation date and held for 12 months. Then, we repeated the study using industry-diversified portfolios in order to reduce biases from industry factors. In this case, we ranked stocks within each of 55 primary industry groups according to size; we put the smallest 10 percent from each industry into the tenth decile, the next smallest 10 percent into the ninth decile, and so forth. We used the BARRA HiCap Universe because it has consistent industry classifications from 1973 through 1992. (The BARRA HiCap Universe consists of, approximately, the 1,300 largest U.S. common stocks.)

The estimates of alpha for the nondiversified portfolios for the 20-year period and for two subperiods are shown in **Table 2**. The estimates were obtained from the standard CAPM regression, with the S&P 500 used as a proxy for the market ($R_{m,t}$). For these portfolios, the biggest difference between calendar-year and February–January year results occurs in the tenth decile. This result is somewhat puzzling and suggests a bid–ask bias problem. The conclusion is reinforced by the fact that the estimates of alpha for the ninth and tenth size deciles are generally closer to zero for the February–January years.

For the 20-year period, the results for the whole sample (HiCap) show an alpha of about 2 percent. Thus, a strategy of simply owning about 1,300 equal-weighted stocks would have beaten the capitalization-weighted S&P 500 by about 2 percent on a risk-adjusted basis and by slightly more on a raw-return basis. That return is attractive and consistent with a positive small-firm alpha, but when the data are partitioned into subperiods, the results become statistically less reliable—although still interesting.

The 1973–82 subperiod was very attractive for small stocks; the alpha was about 12 percent for the ninth and tenth deciles. In contrast, the second subperiod was not at all attractive for small stocks—very negative alphas resulted for the ninth and tenth deciles. These types of results should make researchers question the existence of a long-term, positive alpha associated with small size.

The results for the industry-diversified portfolios are shown in **Table 3**. Note that the alphas for deciles

Table 2. Estimates of Alpha: Nondiversified Series, 1973–92 and Subperiods

Size Decile	1973–92 Calendar Year	1973–92 February–January Year	1973–82 Calendar Year	1973–82 February–January Year	1983–92 Calendar Year	1983–92 February–January Year
10	3.38%	1.58%	14.95%	12.01%	–9.00%	–6.40%
9	4.48	4.57	12.52	12.31	–4.70	–3.59
8	3.02	4.19	8.37	9.33	–5.09	–2.27
7	2.44	0.97	7.07	4.36	–3.64	–1.86
6	2.22	2.66	7.22	6.39	–2.35	–2.17
5	1.94	2.30	6.30	6.51	–2.45	–2.15
4	2.01	1.62	5.01	4.28	–3.20	–1.99
3	1.27	0.81	3.34	2.36	–2.11	–0.97
2	0.32	1.50	0.72	2.44	–1.16	–0.77
1	–0.34	–0.65	–1.07	–1.65	–0.60	–0.35
HiCap	2.08	1.97	6.44	5.82	–3.46	–2.20

Source: Research in progress by Fuller, Kling, and Levinson.

Notes: $(R_{s,t} - R_{f,t}) = \alpha_s + \beta_s (R_{m,t} - R_{f,t}) + e_{s,t}$; R_m = S&P 500; R_s = ninth size decile, not industry diversified.

Table 3. Estimates of Alpha: Industry-Diversified Series, 1973–92 and Subperiods

Size Decile	1973–92 Calendar Year	1973–92 February–January Year	1973–82 Calendar Year	1973–82 February–January Year	1983–92 Calendar Year	1983–92 February–January Year
10	3.70%	2.79%	12.59%	10.91%	−6.43%	−5.35%
9	4.02	3.82	9.76	9.64	−5.06	−3.21
8	3.72	3.74	9.30	8.40	−2.42	−0.83
7	3.01	2.50	9.55	8.03	−4.70	−3.80
6	2.15	2.27	7.77	7.21	−3.81	−2.73
5	1.60	1.75	5.27	4.54	−3.22	−1.03
4	1.79	1.72	4.49	3.84	−2.34	0.40
3	1.64	1.16	4.83	4.32	−1.91	−2.80
2	−0.46	−0.02	0.83	0.98	−2.65	−1.39
1	−0.24	−0.05	0.42	0.45	−1.80	−1.24

Source: Research in progress by Fuller, Kling, and Levinson.

Notes: $(R_{s,t} - R_{f,t}) = \alpha_s + \beta_s (R_{m,t} - R_{f,t}) + e_{s,t}$; R_m = S&P 500 and; R_s = ninth size decile, industry diversified.

nine and ten are generally smaller than was the case for the nondiversified deciles. Also, the use of calendar years has less of an effect on the industry-diversified declines than the use of February–January years. Both of these results could be explained simply by the fact that the average market value of the stocks in the ninth and tenth deciles is larger for the industry-diversified deciles than for the nondiversified deciles. However, as will be explained, industry factors have a significant effect on the return to size.

To calculate the industry effect, we defined DIF as the difference between the annual returns for the nondiversified portfolio and the industry-diversified portfolio for a particular size decile. The correlation between the DIF and RADR for each decile is an indication of how much of the risk-adjusted return is caused by industry factors. The RADR/DIF correlations for the ninth decile (0.53) and tenth decile (0.68) are fairly large, which suggests that a good portion of the spikes in Figure 2 and Figure 3 can be accounted for by industry effects.

Adding DIF to the CAPM regression is a better test of the industry effect than the previous method. Using the simple CAPM regression, we get the results shown in **Table 4**. For the tenth decile, the intercept, or alpha, is 1.58 percent and beta is 0.99 with an R^2 of 0.41. This has a strongly autocorrelated

Table 4. Results for Simple CAPM Regressions

Size Decile	Intercept	Beta	R^2	First-Order Autocorrelation
10	1.58%	0.99	0.41	0.41
	(0.36)	(3.52)		
9	4.57%	1.24	0.64	0.49
	(1.36)	(5.69)		

Source: Research in progress by Fuller, Kling, and Levinson.

residual series, however, which is not what you like to see from a statistical viewpoint. For the ninth decile, the small-cap alpha, 4.57 percent, is larger than for the tenth decile, and beta is also higher. It is a better fit (the R^2 is higher), but that is always the case as firm size increases.

Adding DIF, the variable for the differential return attributable to the industry-diversified portfolio, modifies the CAPM equation:

$$(R_{s,t} - R_{f,t}) = \alpha_s + \beta_s (R_{m,t} - R_{f,t}) + \gamma_s DIF_{s,t} + e_{s,t}.$$

The results are shown in **Table 5**. With the DIF factor, the alpha is 4.44 percent for the tenth decile and 3.21 percent for the ninth decile. This model is better behaved, because if there is a return to size, one would expect the most extreme-sized decile to exhibit the highest alpha. The betas are also better behaved—1.22 for the tenth decile and 0.96 for the ninth decile; as expected, the smaller stocks have higher betas. The slope coefficient on DIF, γ, is positive and highly significant for both the ninth and tenth deciles. The R^2 also rises, and the first-order autocorrelation drops to insignificant numbers.

Table 5. Results for Regressions Using DIF

Size Decile	Intercept	Beta	Slope Coefficient γ	R^2	First-Order Autocorrelation
10	4.44	1.22	2.36	0.70	0.17
	(1.36)	(5.72)	(4.09)		
9	3.21	0.96	1.80	0.77	0.14
	(1.14)	(4.76)	(3.05)		

Source: Research in progress by Fuller, Kling, and Levinson.

The improvement in results with the addition of the DIF factor suggests that much of what appears to be a small-firm effect is attributable to unequal representation of industries in every size decile. This result suggests that forecasts of return to size may, in fact, be simply forecasts of industry returns. The same principle applies to the other factors correlated with size, such as marginal-firm and distressed-firm factors.

Conclusion

The small-firm alpha seen in previous studies is greatly overstated. This research finds that small-firm alphas are typically insignificant, although the methodology contains some problems. The argument in today's literature is that a 2 percent or smaller alpha exists that may or may not be significant statistically. A 2 percent alpha over 20 years is clearly significant in the economic sense, however—if it truly exists.

We could not establish that the observed small-stock alpha is associated with a liquidity premium. The time-varying return to size is large and important, but it is related to bid–ask bias, tax-loss selling, and portfolio rebalancing. One solution for some of the problems in research methodology is to form size-based portfolios not on a calendar year but on a February–January basis. This step reduces the problems associated with tax-loss selling, portfolio rebalancing, bid–ask bias, and so forth. One should also look at factors correlated with size, including marginal firms, distress, industry, and earnings.

Before analysts can forecast the time-varying return to size, they need to understand it better. The historical data, even the purer industry-diversified return series, can be fit fairly well with simple time-series models. In contrast to some causal models, however, simple time-series models depend critically on the assumption that what happened in the past will repeat itself in the future—not a good assumption upon which to build a portfolio.

Question and Answer Session
Russell J. Fuller, CFA

Question: What is the reason for the serial correlation of small-cap returns? Do you expect this effect to continue?

Fuller: We are trying to find an explanation for the serial correlation. We have looked at a number of factors that might explain serial correlation. For example, we even looked at obscure factors such as defense spending as a percentage of GNP as a possible economic explanation for a four- or five-year period when small stocks did poorly relative to large stocks. In a period of high defense spending, large companies, which get the defense contracts, will do well relative to small stocks. Unfortunately, we could not find good causal models.

Question: How is the beta for RADR calculated, and does it change over time?

Fuller: In the material presented, we used a simple ordinary least squares regression of the excess return for a small-cap decile against the excess return for the S&P 500. To see if beta changes over time, one could compare the first and second decades. The betas change somewhat, but not much when the industry difference in return is taken into account. The small-cap group, the tenth decile, tends to have a beta of about 1.3; for the ninth decile, it tends to be closer to 1.0; and the first decile tends to be slightly lower than 1.0.

Question: Do you believe betas are seriously deficient in small-cap research?

Fuller: I like the CAPM, I think it is a great theory, and I believe betas are useful numbers. CAPM is an *ex ante* theory that uses expected returns. None of our studies uses expected returns, so they are not really tests of the theory. One could argue that the CAPM-predicted correlation should not be expected if *ex post* returns are used. The market portfolio cannot be mean–variance efficient for any particular period when *ex post* returns are used because, at the beginning of that period, the market portfolio holding all these assets must be overweighted in the losers of that period and underweighted in the winners of that period. One can always construct some portfolio *ex post* that will be more efficient.

We are dealing with investments in an *ex ante* world. Decisions must be based on what we expect the future to be. Betas, particularly with respect to small stocks, are very useful. On average, small-cap stocks will have high betas *ex ante*. That is the way people should think about them—in terms of risk–return trade-offs and trying to form optimal portfolios.

Question: When computing risk-adjusted differential returns, you suggested the S&P 500 Index as a proxy for the market. With the large-cap and possibly growth bias of the S&P 500, is it a valid proxy and, if not, does that matter?

Fuller: The bias does not matter too much in using a capitalization-weighted index. In our liquidity-premium study, we used the value-weighted CRSP Index. We also reran all the results using the S&P 500, and they were essentially the same. In using an equal-weighted index, the S&P bias will make a difference.

Question: Do you believe small-cap index funds operate at a serious disadvantage because of the bid–ask spread?

Fuller: Small-cap index funds do not have any more serious disadvantage than an active small-cap manager would have. Trading in the small-cap arena means having a bid–ask spread problem. Some argue that liquidity should not matter, that people can form baskets of securities and trade only portions. Some progress is being made in doing that.

Low-P/E Investing: Why It Works and How to Capture the Returns

William E. Jacques, CFA
Partner, Executive Vice President, and Chief Investment Officer
Martingale Asset Management

> People invest in growth stocks because they expect that those companies' earnings per share will grow much faster than the earnings of value stocks. This is generally not the case. Low-P/E investment strategies differ, but those that are industry adjusted appear to outperform those based on simple ranking methods.

The primary determinant of stock performance is earnings. Over the years, empirical studies have shown a strong positive return to low-P/E stocks. Not much research, however, has focused on why the low-P/E stocks do better than high-P/E stocks. This presentation provides a framework for explaining why the low-P/E stocks have achieved and will continue to achieve superior performance. I will describe Martingale Asset Management's study of the return premium of low-P/E stocks and our ideas on how best to capture this superior return.

History of Low-P/E Investing

Many studies have shown that low-P/E stocks tend to outperform high-P/E stocks over time. One of the most careful early studies was done by the BARRA organization, a research and consulting firm based in Berkeley, California. The key to the BARRA study was controlling for company characteristics other than P/Es to determine the pure effect of low P/Es. For instance, low-P/E stocks typically have below-average growth. The difference in growth rates between low-P/E stocks and high-P/E stocks must be controlled to determine whether the stocks' performance difference results from the low P/E rather than the low growth. The BARRA analysis controls for 55 industries and 12 other factors, the most important of which are variability in markets, success, and size. Jacobs and Levy published a paper (1988) examining the pure P/E effect (net of other factors), and their findings confirm the BARRA study.

The results of the BARRA study, updated through June 30, 1992, are displayed in **Figure 1**. The low-P/E factor, net of other factors, has outperformed the market by an average of 3.2 percent a year for nearly 20 years.

Why Low-P/E Investing Works

Low-P/E investing works because growth-stock investors are not as good at forecasting the future as they think they are. Investors are betting that they can find companies that will achieve superior growth over an extended period of time. As a result, they bid up the prices of stocks with good future growth prospects ("growth" companies) and force down the prices of stocks with poor future growth prospects ("value") companies. The superior growth prospects of the growth companies are reflected in their high P/Es, and the poor growth prospects of the value companies are reflected in their low P/Es.

When expectations meet reality, investors discover that the growth companies, on average, grow slightly faster than the average company but not as fast as required to justify their lofty prices. Hence, investors are disappointed, and these stocks underperform. Although value companies grow slightly slower than the average company, their earnings growth is better than expected. Hence, investors are positively surprised, and these stocks outperform.

Growth stocks sell at more than twice the P/E of the value stocks. The implication is that the growth stocks' earnings per share (EPS) will grow at a rate that is 15 percentage points higher a year than the value stocks.[1] This growth rate is not achieved.

---
[1] The assumption is constant superior growth for five years and average growth thereafter.

Figure 1. Return to the BARRA Low-P/E Factor, December 1972–June 1992

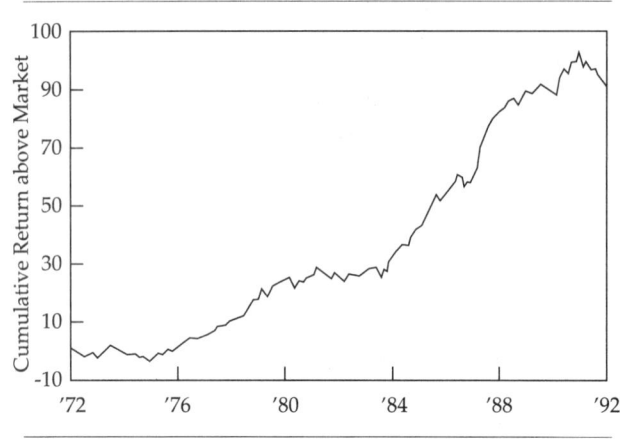

Source: BARRA.

Figure 2 illustrates the difference in P/Es between the top quartile and bottom quartile of the universe of stocks when ranked by simple P/Es. As of December 1979, for example, the average (median) P/E of the stocks in the high-P/E quartile was 11.2, and the average (median) P/E of the stocks in the low-P/E quartile was 5.3. From these two average P/Es, one can infer the expected superior growth rate of the high-P/E companies over the low-P/E companies. In this case, the superior expected growth rate was 16.2 percentage points a year during a five-year period.[2]

Figure 2. Average P/E of Top and Bottom Quartile of Stocks Ranked by Simple P/E, 1979–91

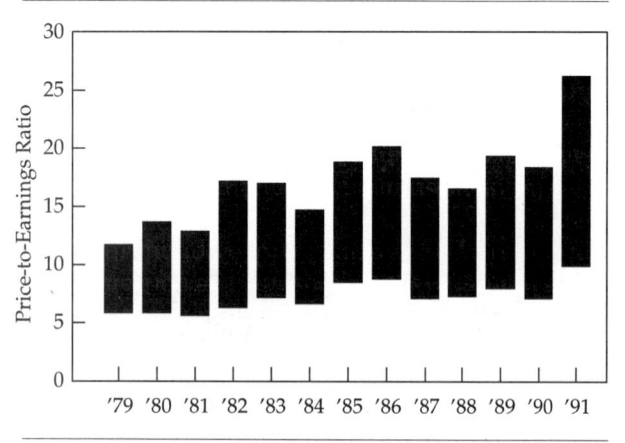

Sources: BARRA and Institutional Broker's Estimate System.

---

[2] These P/Es imply that the average high-P/E stocks were earning 47 cents for every $1.00 earned by the low-P/E stocks (5.3/11.2 = 0.47). To justify their lofty prices, the 47 cents for the high-P/E stocks must have been expected to grow to at least $1.00 over some reasonable time horizon (the next five years). This total growth implies 16.2 percentage points a year superior growth for the high-P/E stocks relative to the low-P/E stocks (0.47 × 1.16^5 = 1.00). This analysis holds even though the EPS for the low-P/E

Stock prices react to the difference between what is expected and what actually happens. Good companies (companies with good future growth prospects) do not always make good investments. Companies doing better than expected make good investments.

Did the top-quartile companies as of December 1979 actually grow as rapidly as necessary to justify their high P/Es relative to the low-P/E companies? As **Figure 3** shows, they were not even close. In the

Figure 3. Actual and Required Increases in Earnings per Share (base year = 1979)

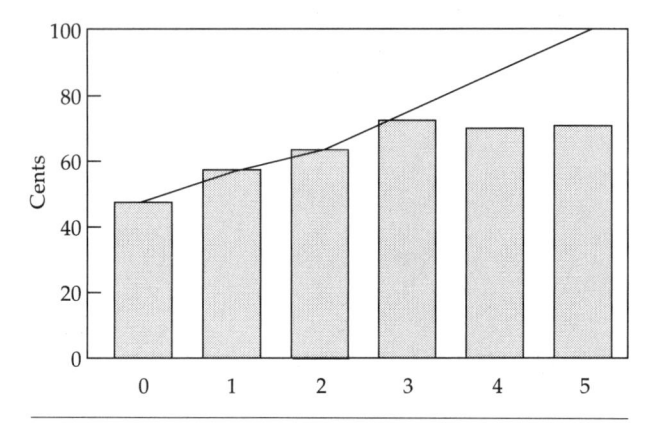

Sources: BARRA and Martingale Asset Management.

base year, the high-P/E stocks were earning 47 cents for every dollar the low-P/E stocks earned. Five years later, they had grown to only 68 cents for every dollar the low-P/E stocks earned. This same analysis holds true for the high-P/E stocks as of each December for the seven years between 1979 and 1986 (see **Figure 4**). This result explains why the high-P/E

Figure 4. Terminal Earnings per Share for Growth Stocks after Five Years

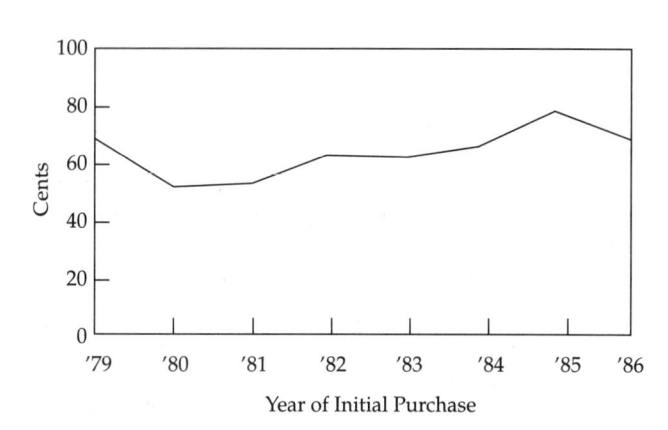

Year of Initial Purchase

Sources: BARRA and Martingale Asset Management.

stocks have significantly underperformed low-P/E stocks by an average of 9.8 percent a year for the past 12 years.

Have growth-stock investors learned their lesson? A reasonable expectation is that this effect would be arbitraged away, but instead, the recent spread between the high-P/E stocks and the low-P/E stocks is at least as large as the historical average (see Figure 2). Outstanding investment opportunities continue to exist in value stocks.

Why Portfolio Construction Helps

Not all low-P/E strategies are the same. The portfolio-construction rules can make a large difference in the returns and risks of different low-P/E strategies. For example, a common way to construct a low-P/E strategy is to rank stocks by P/E and invest in the top of the list, such as the top quartile. We found, however, that this simple ranking scheme typically produces portfolios with unacceptably high levels of tracking error relative to a broad market benchmark. We can produce a low-P/E strategy with higher added value and much lower tracking error by ranking stocks within industries by P/E (which we call the "industry-adjusted P/E"). This strategy avoids the tendency of low-P/E strategies to take very large industry bets, which can overwhelm the P/E factor.

We conducted a study for the period from December 1979 to June 1992 that looked at the returns to companies ranked by P/E. We used month-end price and month-end Institutional Broker's Estimate System (IBES) earnings data to construct the P/Es. The portfolios were constructed monthly and separated into quartiles ranked by P/E. Stocks within the quartiles were equally weighted. The selection universe contained an average of 1,000 stocks during the study period.

The value added by this strategy is the difference between the returns of the top quartile and the bottom quartile—or the "spread." The standard deviation of the performance spread measures the risk of the strategy (which is equivalent to the active risk or tracking error of a strategy against a benchmark such as the S&P 500 Index).

The spread in returns between the top and bottom quartiles of the simple P/E ranking is 9.8 percent a year during the study period, with a tracking error of 10.7 percent. That is, low-P/E stocks outperformed high-P/E stocks by an average of 9.8 percentage points a year. This result is strong evidence of high added value, but the tracking error of 10.7 percentage points a year is also quite high. The spread of the industry-adjusted P/E quartiles is 11.5 percent a year, with a tracking error of 4.3 percent.

Hence, on average across all industries, low-P/E stocks within industries performed 11.5 percentage points a year better than high-P/E stocks within those same industries. The within-industry spread is higher than the unadjusted spread, and the tracking error is significantly less. In summary, low-P/E investing works even better within industries than across the whole universe of stocks.

The year-by-year data are presented in **Figure 5**. The spread of the industry-adjusted P/E quartiles is positive for each of the years, but the spread of the simple P/E ranking is negative in five of the years.

This spread analysis assumes that an investor can capture stock mispricing by going long low-P/E stocks and short high-P/E stocks. Although this method is the most efficient way to capture security mispricing, most investors limit themselves to exploiting the mispricing by buying the low-P/E stocks.

We performed two simulations that mirror this analysis—an optimal long portfolio with and one without industry constraints. The study period was from December 1979 to June 1992. The simulations looked at the returns to optimally constructed portfolios with a low-P/E exposure. The portfolios were optimized monthly using BARRA optimization software.

The unconstrained optimal portfolio used the standardized earnings-to-price ratio (E/P, the reciprocal of the P/E) as the alpha and maximized alpha with respect to tracking error (the S&P 500 Index was taken as normal). The industry-controlled optimal portfolio used the standardized E/P as the alpha, constrained the 55 industry positions to be close to the S&P industry weight, and then maximized alpha with respect to tracking error.

The unconstrained optimal portfolio had an annualized alpha (versus the S&P 500) of 6.4 and a tracking error of 10.1. The corresponding figures for the industry-controlled optimal portfolio were 7.1 and 6.0, respectively.

A Note on Three Kinds of Earnings

Low-P/E strategies add value if they are systematically applied over the long run, but what definition of earnings should be used? The candidates range from the simplest—the trailing 12-month EPS—to a prospective 12-month EPS. BARRA has a measure that is a combination of the trailing and the prospective EPS figures.

A P/E based on the IBES earnings estimates should be superior to a P/E based on the trailing 12-month EPS. When companies report big negative earnings, as the banking industry did in the late

Figure 5. P/E Spreads between Top and Bottom Quartiles: Simple and Industry-Adjusted P/Es, 1980–June 1992

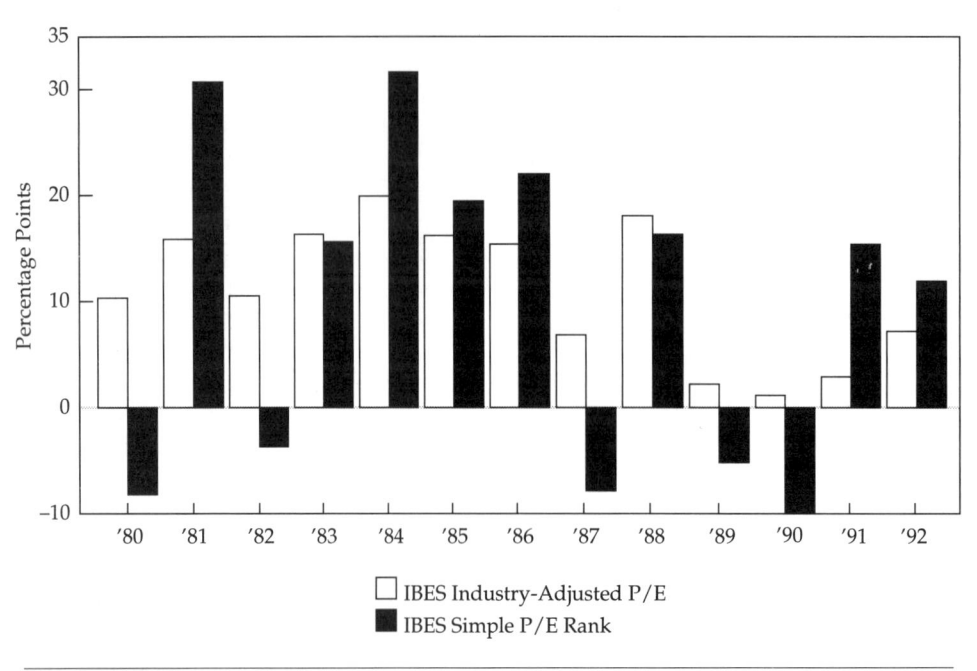

Source: BARRA.

1980s, the E/P factor will be low for some period of time (equivalent to a high P/E). The reason for the negative earnings, however, was a write-down of assets that would allow future earnings to be higher than they would have been otherwise. These stocks would tend to be priced not according to the past reported negative earnings but according to the future earnings. Hence, the IBES estimate of earnings would seem to be a better one to use in calculating the P/E ratio. The BARRA earnings figures would be expected to be somewhere in between, because BARRA uses an average of the IBES and trailing 12-month earnings.

The results of using each of these measures of earnings per share in P/E calculations are reported in **Table 1**. The study period is December 1981 to June 1992 (the longest period for which data are available for all three approaches). The data presented are for the industry-adjusted P/E quartiles.

The IBES-derived P/E, with a compounded added value of 11.4 percent, significantly outperforms the trailing 12-month P/E (7.9 percent at

Table 1. Earnings Spreads and Tracking Errors Resulting from Three Measures of Earnings per Share

Source of Earnings Figures	Spread between Low and High P/E Quartiles (annualized)	Tracking Error (annualized)
IBES P/E	11.4%	4.4%
BARRA P/E	10.1	4.9
Trailing 12-month P/E	7.9	4.4

Source: Martingale Asset Management.

the same tracking-error level). The IBES-derived P/E also outperforms the BARRA P/E by 1.3 percent, with slightly lower risk.

Question and Answer Session
William E. Jacques, CFA

Question: What is your criterion for a low-P/E stock?

Jacques: In this analysis, I used quartiles. So low-P/E stocks are in the bottom 25 percent.

Question: Do cash flows provide a better basis than earnings for valuations?

Jacques: Yes, if estimates of cash flows are available in a historical data base. Trailing 12-month earnings contain a lot of garbage and write-downs. One way I got around that was by not using past earnings. Cash flow is far superior to 12-month trailing earnings, but it is a toss-up between the two when talking about prospective earnings, which tend to be very close to a cash flow number. In an ideal world, the measure does not make much difference to the order of magnitude of the results.

Question: How were the industry adjustments made?

Jacques: We used BARRA's 55-industry classification. If among the 1,000 companies, 80 are utilities, then we would rank those 80 companies by P/E; the top 20 would go into the high-P/E-quartile group, and the bottom 20 into the low-P/E-quartile group.

Question: How do you deal with the fact that high-P/E companies are a mix of growth companies and down-and-out cyclicals? Also, how do you control for depressed cyclical earnings becoming high-P/E stocks?

Jacques: The problem of identifying down-and-out stocks that are only marginally earning money arises mainly in looking at trailing 12-month earnings; normally, the problem would be reduced by looking at forward earnings. I do not know how to differentiate these stocks. IBM was considered a growth stock at one point, and then suddenly, it was down-and-out cyclical. The transition was fairly smooth, which is typical. An investor would probably achieve better results by differentiating the two types of high-P/E stocks, but I'm not sure how to do that.

Question: Was the EPS gap affected by risk-adjusting the low-P/E-company universe for distressed companies?

Jacques: The risk adjustment cuts both ways. Low-P/E stocks have lower betas than high-P/E stocks, so using beta for risk adjustment would enhance the results. If risk is defined as total volatility or earnings volatility, the results might look slightly different. The problem is defining risk properly. The high-P/E group has enormous earnings expectations risk that is not properly adjusted for. That seems to be why the P/E anomaly exists.

Question: In your back-tests, how did you control for survivor bias? If you did not control for it, are the results biased?

Jacques: We did the back-tests both ways—with and without controlling for survivors—just to see what the effect would be. This factor does not seem to affect the results much. The data do tend to have survivorship bias. A company that goes out of business or is taken over drops out of the data base. Those two phenomena were somewhat equally at play. One would think that the low-P/E stocks would be more likely than high-P/E stocks to go out of business and that the high-P/E stocks would tend to be taken over, but that was not clearly true.

Question: Because most portfolio managers are evaluated at least annually, can the gap between high-P/E and low-P/E stocks be eliminated by annual or more frequent rebalancing?

Jacques: A growth stock's growth comes in the first year. A really smart growth manager, always keeping one step ahead, will be out of that stock by then. Annual rebalancing would be a good tactic if these stocks were priced as if they had only a one-year growth premium, but it does not take investors long to determine that the growth in the second year is not coming. So before the manager can get out of that stock, the price is already starting to reflect the disappointment.

Question: Did you consider differentials between ordinary dividend tax rates and capital gains tax rates relative to your BARRA E/P factors? Do you think there is a tax-based explanation for the P/E effect?

Jacques: My viewpoint was that of a tax-exempt investor. I think I uncovered an economic rationale for the P/E effect; whether other effects are occurring is for someone else to prove.

37

Is Beta Dead or Alive?

Josef Lakonishok
*Karnes Professor of Finance
University of Illinois*

> Although noisy returns and lack of sufficient data cloud conclusions about the beta–return relationship, on the downside, high-beta stocks are more risky than low-beta stocks and investors should require additional compensation. The relationship between risk and return has been confounded, however, by institutional factors, including indexation.

Several years ago, few people cared whether beta was dead or alive. Now, because of Fama and French's 1992 paper, beta's vitality seems to be a major issue. Fama and French forced academics and practitioners to reexamine the empirical support for beta. Life without beta would undoubtedly be miserable, because no other widely accepted alternative risk measure exists. In corporate America, people must discount future cash flows and come up with present values, and betas are widely used as risk measures. What to use if not beta? Size and book value to market value are hardly appealing alternatives.

This presentation focuses on the implications of noisy stock returns, standard tests of the CAPM, and behavioral/institutional factors that are driving stock returns and weakening the relationship between risk and return.

Is Beta Important?

Many researchers are using about 20 years of data in testing the CAPM. They think 20 years are more than enough to sort out whether beta is important. In this context, 20 years is a short time span. The stock market is so noisy that, with the existing data, one cannot generally draw clear-cut conclusions—as Fama and French do—that beta is dead.[1] Noise is an issue when comparing returns on high-beta stocks with returns on low-beta stocks; it is also an issue in comparing, for example, the returns on high book-to-market stocks and low book-to-market stocks. Unless the difference in returns is large and the period is long, no conclusive statements can be made.

To examine this point, assume that the CAPM works perfectly. In every period, the compensation per unit of beta is (rm – rf), or the market return minus the return on the risk-free asset. Assume that 20 years of data are used—a very long period in the money management business, where horizons are often measured in months rather than years. (In fact, except for the United States, we have 10 years or more of good data for few countries.) During the past 20 years, the risk premium (rm – rf) was 5.05 percent. In our ideal setting, this percentage is also the compensation per unit of beta. The troublesome part is that this 5.05 percent is not statistically significant; the t-statistic is only 1.36. So, even if the model worked perfectly in the last 20 years, we would not be able to conclude confidently that a positive relationship exists between beta and returns. To continue with the same point, assume that the compensation per unit of beta is 4 percent a year. In that case, one would need 70 years of data before getting a t-statistic of 2.00!

Noisy stock returns are a problem not only when we try to figure out if beta works. Consider a star money manager who beats the market by 200 basis points a year with a tracking error of 5 percent a year (which is below the median tracking error for equity money managers based on the SEI Corporation universe). It would take 25 years to determine whether this money manager is smart or lucky. Needless to say, plan sponsors are not so patient.

Chan and I (1993) examined whether the very noisy and constantly changing environment generating stock returns permits strong statements about the importance of beta. The study used all the available data on the monthly CRSP tapes from 1926 to 1991 to examine the relationship between beta and returns. Using the methodology of Fama and Mac-

---
[1] See also Mr. Ross's presentation, pp.11–13.

Beth (1973), we estimated a slope coefficient (the compensation per unit of beta) of 0.47 percent a month, or about 6 percent a year, which is quite large. The slope coefficient, with a *t*-statistic of 1.84, was marginally significant.

The Sharpe–Lintner CAPM implies that the compensation per unit of beta should be equal to the risk premium. During the 1926–91 period, the risk premium was 0.76 percent a month. Thus, our estimated premium was only 29 basis points away from the "theoretical" risk premium, and this difference is not statistically significant. In fact, the probability that the compensation per unit of beta is zero percent a year is the same as that the compensation per unit of beta is 12 percent a year! Depending on your beliefs, you can pick where you want to be in this very wide range. To pick zero is extreme.

Definition of Risk

The noisy, dynamic environment generating stock returns clouds our ability to reach firm conclusions with respect to the compensation for beta risk. Perhaps a less difficult task would be to verify whether the beta factor is important in driving stock returns. In particular, the case for beta would be more plausible if stocks with high betas did indeed present higher risks than stocks with low betas. Extensive conversations with money managers suggest that downside risk is their major concern; I have not found a single money manager who seems to be concerned about the various multidimensional risk measures consistent with arbitrage pricing theory models. If downside risk is a major concern of investors, beta is a good measure of risk.

Figure 1 illustrates how high-beta stocks and low-beta stocks perform in extreme down markets. Notice that March 1938 was the worst month and October 1987 the second worst month. Take October 1987—a month that is still fresh in our memories—as an example. In October 1987, a portfolio of high-beta stocks (top decile by beta) declined by roughly 35 percent, the market declined by about 23 percent, and the portfolio of low-beta stocks (bottom decile by beta) declined by only 17 percent.

Figure 1 shows clearly that, when the market goes down substantially, high-beta stocks take a much larger beating than low-beta stocks. Therefore, if investors are concerned with downside risk, high-beta stocks are indeed more risky than low-beta stocks, and investors should require compensation for this type of risk.

Figure 2 and **Table 1** summarize the monthly estimated slope (compensation per unit of beta) and excess return ($r_m - r_b$) for months when the market went up and months when the market went down. In both the up-market and the down-market subsamples, the estimated slope is close to the slope expected under the CAPM. The results for the down month illustrate once more that, if investors are concerned with downside risk, high-beta stocks are risky.

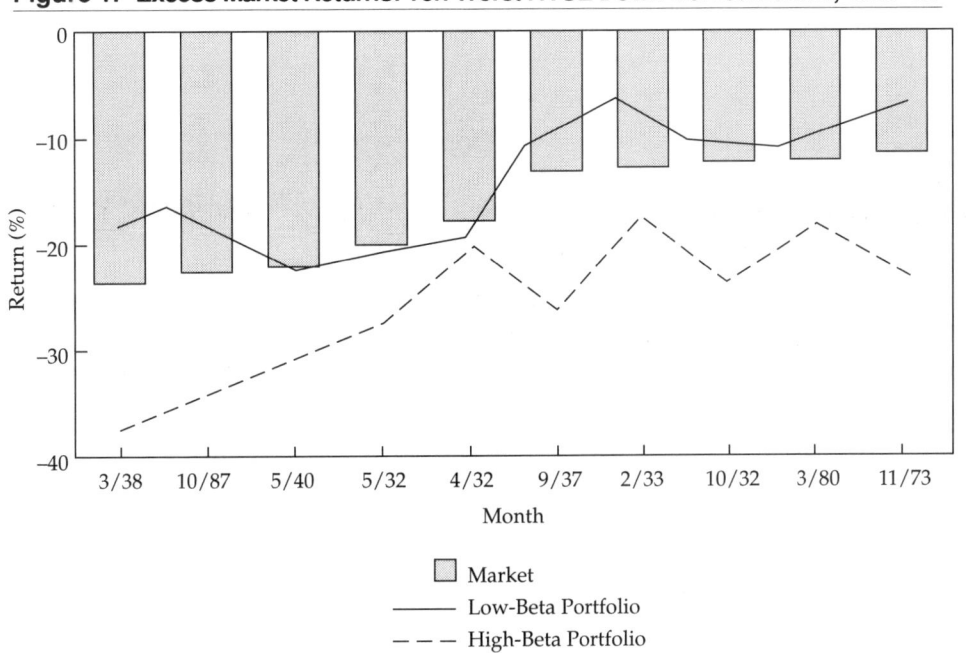

Figure 1. Excess Market Returns: Ten Worst NYSE Down-Market Months, 1926–92

Source: Chan and Lakonishok (1993).

Figure 2. Estimated Slope and Excess Return on Market for All Up and Down Markets, 1932–91

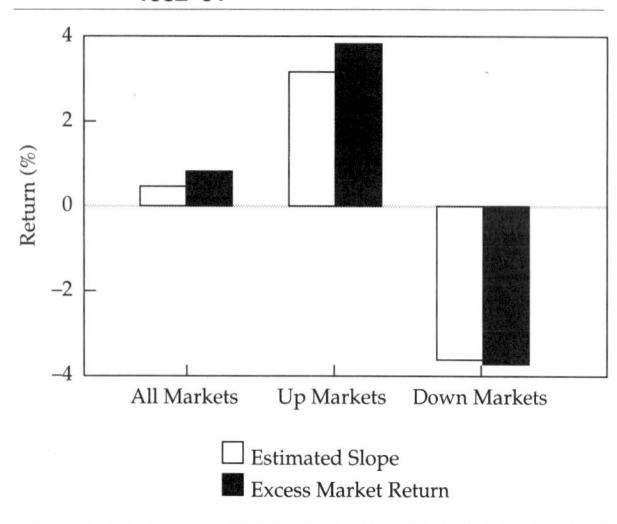

[Bar chart showing Return (%) for All Markets, Up Markets, and Down Markets, comparing Estimated Slope (white) and Excess Market Return (black). All Markets: ~0.5 and ~0.8; Up Markets: ~3.2 and ~3.8; Down Markets: ~-3.6 and ~-3.8.]

Source: Chan and Lakonishok (1993).

The Effects of Indexation

The discussion thus far indicates that burying beta might be premature. If we focus on the point estimates, all the existing evidence suggests that the estimated risk premium is smaller than predicted by the CAPM but positive. Of course, beta may be a poor measure of risk, and better risk measures may be uncovered. An alternative explanation, one that makes much more sense to me, is that behavioral and

Table 1. Estimated Difference in Return between High-Beta and Low-Beta Stocks, 1932–91

Return	All Markets	Up Markets	Down Markets
Realized	0.47%	3.21%	–3.55%
Theoretical	0.76	3.88	–3.81

Source: Chan and Lakonishok (1993).

institutional factors that are unrelated to risk play a major role in generating stock returns, thereby confounding the relationship between risk and return.

Indexation is an example of an institutional factor that may have substantially weakened the relationship between risk and return. Indexation became popular in the 1980s; prior to that time, it was virtually nonexistent. We examined whether stocks in the S&P 500 Index generated extra returns from 1977 to 1991 simply because they are part of this exclusive club. To isolate the S&P 500 effect, we adjusted for all possible differences between S&P 500 stocks and non-S&P 500 stocks—differences in market-capitalization, beta, industries, and book-to-market values. We began in 1977 because Compustat provides information on whether a company be-longs to the S&P 500 Index only since then.

The results are presented in **Table 2**. Each number indicates the extra return in a given year, after adjusting for everything else, associated with a company being part of the S&P 500 Index. For this 15-year period, the average annual extra return to a company in the index was 2.19 percent ($t = 2.33$). The premium for membership in the index is impressive—almost half of the average annualized excess return (5.77 percent) during this period. If we had started in 1980, when indexation really began to catch on, the average extra return would be even more striking—3.03 percent ($t = 3.90$). This extra return is probably totally unrelated to anything other than an extra demand for S&P 500 stocks. This effect is just one example of how institutional and behavioral factors are important in driving stock prices.[2]

Table 2. The S&P 500 Index Effect on Stock Returns, 1977–91

Year	Excess Return on S&P 500 Membership
1977	–3.99%
1978	–4.85
1979	5.33
1980	2.39
1981	3.17
1982	6.94
1983	1.58
1984	4.69
1985	–0.08
1986	2.21
1987	5.92
1988	3.45
1989	4.87
1990	–2.94
1991	4.15
Average	2.19
t-statistic	2.33

Source: Chan and Lakonishok (1993).

Conclusion

Based on available data, no clear-cut evidence supports the interrment of beta. Fama and French probably went too far when they said no relationship exists between beta and returns. Unfortunately, such unqualified conclusions cannot be drawn from the data at hand. For example, even if the CAPM worked "perfectly" with data from the past 20 years, we still would not be able to reject the null hypothesis that betas and returns are unrelated. Moreover, after continuing to accept beta for 20 years without solid empirical support, it would be ironic to discard it now that the move toward portfolio optimization is gaining speed and beta is emerging as an important risk measure.

---

[2] For a thorough discussion of this topic, see Lakonishok, Shleifer, and Vishay (1992, 1993).

Question and Answer Session

Josef Lakonishok

Question: In defense of Fama and French, is it possible that beta is important but these other factors are more important?

Lakonishok: First of all, I would like to point out that the Fama and French 1992 paper is superb and that the debate the paper has generated is a tribute to this work. Second, the market factor is without any doubt an extremely important factor. To sort out what factors are priced in the market is probably an impossible task. Fama and French's results are really not so different from results in other studies. In their Table 3, when beta is the only explanatory variable, they estimate that the compensation per unit of beta is 0.22 percent a month, or about 3 percent a year. Is 3 percent so different from the 4–6 percent that was obtained in quite a few other studies?

Question: What is your response to the notion that a high book-to-market ratio is a proxy for financial distress?

Lakonishok: Without any doubt, high book-to-market stocks are on average more financially distressed than low book-to-market stocks. The question that one should ask, however, is whether a portfolio of high book-to-market stocks is riskier than a portfolio of low book-to-market stocks. This issue is thoroughly examined in Lakonishok, Shleifer, and Vishay (1993). We found absolutely no evidence that a portfolio of high book-to-market stocks is riskier than a portfolio of low book-to-market stocks. For example, high book-to-market stocks underperformed low book-to-market stocks in very few periods. Also, in down markets, high book-to-market stocks outperformed low book-to-market stocks. We think the main reason high book-to-market stocks perform so well is that people extrapolate: High book-to-market stocks are out-of-favor stocks that performed poorly in the past; investors extrapolate from the past and underestimate the future potential of these companies.

Question: In your research, did you notice any cyclicality, such as small-capitalization funds doing well for a while and then large-capitalization funds doing well? Did you notice negative returns to betas followed by positive returns to betas?

Lakonishok: As mentioned in the presentation, even 50 years is a short period from the perspective of statistical significance, and inferences based on much shorter intervals are highly speculative. Such cyclicalities possibly exist. Beta clearly didn't perform well in the past nine years.

Question: Have you done any analysis for 1992?

Lakonishok: No, but I would not change my opinion because of one year. I might not change my opinion for the rest of my academic career.

Question: Might beta be related to the variability of S&P returns over time?

Lakonishok: In extreme up months and extreme down months, the relationship between beta and returns is very tight. When the market does nothing, there is no relationship. On average, the compensation per unit of beta is difficult to sort out; it might be as the model predicts, because 0.47 percent is not very different from 0.76 percent. I doubt that we will ever know the "truth." I would not be so fearful of discarding beta if some alternatives existed, but they don't. Using discount rates based on book value to market value and size is hardly an appealing prospect. Those are anomalies, not risk measures. Fama and French are fond of size, but small-capitalization stocks did nothing in the past nine years. Perhaps a size effect no longer exists. Small-cap stocks were probably neglected for many years, but are they neglected now after the mutual funds have poured billions of dollars into that segment of the market?

Question: To paraphrase your results, beta works well in up and down markets but not in normal periods. Is that correct?

Lakonishok: This result is not a surprise. If the market rises sharply, high-beta stocks will do well; if the market falls sharply, high-beta stocks will do poorly. Whether investors get any compensation for bearing beta-type risk during all the market cycles is not clear, however. The 0.47 percent a month that we obtained is only an estimate. The monthly standard deviation is large, and coming to clear-cut conclusions is impossible.

A Long-plus-Short Market-Neutral Strategy

Bruce I. Jacobs
Principal
Jacobs Levy Equity Management

Kenneth N. Levy, CFA
Principal
Jacobs Levy Equity Management

> Investors who can invest both long and short can benefit from both winners and losers, gaining alpha from both sides. Although the use of short selling is constrained in some institutional portfolios, it offers diversification benefits to portfolios and tends to increase market efficiency. Therefore, long–short strategies deserve serious consideration.

The traditional world of equity investing has focused exclusively on finding stocks to buy long that offer opportunity for appreciation. Over the years, institutional investors have given little thought to incorporating short selling into their equity strategies to capitalize on overvalued stocks. Recently, however, a growing number of investors has begun holding both long and short stock positions in their equity portfolios. Long–short equity investing, more commonly known as market-neutral investing, presents many benefits and opportunities unavailable with traditional methods.

Short selling also has advantages for security markets and society at large. Consider the view expressed by Hoffman (1935) more than half a century ago: "One of the most essential functions of organized markets is to reflect the composite opinion of all competent interests. To admit only opinion looking to higher prices is to provide a one-sided market. To bring together an open expression of both long and short opinion is to provide a two-sided market and . . . a better reflection of prevailing conditions will be shown in the price structure."

When shorts are precluded, according to Sharpe (1990), the result is " . . . a diminution in the efficiency with which risk can be allocated in an economy . . . ," and " . . . overall welfare may be lower."

Long–Short Equity Strategies

Three ways of implementing long–short equity strategies are the market-neutral, equitized, and hedge strategies. The *market-neutral* strategy holds longs and shorts in equal dollar balance at all times. This approach eliminates net equity market exposure, so the returns provided should not be affected by the market's direction. In effect, market risk is immunized. Profits are made from the performance spread between the names held long and the names sold short. These profits are in addition to the interest received on proceeds of the short sales.

The *equitized* strategy, in addition to holding stocks long and short in equal dollar balance, adds an overlay of permanent stock index futures in an amount equal to the invested capital. Thus, the equitized portfolio has a full equity market exposure at all times, and again, profits are made from the long–short spread in addition to the profits or losses resulting from the equity market's rise or fall.

The *hedge* strategy also holds stocks long and short in equal dollar balance but has a variable equity market exposure based on a market outlook. The variable exposure is achieved using stock index futures, and profits are made from the long–short spread. These profits are in addition to the profits or losses attributable to the changing stock index futures position. This approach is similar to typical hedge fund management but is more structured. Hedge funds sell stocks short to hedge their long exposure partially and to benefit from declining stocks. This approach differs from investing the entire capital both long and short to benefit from the full long–short spread and obtaining the desired market exposure through stock index futures.

Equilibrium Models, Short Selling, and Security Prices

The leading equilibrium models, the capital asset pricing model and arbitrage pricing theory (APT), both assume no restrictions on selling stock short. In the real world, however, several impediments to short selling exist.

First, investors have less than full use of the cash proceeds of the short sales. Depending on their clout with the broker, they may or may not receive an interest rebate on the short sales' proceeds. In addition, investors must post cash or securities as collateral for the short positions.

Also, investors may not be able to short certain stocks because the shares are not available for borrowing. The uptick rule, which prohibits shorting a stock when its price is falling, restricts short selling. Finally, institutional investors have concerns about short selling, which will be addressed later, that have caused them to avoid it.

The impact of restricted shorting on market equilibrium depends on whether investors have uniform or divergent opinions about expected security returns. Four cases are shown in **Figure 1.** These cases differ according to whether short selling is unrestricted or restricted and according to whether investor opinion is uniform or diverse.

If all investors have a uniform opinion, they will all hold the market portfolio of all assets. That is, each investor will hold each asset in proportion to its outstanding market value; there will be no short selling, so restricting short selling has no impact. In either case, the market portfolio is efficient, and the CAPM and APT hold.

If investors have diverse opinions and short selling is unrestricted, the market portfolio is efficient and the CAPM and APT hold. Although investors hold unique portfolios, security prices are efficient because arbitrage is unimpeded and security prices reflect the opinions of all investors. If short selling is restricted, however, arbitrage is impeded and the opinion of pessimistic investors is not fully represented. As a consequence, the market portfolio is not efficient and the CAPM and APT do not hold. The real world resembles this last case; investor opinion is indeed diverse, and short selling is restricted.

Miller (1987, 1990) examined the impact of divergence of opinion and restricted shorting on security prices. He showed that restricted shorting leads to security overvaluation because each stock's price is bid up by optimistic investors, while pessimists have difficulty shorting. As a consequence of this overvaluation, a shortfall arises between the returns anticipated by the optimistic investors and what they subsequently receive. Furthermore, the larger the divergence of opinion about a stock, the greater the stock's overvaluation and the eventual disappointment, because the most optimistic investors are the most extreme in their expectations.

An empirical measure of the divergence of opinion about a stock's prospects is the dispersion of security analysts' earnings estimates, often referred to as "earnings controversy." Jacobs and Levy (1988b) found that companies with higher earnings controversies experience lower subsequent returns, which is consistent with Miller's hypothesis.

Miller concluded that overvalued stocks are easier to find than undervalued stocks and that investors should focus their efforts on avoiding holding overvalued stocks in their portfolios. He proposed replacing the standard notion of market efficiency with one of "bounded efficiency." In support of bounded efficiency, Jacobs and Levy (1988a, 1988b) found substantial empirical evidence that the stock market is not fully efficient.

Figure 1. Impact of Divergence of Opinion and Restricted Shorting on Market Equilibrium

	Investor Opinion Uniform	Investor Opinion Diverse
Short Selling Unrestricted	Market Portfolio Efficient CAPM & APT Hold (No one shorts)	Market Portfolio Efficient CAPM & APT Hold
Short Selling Restricted	Market Portfolio Efficient CAPM & APT Hold	Market Portfolio Not Efficient CAPM & APT Do Not Hold

Source: Jacobs Levy Equity Management.

Practical Benefits of Long–Short Investing

Investors who are able to overcome short-selling restrictions and have the flexibility to invest long and short can benefit from both winners and losers. For example, suppose you expect the Yankees to win their game and the Mets to lose theirs. If you wager on baseball, you would certainly not just bet on the Yankees to win. You would also "short" the Mets. The same logic holds for stocks. Why bet on winners only?

Why avail yourself of only half the opportunity?

Another benefit of long–short investing is that, potentially, shorts provide greater opportunities than longs. The search for undervalued stocks is crowded, because most traditional investors look only for undervalued stocks. Because of the various short-selling impediments, relatively few investors search for overvalued stocks.

In addition, security analysts issue far more buy than sell recommendations. Buy recommendations have much more commission-generating power than sells, because all customers are potential buyers but only those customers with the relevant current holdings are potential sellers, and short sellers are few.

Analysts may also be reluctant to express negative opinions. They need open lines of communication with company managers, and in some cases, companies have cut them off and even threatened libel suits over negative opinions. In addition, analysts have been silenced by their own employers to protect their corporate finance business, especially their underwriting relationships. Some analysts have actually been fired for speaking too frankly.

Shorting opportunities may also arise from management fraud, "window-dressing" negative information, or negligence, for which no parallel opportunity exists on the long side. In practice, we have found more opportunity on the short side with our portfolio management systems that capitalize on a large number of market inefficiencies (Jacobs and Levy 1989).

A performance chart is shown in **Figure 2** for equally weighted paper portfolios ranked by predicted returns for the period of our long–short management from June 1990 through December 1992. For this purpose, our universe of 3,000 stocks was ranked from best to worst each month, and then 20 equally weighted portfolios of the top 150 stocks, the next 150 stocks, down to the worst 150 stocks were formed.

The composition of each portfolio was updated monthly, and the points on the chart represent these portfolios' average monthly returns compared with the equally weighted returns of the universe. The point on the far right of Figure 2 represents the superior performance of the portfolio of best liked stocks, which exceeded the universe by about 1.9 percent on average each month. The point on the far left represents the underperformance of the portfolio of worst liked stocks, which lagged by about 2.2 percent on average each month. The chart provides some evidence of enhanced opportunity on the short side. Also, this chart makes apparent the beauty and symmetry of long–short strategies: Profits can be earned simultaneously from winning and losing stocks, thus earning the performance spread.

Portfolio Payoff Patterns

Theoretical portfolio payoff patterns are illustrated in Figures 3 through 7 for separate long and short portfolios (the two building blocks of long–short portfolios), a market-neutral portfolio, an equitized portfolio with a permanent futures overlay, and a hedge portfolio with a variable futures position. In **Figure 3**, a long portfolio's return is graphed against the stock market's return. The market portfolio itself is shown as a 45-degree upward-sloped (dashed) line intersecting the origin. The long portfolio is parallel to the market-portfolio line but higher by the assumed amount of value added, or alpha.

A short portfolio's return is graphed in **Figure 4**.

Figure 2. Average Monthly Relative Performance: Equally Weighted Paper Portfolios Ranked by Predicted Returns, June 1990–December 1992

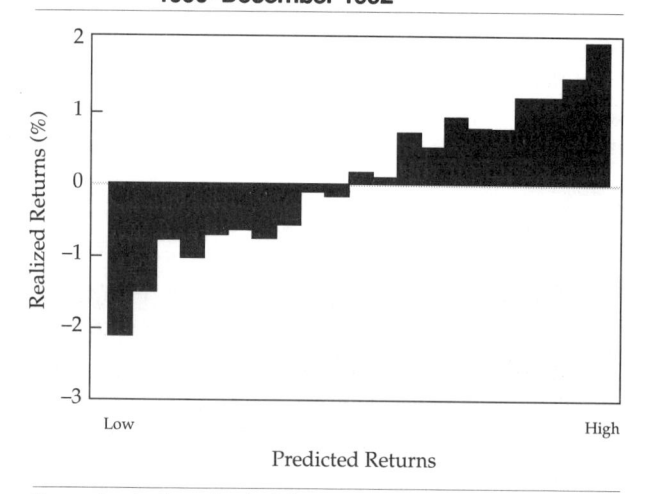

Source: Jacobs Levy Equity Management.

Figure 3. Payoff Pattern: Long Portfolio

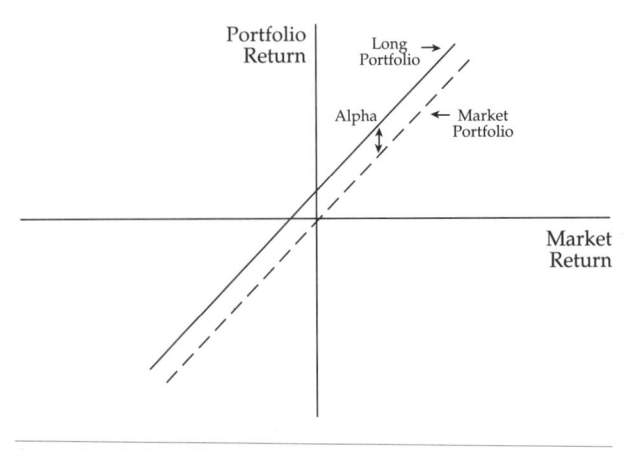

Source: Jacobs Levy Equity Management.

Figure 4. Payoff Pattern: Short Portfolio

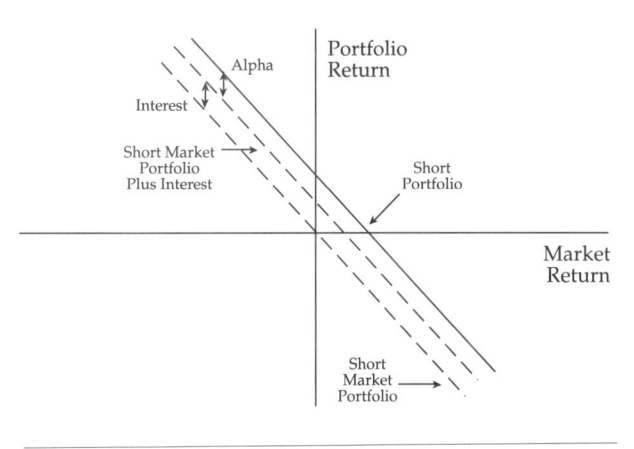

Source: Jacobs Levy Equity Management.

A baseline short market portfolio is a 45-degree downward-sloped (dashed) line intersecting the origin. The short market portfolio plus interest is parallel to the baseline but higher by the amount of interest assumed. The short portfolio is also parallel, but it is higher than the baseline by the sum of interest plus alpha.

A market-neutral portfolio's return, shown in **Figure 5**, is derived from the long and short portfolio payoff patterns shown in Figures 3 and 4. The market-neutral portfolio's payoff line is horizontal at a

Figure 5. Payoff Pattern: Market-Neutral Portfolio

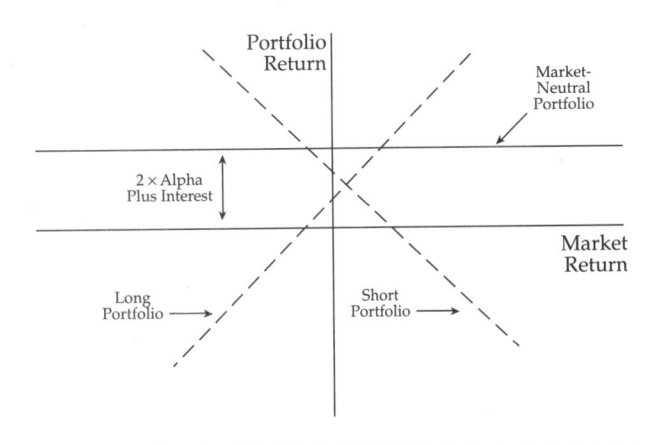

Source: Jacobs Levy Equity Management.

level above the origin by twice the level of alpha plus interest. The implicit assumption is that the full amount of capital is invested both long and short, so alpha is earned from both the long and short sides, providing a "double alpha."

For an equitized portfolio (**Figure 6**), the market portfolio itself is shown as a 45-degree upward-sloped (dashed) line intersecting the origin. The equitized portfolio is parallel to the market-portfolio line but higher by twice alpha. Again, the implicit assumption is that the capital is invested both long and short, so alpha is earned from both the long and short sides.

Figure 6. Payoff Pattern: Equitized Portfolio

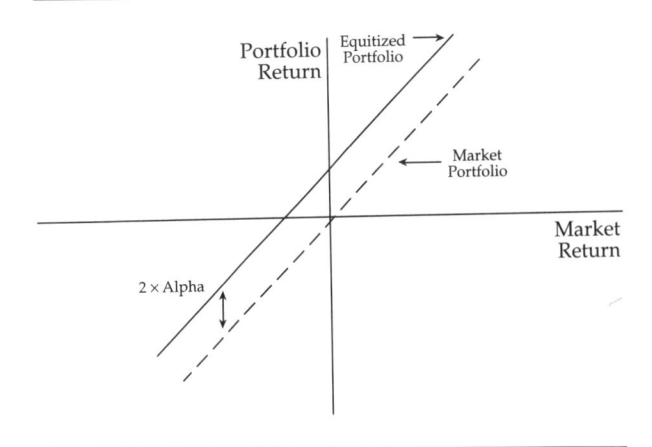

Source: Jacobs Levy Equity Management.

The hedge portfolio illustration (**Figure 7**) assumes perfect market timing. That is, a 100 percent long futures position is established when the

Figure 7. Payoff Pattern: Hedge Portfolio with Perfect Market Timing

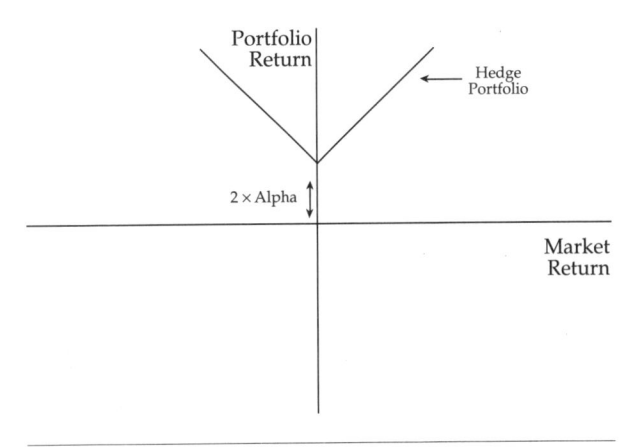

Source: Jacobs Levy Equity Management.

market's return is positive, and a 100 percent short position is established when the market's return is negative. The hedge portfolio line is an upward-sloping 45 degree line in the northeast quadrant intersecting the vertical axis at a height of twice alpha, the mirror image of the line in the northwest quadrant. Again, capital is invested both long and short, so alpha is earned from both the long and short sides.

Market-Neutral Mechanics and Returns

An example of the deployment of capital involved in establishing a $50 million market-neutral account is shown in **Figure 8**.[1] Under Federal Reserve Board regulations, shorts must be housed in a margin account, which requires custody at a brokerage firm. Custodians are referred to as "prime brokers," because they clear all trades and arrange to borrow all stock, irrespective of which brokerage firms execute the trades.

The first step in the deployment of capital is to fund the $50 million account at the prime broker. The actions numbered two through eight occur roughly simultaneously, but they will be discussed sequentially for purposes of exposition.

Typically, 90 percent of the account, or $45 million in this example, is used to purchase attractive securities. These shares are delivered to the prime broker and serve as collateral for the shorts. The prime broker also arranges for the borrowing of the $45 million of unattractive securities that the manager wants to sell short. These shares may come from the broker's inventory of shares held in a street name or may be borrowed from a stock lender. The short sale of these securities results in $45 million of cash proceeds. These proceeds are posted as collateral with the stock lender to provide security for the borrowed shares.

Once these transactions settle, 10 percent of the account, or $5 million, is retained as a liquidity buffer at the prime broker to meet the daily marks to market on the short positions. The collateral posted with the stock lender is also adjusted on a daily basis to reflect the changing value of the shorts. For example, if the shorts rise in price, the mark to market is negative and the lending institution is provided additional capital to remain fully collateralized. If the shorts fall in price, the mark to market is positive and the lending institution releases capital because it is overcollateralized. Also, the short seller must reimburse the stock lender for any dividends paid on the borrowed securities.

Figure 9 illustrates hypothetical performance of a market-neutral strategy in bull- and bear-market scenarios. First consider the bull-market case:

The initial investment of $50 million is deployed as described in the first box. Suppose the S&P 500 return, including dividends, is 30 percent, and assume the long portfolio rises 34 percent, outperforming the market by 4 percent. The result is a $15.3 million gain on the $45 million of long positions. Further assume that the short portfolio, rising 24 percent, underperforms the market by 6 percent. This outcome results in a $10.8 million loss on the short positions. The larger underperformance on the shorts compared with the superior performance on the longs reflects an assumed greater opportunity on the short side. The performance spread of 10 percent

[1] We are indebted to Dennis R. Schwartz of Deere & Company for suggesting and assisting in the development of Figures 8, 9, 11, and 12.

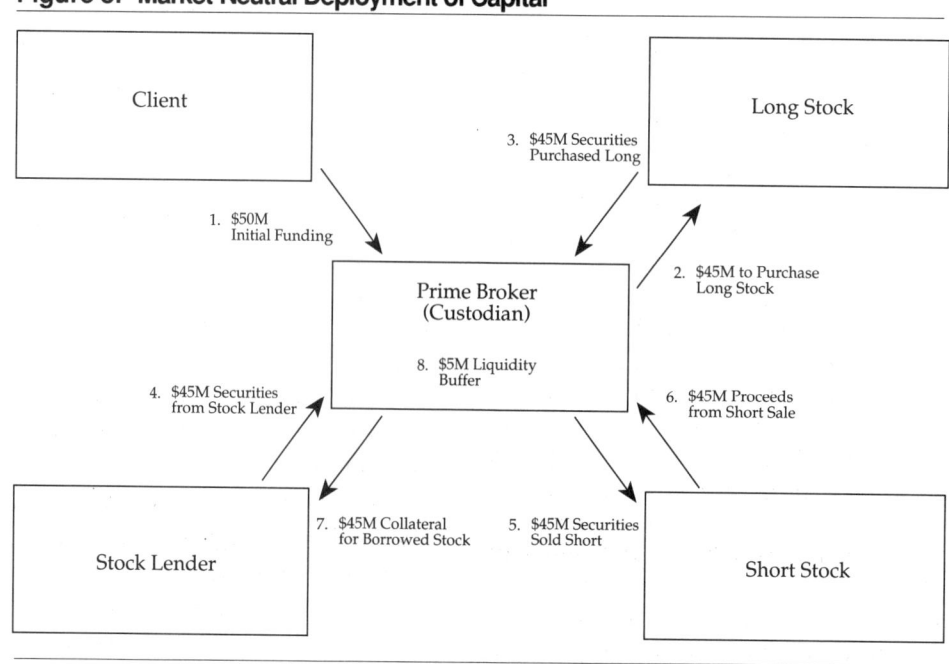

Figure 8. Market-Neutral Deployment of Capital

- Client
- 1. $50M Initial Funding
- 2. $45M to Purchase Long Stock
- 3. $45M Securities Purchased Long
- Long Stock
- Prime Broker (Custodian)
- 8. $5M Liquidity Buffer
- 4. $45M Securities from Stock Lender
- 5. $45M Securities Sold Short
- 6. $45M Proceeds from Short Sale
- 7. $45M Collateral for Borrowed Stock
- Stock Lender
- Short Stock

Source: Jacobs Levy Equity Management.

Figure 9. Market-Neutral Hypothetical Performance: Bull and Bear Markets

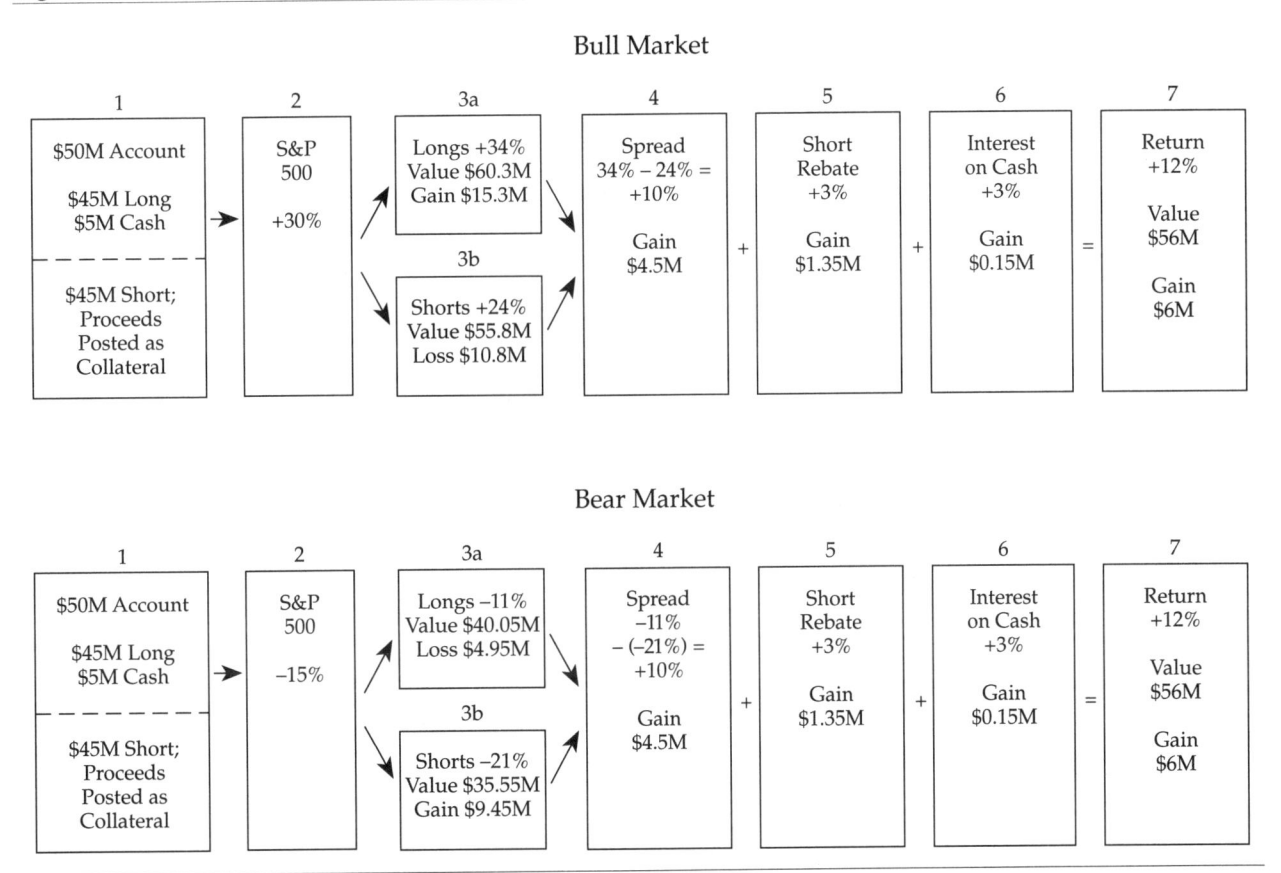

Bull Market

1	2	3a	4	5	6	7
$50M Account $45M Long $5M Cash – – – – – $45M Short; Proceeds Posted as Collateral	S&P 500 +30%	Longs +34% Value $60.3M Gain $15.3M 3b Shorts +24% Value $55.8M Loss $10.8M	Spread 34% − 24% = +10% Gain $4.5M	Short Rebate +3% Gain $1.35M	Interest on Cash +3% Gain $0.15M	Return +12% Value $56M Gain $6M

Bear Market

1	2	3a	4	5	6	7
$50M Account $45M Long $5M Cash – – – – – $45M Short; Proceeds Posted as Collateral	S&P 500 −15%	Longs −11% Value $40.05M Loss $4.95M 3b Shorts −21% Value $35.55M Gain $9.45M	Spread −11% − (−21%) = +10% Gain $4.5M	Short Rebate +3% Gain $1.35M	Interest on Cash +3% Gain $0.15M	Return +12% Value $56M Gain $6M

Source: Jacobs Levy Equity Management.

between the long and short portfolios results in a $4.5 million gain on the $45 million of capital invested both long and short.

The cash proceeds of the short sales, which have been posted as collateral with the securities lender, earn interest. Typically, the lender receives a small portion of this interest as a securities-lending fee, the prime broker retains a portion to cover expenses and provide a profit, and the balance is earned by the investor. The actual split of interest is negotiable. In this illustration, we assume that the short seller receives interest at approximately a T-bill rate—at this time, 3 percent. This interest, or "short rebate," amounts to $1.35 million on the $45 million of short-sale proceeds. In addition, the $5 million of cash retained as a liquidity buffer earns interest—again assumed at a rate of 3 percent—which provides an additional $0.15 million in interest. The total return in this bull market is 12 percent, a gain of $6 million, which has two components: short interest rebate and interest on cash of 3 percent on the full $50 million of capital, and the 10 percent long–short spread on the 90 percent of assets deployed both long and short, which provides an additional 9 percent return on the account.

Now, consider the bear-market case: Suppose the S&P 500 declines 15 percent. As before, assume that the long portfolio outperforms the market by 4 percent and the short portfolio underperforms by 6 percent. The long–short spread remains 10 percent, and the interest earned is 3 percent. The total return on the strategy is thus, again, 12 percent.

The market-neutral strategy produces the same return in the bull and bear markets. The return depends solely on the performance spread between the long and short portfolios and the interest rate received. The return is independent of the market's direction, which is why the strategy is termed "market neutral."

Because the market-neutral strategy produces approximately a T-bill rate of return in the absence of a performance spread between the longs and shorts, an appropriate benchmark for the strategy is the T-bill rate. **Figure 10** is a scatterplot of our live monthly market-neutral returns versus the monthly returns of the S&P 500 Index. As can be seen, the market-neutral strategy lives up to its name: Its returns are uncorrelated with the stock market.

Figure 10. Market-Neutral versus S&P 500 Monthly Returns, June 1990–December 1992

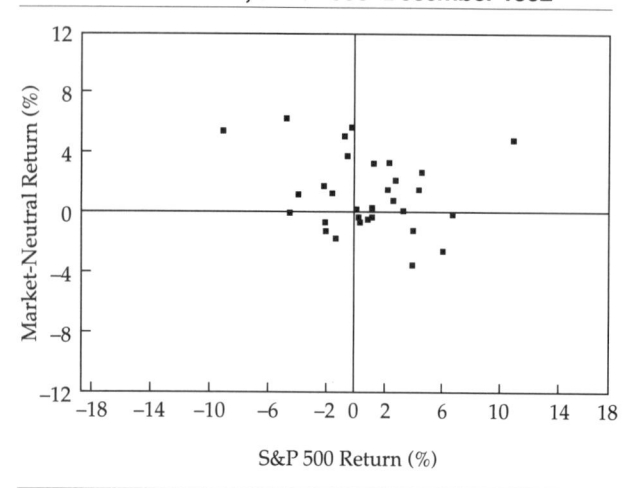

Source: Jacobs Levy Equity Management.

Equitized Mechanics and Returns

An example of the deployment of capital in establishing a $50 million equitized account is shown in **Figure 11**. The deployment is identical to that of the market-neutral strategy except for the stock index futures overlay, shown as step nine. To "equitize" the account, $50 million of S&P 500 futures are purchased. Buying futures does not require an outlay of cash except to post margin. As a margin for the futures, $2 million of T-bills are purchased, which leaves a $3 million liquidity buffer. This buffer is smaller than in the market-neutral case, but it is adequate because the daily marks to market on the long futures tend to offset the daily marks on the short portfolio.

Figure 12 illustrates the hypothetical performance of an equitized strategy in bull and bear markets. The performance is similar to the market-neutral case except for the impact of the futures overlay. S&P 500 futures contracts are priced so that they provide approximately the return of the S&P 500 Index, including dividends, less the cost of carry at about a T-bill rate. The short rebate interest earned on the $45 million of shorts, plus the interest earned on the $2 million of T-bill margin and $3 million of cash, in conjunction with the price change on $50 million of S&P 500 futures, should provide a return similar to $50 million invested in the S&P 500 Index.

In the bull-market case, the 3 percent short rebate plus the 3 percent interest on T-bill margin and cash and the 27 percent price change in futures (as shown in boxes five, six, and seven) provide the 30 percent S&P 500 return. In the bear-market case, the 3 percent interest on capital and the –18 percent price change in futures provide the –15 percent S&P 500 return.

The total return in the bull-market scenario is 39 percent, or 9 percent more than that provided by the S&P 500. The total return in the bear-market scenario is –6 percent, again 9 percent more than the index return. This 9 percent added value is the same as that achieved in the market-neutral strategy. The futures overlay transports the long–short added value to the S&P 500 benchmark. In the same way, bond futures can be used to transport the long–short added value

Figure 11. Equitized Deployment of Capital

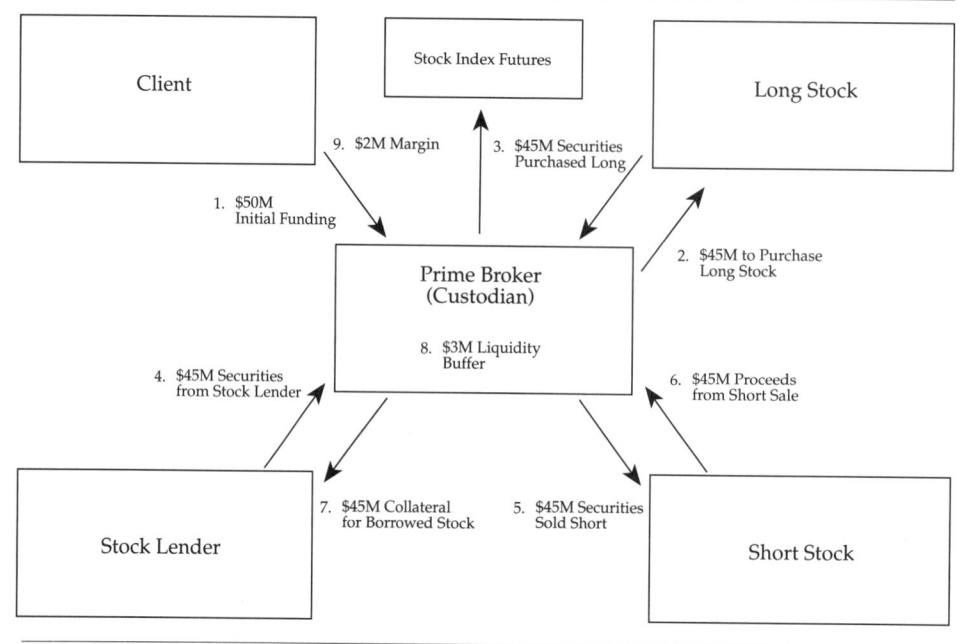

Source: Jacobs Levy Equity Management.

Figure 12. Equitized Hypothetical Performance: Bull and Bear Markets

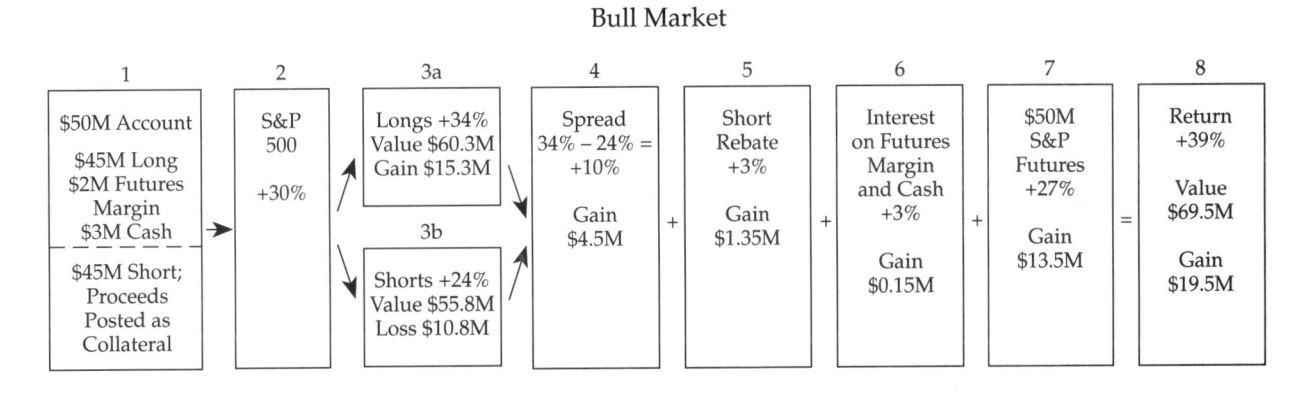

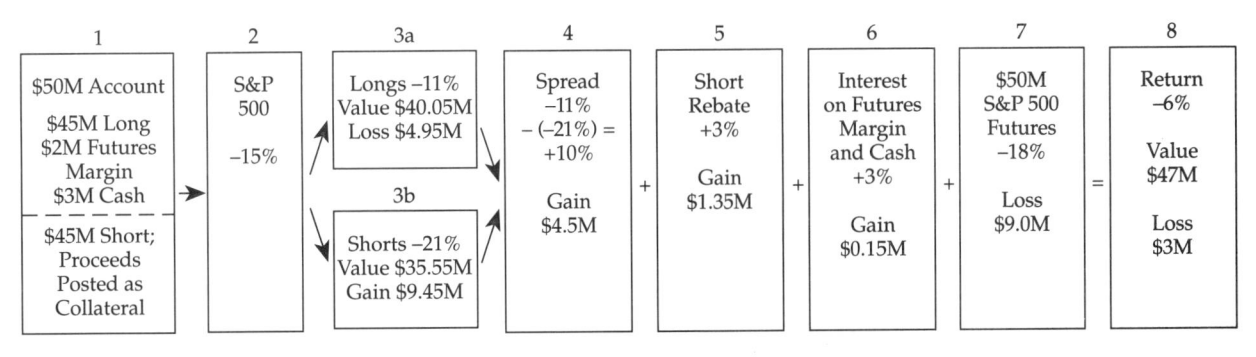

Bull Market

1	2	3a / 3b	4	5	6	7	8
$50M Account $45M Long $2M Futures Margin $3M Cash $45M Short; Proceeds Posted as Collateral	S&P 500 +30%	Longs +34% Value $60.3M Gain $15.3M Shorts +24% Value $55.8M Loss $10.8M	Spread 34% − 24% = +10% Gain $4.5M	Short Rebate +3% Gain $1.35M	Interest on Futures Margin and Cash +3% Gain $0.15M	$50M S&P Futures +27% Gain $13.5M	Return +39% Value $69.5M Gain $19.5M

Bear Market

1	2	3a / 3b	4	5	6	7	8
$50M Account $45M Long $2M Futures Margin $3M Cash $45M Short; Proceeds Posted as Collateral	S&P 500 −15%	Longs −11% Value $40.05M Loss $4.95M Shorts −21% Value $35.55M Gain $9.45M	Spread −11% − (−21%) = +10% Gain $4.5M	Short Rebate +3% Gain $1.35M	Interest on Futures Margin and Cash +3% Gain $0.15M	$50M S&P 500 Futures −18% Loss $9.0M	Return −6% Value $47M Loss $3M

Source: Jacobs Levy Equity Management.

to a bond index, and so forth.

Because the equitized strategy produces approximately a S&P 500 return when no performance spread exists between the longs and shorts, an appropriate benchmark for the strategy is the S&P 500 Index. **Figure 13** is a scatterplot of our live monthly equitized returns versus the monthly returns of the S&P 500 Index. As expected, the strategy's returns are highly correlated with the stock market.

Theoretical Tracking Error

In addition to return considerations, the theoretical tracking errors of long–short portfolios relative to their benchmarks are instructive. Assume the standard deviation of the long portfolio's alpha, or added value, is 4 percent and the short portfolio alpha's standard deviation is also 4 percent. Now, consider two correlations between values added by the long and the short portfolios. First, assume the correlation is zero. In this case, the standard deviation of the market-neutral (or equitized) portfolio's added value is the square root of 2 times 4 percent, or 5.7 percent. Next, assume the correlation of the values added by the long and the short portfolios is 1. In this case, the standard deviation of the market-neutral (or equitized) portfolio's added value is 2 times 4 percent, or 8 percent. A reasonable assumption is that the correlation lies somewhere between zero and

Figure 13. Equitized Portfolio versus S&P 500 Monthly Returns, June 1990–December 1992

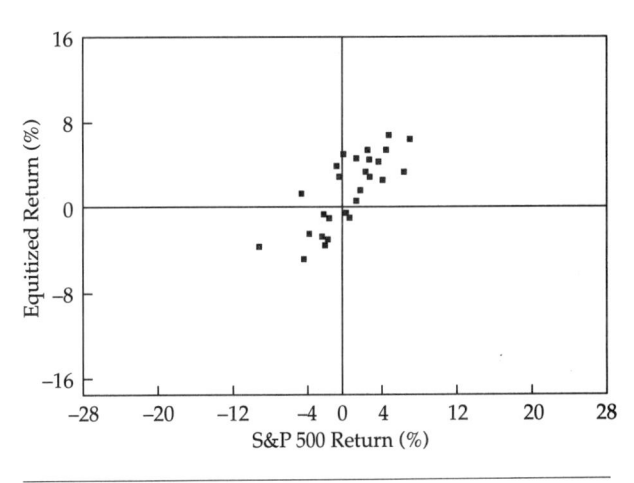

Source: Jacobs Levy Equity Management.

1, in which case the standard deviation of the tracking error will lie between 5.7 percent and 8 percent.

Advantages of Different Strategies

Using a market-neutral strategy rather than separate long and short managers has several advantages. The market-neutral strategy coordinates the names held long and short to maximize profits while controlling risk. It avoids the situation in which one manager is long a stock while the other manager is short the same stock, which wastes assets. It also precludes excessive risks arising when one manager is, for example, buying oil stocks while the other is shorting airlines, which magnifies the oil price risk.

A market-neutral strategy also enables the capital to work twice as hard as with separate long and short managers. Each dollar of capital is invested both long and short, with the longs collateralizing the shorts. With separate long and short managers and $1 of capital, each would have only 50 cents of capital to invest.

In addition, a single manager fee is likely to be more economical than fees for two managers, especially in a performance-fee setting. A market-neutral manager would earn a performance fee only if the entire strategy added value. With separate managers, if either is ahead, an incentive fee must be paid, even if the combined strategy is behind.

The equitized strategy has several advantages over traditional long equity management. It can profit from winners and losers. Why tear the *Wall Street Journal* in half and focus solely on good-news stories? Bad news presents potentially greater opportunity. Also, investment insights can be levered without any borrowing, which results in a double alpha. Of course, the key to good performance is good insight.

The flexibility afforded by having longs and shorts in a portfolio increases one's latitude in implementing investment ideas. Thus, investment insights are more likely to be productive and to produce more profits than when the range of implementation is limited. An important consideration is that overvalued companies and industries may be underweighted without the usual constraints associated with long equity management. For example, the automobile industry today is 2 percent of the capitalization weight of the S&P 500 Index. A traditional long manager who is bullish on automobiles can overweight the industry as much as desired but can underweight the industry by no more than 2 percent. By shorting, when bearish, the manager may underweight companies and industries beyond the usual constraints. The portfolio manager's flexibility to overweight and underweight becomes symmetrical.

Managers who invest long and short can focus solely on market sectors in which the most significant misvaluations exist and ignore the fairly priced sectors without incurring any risk. For example, if all health care stocks are fairly priced, there is no need for, nor any potential benefit in, holding any, long or short. Assets are not wasted on these fairly priced stocks. The full market exposure to health care stocks can be obtained with the futures overlay. A traditional long manager, however, would probably include some fairly priced, or even overpriced, health care stocks in the portfolio to avoid a substantial industry underweight. By holding some stocks in the health care sector, the long manager simply reduces risk; there are no perceived profit opportunities.

In addition, managers investing long and short can target desired bets and reduce incidental bets better than traditional long managers. For example, a traditional long manager emphasizing low-P/E stocks will wind up with incidental bets on related attributes, such as high dividend yield, and on low-P/E industries, such as utilities. In a long–short portfolio, however, related attributes and industries can be effectively neutralized, which allows a "pure" low-P/E bet without incidental biases.

Implementation of Long–Short Strategies

Any active equity management style can be implemented in a long–short mode. To date, however, most long–short managers have been quantitative rather than judgmental in their investment approaches. Quantitative models can generally be applied to a large universe of stocks, which promotes the identification of a large long–short spread. Shorts naturally fall out of a quantitative process as the lowest ranked stocks. Quantitative styles are also amenable to simulation and back-testing, the results of which are helpful in developing and marketing a novel investment approach. Moreover, most quantitative managers use structured portfolio-construction methods, which are important in order to control risk taking in a long–short portfolio.

In contrast, judgmental approaches generally rely on in-depth company analyses, but of a limited universe of stocks, which restricts the range of opportunities and potentially reduces the performance spread. Also, traditional security analysts are generally not accustomed to recommending stocks to sell short. Judgmental analysis should help, however, in detecting fraud, negligence, and financial window dressing, which can provide exceptional short-sale opportunities.

Long–short managers use a few primary portfolio-construction techniques to control risk. Simplest to implement is "pairs trading," which identifies mispriced pairs of stocks with returns that are likely to be highly correlated. For example, if Ford Motor Company and General Motors Corporation stock are identified as mispriced relative to each other, the underpriced stock can be bought and the overpriced stock sold short.

Some managers neutralize industry exposures by investing the same percentage of capital both long and short within each industry. A few even restrict their attention to a single industry that they know well. Others neutralize industries and common factors such as beta or average company size. Some managers coordinate long and short portfolio characteristics statistically to control risk taking but are not necessarily neutral toward characteristic or industry; hence, the term "statistical arbitrage" is applied to their strategy.

Practical Issues and Concerns

A long–short strategy gives rise to a variety of issues not encountered in traditional long management—issues relating to shorting, trading, custody, legality, and morality.

Shorting Issues

Investors sometimes ask whether short selling is an appropriate activity for those with long-term horizons. Dedicated short managers must fight an uphill battle because of the stock market's long-term upward trend. They are short the equity risk premium that the market provides for bearing equity risk. Market-neutral strategies, having no net exposure to the market, neither pay nor earn the equity risk premium. Equitized strategies are fully exposed to the market and, similarly to traditional long investing, earn the equity risk premium. Hedge strategies are opportunistic with respect to the equity risk premium. Thus, short selling can be incorporated as part of a long-term equity program to meet different investment objectives.

Another concern is that a rising market can force the covering of shorts as losses mount. Those who engage solely in short selling without offsetting long positions can indeed find themselves forced to cover as the general market rises and their shorts go against them. In a long–short approach, however, as the market rises, the losses on the shorts are offset by gains on the longs.

Another common concern regards the unlimited liability of a short position. Although one cannot lose more than the original capital invested in a long position, the potential loss on a short position is, in theory, unlimited because the price of a stock can rise without bound. Long–short managers generally mitigate this risk by holding widely diversified portfolios with many stocks and small positions in each and by covering their shorts as position sizes increase.

Another question often asked is whether the market can accommodate the growing volume of shorting. This is an issue of market depth. The current market capitalization of the U.S. stock market is approximately $4.4 trillion. The current volume of short open interest is approximately $45 billion, or about 1 percent of the market capitalization of stocks held long. The amount of shorts outstanding thus remains small relative to the depth of the stock market.

Not all stocks can be borrowed easily, and brokers maintain a list of "hard-to-borrow" names. The lack of supply on these names is generally not an impediment for quantitative managers because they can select from a broad universe of stocks and have the flexibility to substitute other stocks with similar characteristics. Hard-to-borrow names can be a serious problem for dedicated short sellers, however. They often specialize in illiquid names and make concentrated bets, such as on fraud situations, for which no near substitutes exist.

Shorting a name that is hard to borrow runs the risk of being forced to cover the short if the lender demands the return of the security. This situation can occur if the lender simply decides to sell the security, for example, and so needs it back. If the prime broker cannot locate an alternative lender, the result is a "buy-in," or forced cover. Our experience is that buy-ins are rare, especially for typical institutional-quality stocks.

A "short squeeze" is a deliberate attempt by some investors to squeeze the short seller by reducing the lendable supply of a stock while simultaneously pushing the stock's price up through purchases. A successful short squeeze can force the short seller to cover at inflated prices. This problem is more a concern for dedicated short sellers than for long–short managers, because the latter generally have many small positions and focus on larger institutional names for which stock lending and share price are difficult to manipulate.

Trading Issues

Managing long–short strategies entails some special trading considerations. SEC Rule 10a-1, adopted in 1938, requires that exchange-listed securities be sold short only on an uptick (higher price than the last trade) or a zero-plus tick (same price as the last trade but higher than the last trade at a different price). We find that the uptick rule need not be restrictive, especially for those with patient trading styles.

Also, managing two interrelated portfolios requires substantial care in execution and rebalancing to maintain long–short dollar balances. Controlling transaction costs is especially important because turnover runs about twice that of traditional long management. Some new electronic trading systems are especially conducive to long–short management; they are inexpensive and allow simultaneous execution of large programs with dollar trading constraints to maintain the long–short balance.

Custody Issues

The Federal Reserve regulations that require short selling in a margin account necessitate custody at a prime broker. Because assets are custodied away from the master trust bank, safety and soundness issues must be addressed and due diligence is required.

Also, although some master trustees can account for shorts and maintain a set of books at this time, others cannot. Even when a master trustee can account for shorts, some plan sponsors rely on a reconciliation of the prime broker's accounting records with the manager's to avoid paying the master trustee for a triplicate set of books.

Legal Issues

Long–short management gives rise to two fundamental legal issues. One is whether these strategies are prudent for ERISA plans, public-employee retirement systems, endowments, and foundations. Several institutional investors have concluded that these strategies are prudent and do diversify risk for the overall plan.

The other issue is whether shorting gives rise to unrelated-business taxable income (UBTI). In 1988, the Internal Revenue Service (IRS) issued a private letter exempting long–short strategies used by one large institutional investor from UBTI.[2] In 1992, the IRS approved regulations specifically exempting swaps, for which the tax issues are similar. The IRS has not commented any further, despite the growing use of long–short and hedge strategies by tax-exempt investors. Nonetheless, this issue is not settled, and tax counsel should be consulted.

Morality Issues

The use of shorting raises moral issues for some investors. Although selling something that one does not own may appear to be immoral, it is common commercial practice. Farmers sell wheat before it is grown, and home builders sell houses before they are built.

Some fear that short selling destabilizes security prices. Although this effect might have been possible prior to the uptick rule and SEC oversight, today most agree that short selling stabilizes prices by checking speculative bubbles, equilibrating day-to-day supply and demand, and increasing liquidity.

Others charge that short selling depresses prices. During the collapse of the Dutch East India Company stock bubble in the year 1610, some claimed that short selling hurt "widows and orphans." Because shorting allows countervailing negative opinion to balance positive opinion, however, prices in the presence of short selling can reflect the consensus of all investors, which provides a better indication of value than if negative opinions are ignored.

Short sellers are often accused of rumormongering. Although dedicated short sellers are sometimes alleged to spread unsubstantiated rumors about their target companies, long–short managers are not adversarial. They go long and short various stocks to exploit subtle mispricings, not because they want or expect a particular company to go bankrupt.

Some have suggested that short selling is anti-management or anti-American, but shorting actually promotes all-American values by checking management abuses, improving market efficiency, and raising social welfare.

What Asset Classes Are Long–Short Strategies?

Using risk-and-reward comparisons, one can categorize the long–short strategies by asset class so that their fit in an overall investment program becomes apparent.

Figure 14 shows experienced risk, measured by annualized standard deviation, and annualized return for our market-neutral, equitized, and hedge strategies and their respective benchmarks from the inception of live performance in June 1990 through December 1992. The market-neutral strategy added substantial value over T-bills, and its risk was between that of T-bills and the S&P 500. The equitized strategy added roughly the same value versus the S&P 500 as the market-neutral strategy did versus T-bills. The stock index futures overlay transported the long–short spread to the stock market. The equitized strategy had about the same risk as the S&P 500. The hedge strategy was between the market-neutral and equitized strategies in terms of risk and reward.

The market-neutral strategy has an absolute return objective, because its returns are not correlated

---

[2] IRS private letter ruling 8832052 to The Common Fund, May 18, 1988.

Figure 14. Risk–Return Comparisons: Long–Short Strategies versus Benchmarks, June 1990–December 1992

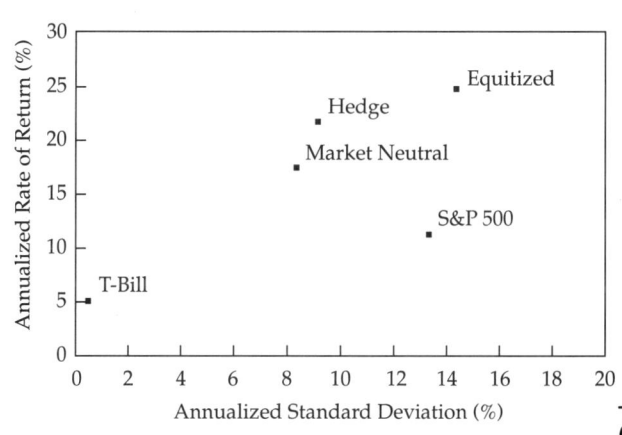

[Scatter plot: Annualized Rate of Return (%) vs Annualized Standard Deviation (%). Points: T-Bill (~0, 5), Market Neutral (~9, 17), Hedge (~9, 22), S&P 500 (~13, 11), Equitized (~14, 25).]

Source: Jacobs Levy Equity Management.

Note: Live hedge returns commence October 1991.

with those of the stock market. It has about half the volatility of the market and is obviously riskier than cash. We categorize the market-neutral strategy as an "alternative equity."

The equitized strategy has a relative return objective because its returns are highly correlated with those of the stock market. Although it has about the same volatility as the market, its tracking error will generally be higher than that of traditional long strategies. We categorize the equitized strategy as "flexible equity," because it allows more flexible portfolio management than traditional long investing.

The hedge strategy can arguably be assigned an absolute or a relative return objective because its returns are somewhat correlated with those of the stock market. Its volatility is between that of the market-neutral and equitized strategies. We categorize hedge as an "alternative equity."

Conclusion

The institutional acceptance of long–short strategies is increasing rapidly (White 1991 and Williams 1991). Current estimates of long–short assets under management in U.S. equities range from $3 billion to $5 billion. Long–short strategies merit serious consideration as part of an overall investment program.

Question and Answer Session

Bruce I. Jacobs
Kenneth N. Levy, CFA

Question: Why do you use futures in the equitized long–short strategy instead of holding a larger long position and a smaller short one?

Jacobs: The beauty of the long–short strategies is that they can earn a double alpha. If an investor wants equity market exposure, that can be achieved with derivatives while the investor is fully levered both long and short to earn the full double alpha. The manager of a more traditional hedge fund may hold 100 percent of the portfolio long and 40 percent short, thereby having a net 60 percent exposure to the market. That manager is giving up the opportunity to earn a full alpha on the short side of the market, however, because the strategy is only 40 percent rather than 100 percent short.

Question: In the short strategy, do you deduct from returns the dividends paid to the security lender?

Jacobs: Yes. On traditional long positions, dividends are received. On shorts, dividends are paid out. In long–short strategies, the dividends have to be accounted for on both sides. Unless the portfolio has a yield tilt, the long and short dividends will wash out.

Question: Have you added liquidity, borrowing constraints, uptick requirements, and so forth on top of your anomaly results? If so, what have you found out about the relationship?

Levy: We have added those factors, and we found out a lot. For example, an important question is whether the extent to which a stock has been borrowed and sold short previously has any correlation with subsequent return. One hypothesis says that a large existing short interest in a stock represents potential pent-up buying pressure; that stock will subsequently outperform the market as those shorts are forced to cover at some point. The alternative hypothesis is that, because of all the constraints and difficulties short selling involves, the short interest is generally smarter money than the long money, in which case a stock with a large short interest would subsequently underperform the market. We found no support for the first hypothesis but some support for the second, namely, that stocks with a large short interest subsequently underperform somewhat, which is consistent with smarter money.

Question: You apparently switched from 2 percent alphas in your earlier discussion to 4 percent alphas on longs and 6 percent alphas on shorts in your market-neutral example. What happens to market-neutral returns when the alphas are reduced to the 2 percent level noted earlier?

Jacobs: The 2 percent alphas shown in Figure 2 are average monthly alphas for the 150 best stocks represented by the rightmost bar and 150 worst stocks by the leftmost bar. In practice, however, those alphas are not fully obtainable. Our relative return chart, derived by reranking all the names in our universe monthly, illustrates the ability of our system to discriminate among stocks and also shows the power of exploiting the long and short sides simultaneously. Implicit in this chart, however, is monthly turnover that may reach 100 percent round trip, an equal weighting of stocks that may not be possible or desirable, and an acceptance of possibly concentrated bets that may be present in the right- and leftmost bars. Once optimal portfolios are structured to take into account turnover costs, illiquidity, and risk taking, the retrievable return will be much less than 2 percent monthly per side. We assumed in Figures 9 and 12, for illustrative purposes, an annual alpha of 4 percent on the long side and 6 percent on the short side. This 10 percent spread between longs and shorts is in keeping with our actual annualized performance, and here we are assuming more opportunity on the short side. Using these alpha assumptions, we show how the added values flow through to achieve market-neutral and equitized results.

Question: What are the risks of a market-neutral strategy?

Levy: Risk depends on the implementation; different management styles give rise to different risks. Our experience has been about an 8 percent annual standard deviation for our market-neutral approach.

Question: What criteria were used to generate the return expectations for the 3,000 stocks in your universe?

Jacobs: We used our own proprietary model. (For the conceptual foundation of our approach, see Jacobs and Levy 1988a, 1988b.)

Question: Have you lowered your expected return estimates based on the recent decline in short rates?

Levy: The market-neutral approach provides a return from two sources: short-term interest rates and the long–short spread. Interest rates are beyond our control. Our objective is to add a positive long–short spread over contemporaneous short-term interest rates. In an era of lower short-term rates, the total absolute return on market-neutral strategies will be lower because the interest rate component of return is lower. There is no reason, however, to expect the excess return above the contemporaneous short rates to differ.

Question: What are the pros and cons of using beta to measure market neutrality?

Levy: Beta is only one potential measure of both risk and opportunity in the marketplace. Risk is multidimensional, and beta is a rather narrow construct. Although it has some theoretical appeal, it does not have much practical usefulness.

Question: Generally, do market anomalies that create shorting opportunities arise from factors or considerations that are different from those that create buying opportunities?

Levy: The answer is often yes. Many effects in the market are not symmetrical. Certain opportunities are present only on the short side of the market. If the characteristics of the short portfolio are a mirror image of those of the long portfolio, the opportunity for a double alpha is created at the cost of doubling the level of risk—the case in which the long and short value-added amounts have a correlation of 1. Making different bets in the long and short portfolios lowers the correlation and improves the ratio of reward to risk. Even more important to exploit the opportunities at hand fully is that if the opportunities are asymmetrical, the bets should be also.

Question: Please comment on the reversal effect (residual return reversal) popularized some time ago. Is it still there on either the short or the long side, or has it been arbitraged away?

Levy: The reversal effect was a well-researched anomaly, and a lot of money went into exploiting it. Much of the money that went into playing return reversal was traditional long money. Those investors would look for stocks that had dropped more than would be justified by news events and anticipate a small bounce back to fair value. They would buy the stock to capture part of that return reversal.

As more money went into this strategy in the mid- to late 1980s, stocks that dropped did not drop as much as before, because more investors were rushing in to buy them. Later, those investors had to get out of that name and move on to the next reversal situation. They would all get out at the same time, which resulted in another down leg, and return reversal became treacherous to play on the long side of the market.

Much less emphasis was placed on return reversal as a short-selling model, simply because few people sell short, so the opportunity on the short side did not diminish as much. That is one example of an asymmetrical opportunity in the market.

Question: What are the advantages or disadvantages of using a long–short strategy as opposed to a strategy of buying equal amounts of put and call options to obtain full exposure and investing the cash in T-bills?

Levy: You must be assuming the investor would be adding alpha through the put and call options similar to the alpha that would be added by owning the underlying securities. The options markets have less liquidity than the equity markets; options are not available on all stocks, and options have fixed expirations. If you can identify over- and undervalued securities, however, you can go long and short derivatives rather than the securities themselves. It will work if you can establish for any position that is held long or short a similar position in the options market.

Global Investment in a CAPM Framework

Denis S. Karnosky
Managing Partner
Brinson Partners, Inc.

> Increased globalization broadens the definition of the market for all investors. In theory, global integration of markets should reduce risk premiums. Portfolio globalization is efficient in terms of risk–reward opportunities, but attractive transient returns may be available in those markets that are still segmented.

The capital asset pricing model comes under frequent criticism for its apparent failure to produce reliable forecasts of near-term market conditions. Some practitioners and quantitative analysts, taking a very pragmatic approach to judging the merit of any theory, ask: If it cannot forecast market prices, what good is it? That criticism of the CAPM, however, is off the mark. Like all theories of behavior, the CAPM attempts to explain relationships among variables rather than to forecast the pattern of a variable over time. It is a framework that attempts to define the equilibrium conditions that dominate asset pricing. As such, it provides the foundation for development of models that generate expected future asset prices and returns. The CAPM itself is not such a model, however. The CAPM has never claimed to be able to forecast expected returns. It is not a trading mechanism, and it does not indicate how to manage a portfolio actively.

Comparing the CAPM with an alternative, such as arbitrage pricing theory (APT), on the basis of relative ability to replicate historical data or ability to forecast market prices is a fundamentally flawed exercise. The CAPM and APT are not alternatives; they have nothing in common other than the fact that they both involve relationships that have asset returns to the left of the equal sign. The APT attempts to explain current market conditions, while the CAPM is concerned with the fundamental relationships that underlie markets. They should be judged accordingly.

The CAPM should thus be judged on the merit of the insight it can provide in the analysis of asset markets. Discrediting the theory on the basis of failed forecasts would leave a large void in our ability to comprehend the basic structure of markets and their equilibrium conditions.

The recent shift to analysis of portfolios in a global context is an excellent example of the power of the CAPM in providing a coherent framework for analysis of multiple markets and currencies within an integrated portfolio. The CAPM implies, for example, that globalization of investment portfolios is an equilibrating process reflecting the distortions in asset pricing that offer attractive rewards in relation to risks. The following analysis uses historical data to illustrate the manner in which the CAPM can be applied to the analysis of global markets. While the historical data can only be suggestive of underlying structure, this approach is a convenient way to illustrate the analytical process. The development of working estimates of equilibrium risk premiums would require a more thorough treatment.

What Is the CAPM?

The CAPM is an analytical framework, an equilibrium paradigm. It provides a foundation for evaluating investment issues. It does not describe a market or security at any moment in time or across periods of time. It simply specifies an equilibrium condition:

$$R_i - C = \beta_{i,m}(R_m - C).$$

"Beta" relates an asset's return (R_i) in excess of cash (C) to the return of "the market" (R_m) relative to cash in equilibrium. There is no "alpha" or "epsilon," and the relationship is not amenable to estimation through regression analysis. Because asset market

---

Note: The author acknowledges Brian D. Singer, CFA, of Brinson Partners for his contribution to this presentation.

prices can deviate from equilibrium, the CAPM seeks to explain the equilibrium state to which markets converge. It is a general relationship, applicable to all assets.

In practice, however, beta has become effectively an equity concept and the "market" has typically been narrowed to specific universes, such as large- or small-cap stocks or broad equity indexes like the Wilshire 5000 or Russell 3000. (Bond analysis, on the other hand, tends to concentrate on duration as the quantifiable measure of risk within the market. From both the analytical and the equilibrium perspective, however, the notion of a bond beta is a viable and meaningful concept.)

Treating beta as an equity concept introduces another danger into the application of the CAPM to portfolio analysis: treating a portfolio as a collection of distinct assets rather than as an integrated total. For an investor whose portfolio consists of equities only, some index of stocks might be appropriate as a benchmark. The same would be true of a bond investor, who could focus on a bond index as the representative alternative. In neither case, however, are risk premiums that might be derived relative to these benchmarks accurate estimates of the equilibrium risk premiums. The relevant market for equilibrium analysis is more broadly defined. Invoking separation theorems and applying a CAPM framework to each of the component markets of the portfolio necessarily ignores intermarket relationships and gives a distorted view of the risk–return properties of the total portfolio. As will be seen later in considering global markets, such an adding-up approach to portfolio analysis implies a degree of market segmentation that is inappropriate for an individual investor.

In reality, the CAPM requires that investors define the market as broadly as possible rather than focus on the market segments. The complexities of covariance most often mean that understanding of the pieces does not imply understanding of the total. The situation is similar to that of economists in the late 1960s as they adopted newly available computer technology. As computing facilities became readily available, economists were better able to estimate equations, and by the early 1970s, the object was to have the macroeconomic model with the most equations. The idea was that if they could explain more of the pieces of the economy, they would have a better understanding of the total. Unfortunately, the total has seldom been the sum of the parts; high explanatory power in individual equations has not been translated to meaningful understanding of macroeconomic conditions.

Global Investing Using the CAPM

The CAPM is a particularly useful tool in global analysis; it provides a consistent framework for evaluating diverse markets and multiple currencies within a single portfolio. As always, the key consideration is the definition of "the market." Although barriers to international capital flows have been coming down, many asset markets have been segmented by national borders. These restrictions on capital inflows and outflows tend to create conditions whereby individual country markets are dominated by local investors. Such segmentation implies opportunity, however, which encourages outside investors to seek means to weaken or circumvent the barriers. That pressure is an equilibrating process moving global markets toward integration. The degree of global integration will define the relevant market, in CAPM terms, for the investors in each country. The implications of applying the CAPM to global analysis can be illustrated by considering global markets within the context of increasing degrees of integration, starting with a condition of total segmentation.

Segmented/Segmented Markets

Before the CAPM, financial analysis assumed that segmentation prevailed both across and within national markets. In such a segmented/segmented structure, each market is distinct and independent of all other markets. Bond markets are evaluated independently of stock markets, and in the extreme, stocks are evaluated independently of each other. Extreme segmentation still pervades analysis within the bond market, especially within the government component, where duration is used as the only relevant measure of risk.

In a segmented/segmented environment, compensation for risk is based on the absolute risk of each asset or asset class. The equilibrium risk premium of an asset is defined as a unit price of risk times the segmented risk—typically, its volatility.

Table 1 shows historical segmented/segmented risk premiums for stock and bond markets in Canada, Germany, Japan, the United Kingdom, and the United States. In each case, the annualized quarterly standard deviation of total local currency returns is used as the measure of historical risk. The price of risk is the compensation the market demands for assuming additional units of risk and is assumed to be 40 basis points in each country. In the case of Canadian equity, for example, 40 basis points times 17.5 percent volatility produces a risk premium of 7 percent. That is, in equilibrium within a totally segmented world, Canadian equity should offer 7 per-

Table 1. Historical Segmented/Segmented Risk Premiums for Selected Global Markets, 1970–92

	Equity		Bond	
Market	Volatility	Risk Premium	Volatility	Risk Premium
Canada	17.5%	7.0%	8.8%	3.5%
Germany	20.2	8.1	4.8	1.9
Japan	21.9	8.8	5.1	2.0
United Kingdom	22.9	9.2	9.8	3.9
United States	17.6	17.0	6.1	2.5

Source: Brinson Partners.

cent in Canadian dollars in excess of Canadian cash.

Segmented/Integrated Markets

Although global markets are not completely segmented, neither are they totally integrated. A segmented/integrated case can be considered an interim state. In this case, markets are integrated within each country, but segmentation exists among countries. In a CAPM framework, therefore, "the market" in each country is defined by local investors and risk is perceived within a domestic context. The risk premiums for all assets in a specific country are determined by the local investors.

In a segmented/integrated structure, the compensation for risk within the CAPM framework is based on that portion of an asset's risk that is correlated with the local investor's reference market:

Risk premium = Price of risk × Beta (with respect to reference market) × Risk (volatility of reference market).

In this formulation, the reference market in each country is the relevant market for determining the equilibrium risk premium for each local asset. For a U.S. investor, the reference market includes U.S. stocks, U.S. bonds, non-U.S. stocks, non-U.S. bonds, venture capital, and real estate. If an investor is evaluating U.S. stocks, the risk premium for U.S. stocks is relative to a market that is broadly defined in terms of what the typical U.S. investor owns.

In a segmented/integrated state, the CAPM would describe equilibrium within national markets but disequilibrium across national markets. Thus, an investor's required risk premium for a foreign asset could be different from the available risk premium. That is, the array of risk premiums that are available to a global investor are dominated by the behavior of local investors in each market, but the required risk premiums are determined in the context of a global investor's own reference market. For example, German investors would determine the risk premiums offered by German assets based on the German reference portfolio; the risk premium that a U.S. investor requires from German assets would be based on the U.S. reference market. If segmentation among global markets is meaningful, the equilibrium risk premiums prevailing in a particular market will not necessarily be equal to the required risk premiums of all or even most investors.

Examples of local reference markets in the 1980s are shown in **Figure 1**. They are based on typical portfolios in each of the five countries. Canadian equities and bonds, for example, were about 90 percent of what Canadians held during the late 1980s. (Until 1992, Canadians could not hold more than a 10 percent position outside Canada.) Germans typically had very small German equity and very large German bond holdings; the 10 percent in investments outside Germany were about evenly split. The Japanese had a little larger share in foreign equities than Germans or Canadians. The United Kingdom was evenly split between U.K. bonds and U.K. equities, with a large component of foreign investments. U.S. investors held a mix of U.S. and foreign stocks and bonds that would generate risk equal to about a 60/40 balanced U.S. portfolio.

Figure 1. Examples of Local Reference Markets

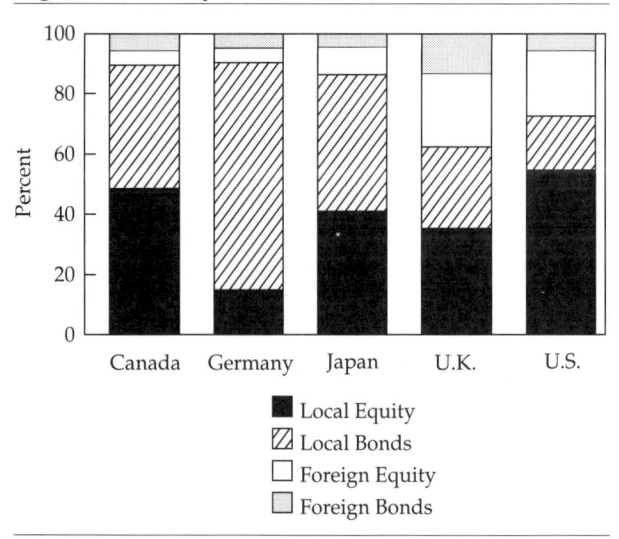

[Bar chart showing percentages for Canada, Germany, Japan, U.K., U.S. with categories: Local Equity, Local Bonds, Foreign Equity, Foreign Bonds]

Sources: Brinson Partners and Goldman Sachs & Co.

The risk premiums for each market were estimated, again based on historical data, by using the market mixes in Figure 1, a universal price of risk of 40 basis points, and estimates of each beta. **Table 2** presents the matrix of risk premiums for equity markets and risk premiums for fixed-income markets based on betas and volatility experienced during the 1970–92 period. The diagonal shows the risk premium each country made available to outside invest-

Table 2. Historical Segmented/Integrated Risk Premiums Required by Investors in Selected Global Markets, 1970–92

	Canada		Germany		Japan		United Kingdom		United States	
Market	Beta	Risk Premium	Beta	Risk Premium	Beta	Risk Premium	Beta	Risk Premium	Beta	Risk Premium
Equity Markets										
Canada	1.47	6.6%	1.57	3.7%	0.88	3.8%	0.79	5.1%	1.11	6.0%
Germany	0.76	3.4	2.62	6.1	0.82	3.5	0.64	4.2	0.93	5.0
Japan	1.09	4.9	2.00	4.7	1.99	8.5	0.94	6.1	1.25	6.8
United Kingdom	1.15	5.2	2.14	5.0	1.14	4.9	1.37	8.9	1.29	7.0
United States	1.17	5.3	1.92	4.5	0.98	4.2	0.94	6.1	1.23	6.7
Bond Markets										
Canada	0.51	2.3%	0.90	2.1%	0.23	1.0%	0.29	1.9%	0.39	2.1%
Germany	0.24	1.1	0.65	1.5	0.10	0.4	0.09	0.6	0.33	1.8
Japan	0.31	1.4	0.72	1.7	0.24	1.0	0.21	1.4	0.39	2.1
United Kingdom	0.38	1.7	0.62	1.4	0.10	0.4	0.37	2.4	0.40	2.1
United States	0.22	1.0	0.70	1.6	0.16	0.7	0.23	1.5	0.23	1.3

Source: Brinson Partners.

ors. As an example, the risk premium a Canadian investor demands from Canadian stocks in a segmented/integrated Canadian market is 6.6 percent. This percentage is the equilibrium risk premium the Canadian market offers to all global investors.

Notice, however, that a free lunch is implied by the segmentation among national markets. Consider a U.S. investor with the specified U.S. reference portfolio confronting Canada's 6.6 percent equity risk premium. The U.S. investor requires a risk premium of only 6 percent from Canadian equity, but the U.S. investor receives a 6.6 percent risk premium relative to a beta of 1.11 with respect to the U.S. reference portfolio and the framework of a U.S. reference portfolio premium. The implication is that the U.S investor investing in Canada would receive a price of risk of 0.44 percent, not 0.40 percent. That is, the U.S. investor would receive a 10 percent higher compensation per unit of risk from Canadian equity than a Canadian investor would receive. In other words, the actual risk premium offered to the U.S. investor is higher than is required.

The higher compensation per unit of risk accruing to the U.S. investor occurs because the Canadian market offers a risk premium consistent with Canadian equilibrium. That premium is different from the risk premium required by a U.S. investor, who is evaluating the situation in the framework of U.S. capital market equilibrium.

If the assumption of segmentation across national borders is maintained, the result is inconsistencies or the appearance of free lunches. Canadians demand the risk premium of 3.4 percent for German equities, while the German market offers 6.1 percent; they demand 4.9 percent from Japanese equities, and the Japanese offer 8.5 percent. The Japanese require 3.8 percent from Canadian equity, while the Canadian market offers 6.6 percent; they need 3.5 percent from German equity, and that market offers 6.1 percent. In fact, each market offers a higher risk premium than the risk premium outside investors require.

Integrated/Integrated Markets

These distortions between equilibrium risk premiums and the risk premiums required by outside investors point to the conclusion that a truly global CAPM requires integration both within markets and across national markets; that is, an integrated/integrated equilibrium framework. Such a framework involves determining consistent estimates of risk premiums for every asset relative to the global market—broadly defined. In this framework, the global riskless asset is expressed in terms of the global currency *numeraire*, and the global market is defined to include the full range of investable assets, each expressed in terms of the global currency *numeraire*. The global CAPM is

Risk premium = Price of risk × Beta (with respect to global market) × Risk (volatility of global market).

Beta estimates are now relative to the global market—all the investable stocks, bonds, and other assets—and that market is the same for everybody.

Table 3 presents the risk premiums for the five countries when an integrated/integrated global capital market is assumed. In an integrated/integrated equilibrium context, the risk premiums are the same internally and externally.

59

Table 3. Historical Integrated/Integrated Risk Premiums for Selected Global Markets, 1970–92

Market	Equity Beta	Equity Risk Premium	Bond Beta	Bond Risk Premium
Canada	1.40	5.4%	0.52	2.0%
Germany	1.20	4.7	0.29	1.1
Japan	1.70	6.6	0.40	1.6
United Kingdom	1.70	6.6	0.44	1.7
United States	1.57	6.1	0.30	1.2

Source: Brinson Partners.

Market Comparisons

Obviously, the global capital market is not yet fully integrated, and the degree of segmentation of markets affects available risk premiums. Integrated/integrated analysis still provides useful information, however, about the nature of the equilibrium to which global markets are converging. **Table 4** summarizes the historical results based on a segmented/segmented market perspective, the more re-

Table 4. Comparison of Historical Risk Premium Estimates by Degree of Segmentation, 1970–92

Market	Segmented/ Segmented	Segmented/ Integrated	Integrated/ Integrated
Equity markets			
Canada	7.0%	6.6%	5.4%
Germany	8.1	6.1	4.7
Japan	8.8	8.5	6.6
United Kingdom	9.2	8.9	6.6
United States	7.0	6.7	6.1
Bond markets			
Canada	3.5	2.3	2.0
Germany	1.9	1.5	1.1
Japan	2.0	1.0	1.6
United Kingdom	3.9	2.4	1.7
United States	2.5	1.3	1.2

Source: Brinson Partners.

alistic segmented/integrated market perspective, and the global CAPM integrated/integrated market state, which does not yet exist. Taking the Canadian example again, note that the risk premium for Canadian equities in a segmented/segmented market is 7 percent; for a segmented/integrated market, 6.6 percent; and for an integrated/integrated market, 5.4 percent. Increasing integration appears to reduce equilibrium risk premiums of all asset classes and all countries, with the exception of Japanese bonds. For this asset, the risk premium is 2.0 percent in a segmented/segmented market and 1.0 percent in a segmented/integrated market; in an integrated/integrated market, it is 1.6 percent. On a statistical basis, however, the estimated betas for Japanese bonds are indistinguishable from each other. Thus, the significance of this exception is not clear.

Because global assets require investors to address the practical problem of exposure to exchange rate risk, a final note about currencies is in order. Recall that the CAPM focuses on returns relative to cash. This risk premium is the factor that distinguishes among assets. Thus, the risk premium for German equity involves the deutsche mark (DM) return from German equity in excess of the DM return from German cash. If a U.S. investor in German equity hedges the DM exposure into U.S. dollars, the implicit transaction involves selling DM cash and buying dollar cash. The hedged return is then equal to the return from U.S. cash plus the German equity risk premium. The unhedged return involves the risk premium plus the dollar return from DM-denominated cash. In other words, the global cash market completely defines the exchange rate choices facing the global investor. Within the CAPM, this situation is reflected in the global cash *numeraire* that is applied to all markets.

Conclusion

The estimates discussed in this presentation imply that, in theory, the market pressure of portfolio globalization should drive global risk premiums down. Although the direction of this effect is clear, the magnitudes and the pace of the adjustments are unknown. As is typically the case with CAPM analysis, immediate trading implications are lacking. More fundamental implications, however, abound. Among them is, first, a strong suggestion that expansion of portfolios into foreign markets is efficient in terms of the risk–reward opportunities. Second, particularly attractive transient returns may well be available in markets where a meaningful degree of intermarket segmentation remains. Third, equilibrium returns are likely to be less than is implied by recent history, because increased globalization broadens the definition of the market for all investors.

Question and Answer Session

Denis S. Karnosky

Question: What you calculated were more indicators than statistics. Did you do any statistical measurements of the differences in market betas or risk premiums?

Karnosky: No. The primary purpose was to illustrate the applicability of the CAPM to the global market. The estimates use historical data directly and are, at best, suggestive. Some statistical tests were performed to see whether the betas were different among the three cases, and only in the case of Japanese bonds could the hypothesis be rejected.

Question: Because the Japanese bond market is underdeveloped, small, and subject to government influence, many consider it inefficient. Was this the problem with your results for Japan?

Karnosky: I would not hold the Japanese bond market up as an example of efficiency, openness, or understandability. Within the framework discussed here, this market has probably the largest confidence bands around the estimates of beta because it is heavily regulated. These observations relate to the changing degree of market segmentation, which underscores the limits to using historical data in the estimation of equilibrium betas and risk premiums.

Question: Where does the free lunch come from?

Karnosky: The free lunch arises because of segmentation among countries. If resources cannot flow freely into or out of a market, the available returns on assets will tend to be dominated by local investors. Those investors have reference portfolios that can differ from the reference portfolios of outside investors. Thus, local and outside investors can require different risk premiums for the same assets. Because the reference portfolio within each market will tend to be dominated by local assets, market risk will tend to be higher than for more broadly defined markets.

Question: Do opportunities to profit from segmentation exist in addition to what would be available to a professional arbitrageur?

Karnosky: The analysis presented here suggests that, in an equilibrium sense, if a broadly based portfolio of non-U.S. assets were added to a domestic portfolio, then over the long run, the result would probably be the same dollar return from those global assets as from the U.S. portfolio. The difference is not great, on average, because the differences in inflation rates are canceled through the spot and forward exchange rate mechanisms. What is gained, however, is a significant drop in the volatility of the portfolio. Transitory extra returns, however, are suggested by the segmented/integrated analysis.

Question: Is the concept of local investors setting available risk premiums likely to break down as investors become increasingly global and local-market frictions decline?

Karnosky: Without a doubt. Such a phenomenon is currently visible within Europe, where actual integration continues despite the inability of governments to develop programs that coordinate economic policies. Resources will seek the highest perceived reward, and to the extent that remaining segmentation produces distortions among asset prices, resources will seek ways to take advantage of the perceived opportunities or to avoid the uncompensated risks.

Question: What is Brinson Partners doing to develop strategies to take advantage of what is happening?

Karnosky: The type of analysis presented here is the foundation for all our global analysis. This methodology provides us with a means to develop consistent estimates of value in global markets, which provides a basis for evaluating the opportunities that are given by current market prices. By focusing on individual markets as parts of a large global market, we believe we can develop a better understanding of the markets' interrelationships and reduce the risks associated with analyzing markets in isolation.

Question: Please discuss to what extent currency risk, high trading costs, increasing custody costs, and so forth add to the cost of the free lunch. Are these risks and costs accounted for?

Karnosky: Investing in non-U.S. assets is more expensive than investing in domestic markets in terms of transaction costs, custody charges to the client, and the inconvenience of diverse settlement procedures. These issues do affect the returns available from these markets.

International Capital Market Integration and Global Asset Allocation

Richard A. Weiss
Senior Vice President
MPT Associates

> Global capital markets today exhibit varying degrees of integration. Some are highly integrated; others are still highly segmented and have a domestic focus; many are somewhere between these two extremes. Global investing strategy should differ according to these characteristics.

The degree of integration among capital markets has importance for valuing assets in the global context. In turn, asset valuation methodology has a large effect on how global asset-allocation strategies are structured.

Capital Market Integration Theory

Capital market integration theory concerns the degree to which worldwide financial markets behave as a single, unified market. In order to understand the concept fully, one might envision capital market integration as a spectrum: On one end, capital markets are assumed to be completely segmented from one another, and at the other extreme, they are assumed to be perfectly integrated with one another. Suppose, for example, two capital assets have exactly the same risk characteristics but are traded in two different national markets. In a perfectly integrated world capital market, these two assets would be priced to yield exactly the same return. In a world of segmented markets, however, these two assets would not be priced to yield the same return. In fact, it would be a coincidence if they were.

The market integration spectrum has implications for global asset allocation as shown in **Table 1**. The middle column indicates which aspect of global asset allocation is affected, and the outside columns list what the implications are for either segmented or integrated markets. As to strategy type, if markets were completely segmented from one another, the most appropriate global asset-allocation strategy would focus on each country or region or, in the extreme case, on each market in isolation. Any knowledge used to evaluate securities in one market might not be applicable to analysis in another.

Factor type means factors in their most general sense—any economic, political, regulatory, or financial event affecting asset prices or asset-class returns. (Note that this schematic assumes that the capital market integration or segmentation mimics the underlying economic integration or segmentation.) The factors that play a major role in a world in which markets are segmented are domestic in nature, and only domestic factors will have relevance for domestic asset returns. If markets are perfectly integrated, however, the types of factors affecting asset-class returns will be of both an international and domestic nature.

What about the implications for factor importance? In arbitrage pricing theory, factor importance is known as factor pricing—the relative weights of the different factors in influencing asset-class returns worldwide. In a segmented world, factor importance may vary significantly from market to market, whereas in an integrated world, the cross-border marginal investor will ensure that these factors are all equally priced across markets.

Asset Valuation Approaches

This theoretical framework provides three basic alternatives—depending on whether markets are segmented, integrated, or partially integrated—for valuing asset classes in the global context. I will illustrate these alternatives with some examples.

Note: Mr. Weiss is currently senior vice president of Vantage Global Advisors.

Table 1. Capital Market Integration Theory

Complete Segmentation	Implications for Global Asset Allocation	Perfect Integration
Regional or country by country	Strategy type	Worldwide or global industry
Domestic	Factor type	International and domestic
May vary significantly from market to market	Factor importance	All factors priced equally

Source: Richard A. Weiss.

Segmented Market Strategies

Consider this quote from a Salomon Brothers research report: "Facing poor earnings prospects... [U.S. and U.K.] equities will make no headway." Another quote from this source says, "[We] recommend reduced exposure to Japanese equities where the overvaluation relative to bonds is currently extreme." Finally, "... interest rate cuts will fuel a rally in Spanish equity prices...."

This research report illustrates a specific type of global asset-allocation strategy. The research department is making recommendations on four separate equity markets. For each recommendation, the analysts are relying on a single, domestic factor. Their bearish outlook for the U.S. and U.K. equity markets is related to domestic earnings prospects. For Japan, they use a valuation concept for their negative forecasts. In Spain, domestic interest rate cuts have fueled their bullish recommendation for the market.

This segmented approach is also applicable in the bond markets. A Merrill Lynch report included the following forecasts for three different government long-term bond markets: "Technical factors favor the 3-year issue over the 30-year [U.S.] bonds." "The long end [U.K. gilts] will continue to be adversely affected by concern about underlying inflation." "The 10-year area of the German curve continues to look a little expensive relative to the short maturities." Again, the global bond-allocation strategy and the individual forecasts critically depend on unique domestic factors. In the United States, the factors are technical; in the United Kingdom, domestic inflation; in Germany, valuation or a term premium notion—comparing yields on the long end to yields on the short end of the yield curve.

These illustrations are examples of global asset valuation with the implicit assumption that the markets are segmented from one another. Most firms using this approach have separate research groups worldwide making their own forecasts on their respective markets. Then, these forecasts are pulled together into one research report.

These segmented approaches are typically characterized by several attributes:
- They identify one key factor affecting each country.
- They base market opinions directly on that factor.
- The factors are almost always local or domestic in nature.
- The factors change frequently—a necessity for a segmented approach.
- The asset and currency decisions are typically combined.

A quantitative model for this approach might look as follows:

$$E(R_x) = (100\%) \times (\text{Factor}_x)$$
$$E(R_y) = (100\%) \times (\text{Factor}_y)$$
$$E(R_x - R_y) = \text{Factor}_x - \text{Factor}_y,$$

where

$E(R_x)$ = expected return on asset x,
$E(R_y)$ = expected return on asset y, and
Factor_x (or $_y$) = financial event affecting the returns of asset x (or asset y).

In this case, the expected return for the market in country X depends (100 percent) on factor X, and the return for the market in country Y depends (100 percent) on factor Y. To make a cross-border decision or a global asset allocation, analysts compare factor X with factor Y.

Some of the potential problems with this approach are fairly obvious. The analyst could be focusing on the wrong factor, particularly if only one factor is used. The implicit 100 percent weighting can be a problem. The primary focus tends to be on the country—that is, "we like Japan, we don't like the United Kingdom"; or "we like Europe, we don't like Australia." They do not specify to which financial markets they are referring—equities, bonds, currencies, real estate, or so forth. To the degree that markets are integrated to any extent, this approach will have some bias in its forecasts.

Integrated Market Strategies

A Phillips & Drew report said, "In equities, the recent gains in the U.K. and Japan may now leave them vulnerable to a setback." This global strategy recommendation is subtly different from the previous market-special recommendations. It focuses on one factor and compares that factor directly across two or more countries. Because the U.K. and Japanese markets have risen dramatically in the recent past, the analysts are basing their bullish recommendations on those markets. They are looking at a technical factor across markets.

Another example is Salomon Brothers' recently introduced global telecommunications index. This index is a great example of a global strategy that assumes markets are fully integrated, because it reduces the emphasis on a single country. Salomon is looking at global industries, while essentially dissolving national borders altogether.

As another example, consider a Morgan Stanley report comparing five different European equity markets as shown in **Table 2**. The markets are compared on three different bases: P/E, dividend yield, and earnings per share (EPS). Instead of looking at a single domestic factor to drive each forecast, the analysts are looking at three factors and comparing them directly across several markets. The implicit assumption is that the importance of these three measures is equal among these markets. In other words, an investor can read this table and discern that Belgium is more attractive than Germany on a P/E basis.

These research reports from Phillips & Drew, Salomon Brothers, and Morgan Stanley are good examples of asset valuation with the implicit assumption that markets are highly, if not fully, integrated. The recommendations identify several key factors for each asset class. They compare these factors across borders under the assumption that the factors are equally important across markets. Finally, they apply equal or subjective weights to each comparison. A model for this type of approach might look as follows:

$$E[R(x)] = \beta_1[\text{Factor}(x1)] + \beta_2[\text{Factor}(x2)] + \ldots + \beta_N[\text{Factor}(xN)]$$

$$E[R(y)] = \beta_1[\text{Factor}(y1)] + \beta_2[\text{Factor}(y2)] + \ldots + \beta_N[\text{Factor}(yN)]$$

$$E[R(x)] - R(y)] = \beta_1[\text{Factor}(x1) - \text{Factor}(y1)] + \beta_2[\text{Factor}(x2) - \text{Factor}(y2)],$$

where

$E[R(x)]$ = expected return on asset x,
$E[R(y)]$ = expected return on asset y, and
Factor(x) = economic, political, regulatory, or financial event affecting the returns of asset x.

These models are specified as linear, but they do not necessarily have to be that way. The expected return for the market in country X now depends on several different factors, possibly both domestic and international in nature. Now, however, these factors are weighted by the betas, or the factor prices, and these

Table 2. Market Strategy and European Model Portfolio Weightings, 1990

Country	P/E	Dividend Yield	EPS
Belgium	12.12	4.34%	$ 7.00
France	12.90	2.99	14.00
Germany	16.57	3.01	12.50
Italy	12.89	2.72	11.00
Spain	12.43	4.50	10.00

Source: Morgan Stanley, *Eurostrategy* (Winter).

factor prices are not subscripted to have the country notation, so they are the same in country X and country Y even though the factors might be different. When making a cross-border comparison or global asset allocation, the formula reduces to one factor price for each comparison.

Again, this construct is not without potential problems. For example, differences in accounting standards effectively preclude naive direct comparisons of P/Es. Unequal weights also present a problem. To the degree that segmentation exists to any extent, the weights will not necessarily be equal, so these integrated techniques will introduce some bias. Determining which factors are important in one country and then blindly applying them to every other country is not an optimal approach if segmentation exists among those markets. Finally, the primary focus of these integrated approaches is usually the asset class, rather than the country, so any country effect that may be present is ignored.

Partially Integrated Market Strategies

Table 3 is from a Barings Securities research report. Like Morgan Stanley's *Eurostrategy*, the Barings report examines several different markets—in this example, five major equity markets—across several categories of factors. For each market, each factor is scored from one to ten (with ten being "best"). For the United States, for example, the equity market is ranked five in valuation. At that time, Barings' analysts considered the U.S. stock market fairly valued. Japan ranked a six in this category, so it was slightly undervalued when compared with the U.S. market.

The Barings approach is similar to Morgan Stanley's except that Barings estimates weights (the percentages in parentheses) that should be applied to each of the scores in making a final evaluation of each market. In the United States, for example, the market is considered to be fairly valued and that factor is weighted as 25 percent of the total weight for these seven factors—much more than an equal weight. In Japan, only 10 percent of the weight is placed on valuation factors. Thus, Japan is relatively undervalued, but that is considered not very import-

Table 3. Factor Scores and Weights of Major Equity Markets

Factor	United States	Japan	United Kingdom	Germany	France
Valuation	5 (25%)	6 (10%)	9 (25%)	8 (20%)	3 (15%)
Technical	2 (5)	2 (40)	1 (5)	1 (5)	4 (5)
Inflation	9 (10)	8 (5)	4 (15)	10 (25)	5 (15)
Economic growth	7 (15)	9 (5)	3 (10)	5 (20)	9 (25)
Monetary policy	9 (35)	3 (25)	5 (20)	1 (15)	6 (25)
Fiscal policy	5 (5)	9 (10)	4 (10)	4 (5)	4 (10)
Trade balance	3 (5)	7 (5)	6 (15)	5 (10)	2 (5)
Composite	6.85	4.25	5.50	6.00	5.65

Source: Barings Securities.

ant. In contrast, technical factors in Japan are ranked two and have a 40 percent weight. As a result, the composite score for Japan is lower than that for the United States.

The Barings approach is one of the few examples of global asset allocation that assumes markets are partially integrated. The analysts identify several key factors, both international and domestic. As in the segmented approach, they then determine the proper weights, or factor prices, from a local-market perspective, which allows cross-border comparisons involving different factors and weights. This approach recognizes that various markets may have different sensitivities to the same factor, whereas the examples of the extreme approaches to global asset allocation export a manager's domestic bias. This strategy that views markets as partially integrated attempts to reconcile the two extreme views.

This model specification is the most general of the three. One could argue that the other two are just subsets of this specification:

$$E[R(x)] = \beta_{x1} [\text{Factor}(x1)] + \beta_{x2} [\text{Factor}(x2)] + \ldots + \beta_{xN} [\text{Factor}(xN)]$$

$$E[R(y)] = \beta_{y1} (\text{Factor}(y1)) + \beta_{y2} [\text{Factor}(y2)] + \ldots + \beta_{yN}[\text{Factor}(yN)]$$

$$E[R(x) - R(y)] = (\beta_{x1} [\text{Factor}_{(x1)}] + \beta_{x2} [\text{Factor}_{(x2)}] + \ldots) - (\beta_{y1}[\text{Factor}_{(y1)}] + \beta_{y2}[\text{Factor}_{(y2)}] + \ldots)$$

The expected return for country X depends on several different factors, but now the beta coefficients or the factor prices are subscripted so that they have the country notation. In making a cross-border decision using the third equation, which does not reduce at all, one must estimate all of the parameters, the factor prices, and the factors themselves.

As with the extreme approaches, this approach is not without problems. Factors and factor prices are not stable over time, which presents more of a problem for this approach than for either of the other two. To the extent that relationships are too unstable to model accurately, this approach, rather than increasing accuracy, may introduce more error into the equations and the forecasts of expected returns.

The existence of regional integration or global industries also presents a problem for this approach to the degree that integration is not uniform across regions and industries. Perhaps selective use of the segmented/integrated approaches is appropriate in this situation. For example, if the Pacific Basin markets are fairly highly integrated, an integrated approach might be used to forecast their relative returns, but a more segmented approach might be appropriate for making European and cross-regional allocations.

Another potential problem is the illusion of accuracy. A partially integrated approach is more quantitative than the others because of all the estimation it requires. Many times, issuers of recommendations based on a partially integrated approach publish global equity and bond market forecasts to the second or third decimal place. Be aware, however, that although the forecasts may be very precise, they are not necessarily very accurate. The data are noisy, and the statistical techniques have large confidence intervals; so these approaches are not necessarily any more accurate than the other two types.

Conclusion

The theory of international capital market integration is relevant to global asset-allocation strategies and global investing. Theory cannot be ignored; when investors make a global investment or cross-border decision, they implicitly take a stand on the capital market spectrum of integration.

Currently, the world is somewhere in the middle of the spectrum. Certain regions have pockets of integration, and certain industries are more highly integrated than others. Today's statistical methodologies are simply not powerful enough to distinguish between the two extremes, and so far, we lack a definitive empirical method for determining whether or to what extent capital markets are integrated or segmented.

Question and Answer Session

Richard A. Weiss

Question: What role does the multinational company play in the whole scheme of capital market integration?

Weiss: It is important to distinguish between economic integration, and capital market integration. Although, in practice, one tends to follow the other, the relationship is by no means perfect. Two countries may be integrated economically (e.g., because they have similar industrial bases or through the existence of multinationals operating in both countries), but their capital markets may be segmented because of frictions that limit domestic capital market accessibility.

Question: A recent study shows that correlations among the world's equity markets have increased significantly over the past couple of decades. Isn't that proof of increasing capital market integration and, therefore, of decreasing benefits to international diversification?

Weiss: No, on both counts. Although higher correlations among national equity markets are consistent with the notion of increased capital market integration, they are not proof. High correlations indicate a stable world element in returns, which could simply be the result of economic links, not capital market links. Even in a perfectly integrated world capital market, correlations might still not be perfect. National random factors could selectively affect the production activities (thus, stock returns) of any one nation without evidence of market segmentation.

As for the second part of the question, rising correlations do not eliminate the benefits to international diversification. As long as markets are not perfectly correlated, international investing will provide some benefit, whether it be in terms of risk reduction or return enhancement.

Question: You mentioned that today's statistical techniques are not powerful enough to prove conclusively whether or not markets are segmented. Is the reason a lack of sufficient historical data?

Weiss: Partly. The real problem is that testing for capital market integration requires a triple-jointed hypothesis; every time you test for market integration, you are also testing for the validity of your asset pricing model and for market efficiency. If, subsequently, the statistical tests for market integration fail, you cannot be certain why. The problem could be a poorly specified asset pricing model, market inefficiencies, or market segmentation. You have no way of knowing which of the three hypotheses proved false.

Currency Anomalies: Strategy Opportunities and Hedging Implications

Mark P. Kritzman, CFA
Partner
Windham Capital Management

> Currency returns have been characterized by nonrandomness, or trends, and forward-rate bias, in which the forward rate systematically overestimates changes in the spot rate. Both anomalies are exploitable with the application of appropriate strategies.

Currency markets are characterized by two alleged anomalies: nonrandomness and forward-rate bias. Nonrandomness refers to the fact that currency returns have historically been positively correlated with their prior values. Forward-rate bias refers to the fact that the forward rate has historically overestimated subsequent changes in the spot rate. This presentation provides evidence of these anomalies and discusses some strategies designed to take advantage of them.

Nonrandomness

Nonrandomness is a well-documented phenomenon. In 1989, I presented some test results of serial dependence in currency returns, and others have since updated and extended those results. For my study, I performed a runs test using the returns of one-month currency forward contracts. In this test, four consecutive positive returns constitute one run, whereas four differing observations—positive, negative, positive, negative—constitute four runs. For any given number of observations, a certain number of runs are associated with a random sequence. Finding fewer runs then expected suggests positive serial correlation. It means the duration of the typical run is longer than it would be if the series were random. If there are more runs than expected, then the process is mean reverting.

Table 1 shows the expected number of runs compared with the actual number of runs. All the *t*-statistics are negative, which indicates that the number of runs is smaller than one would expect from a random sequence. The test period was from 1977 to 1988. I have updated these results through 1992, and the nonrandomness has persisted.

The runs test is somewhat limited because it deals only with direction; it does not incorporate magnitude. Another test, one that incorporates magnitude, is the variance-ratio test.

In the variance-ratio test, if the returns sequence is random, the variance of quarterly observations should be three times as large as the variances of monthly observations for the same measurement period. The variance-ratio test statistic is normalized to 1 by dividing by 3; if six-month returns are being compared with monthly returns, one divides by 6. If the sequence is random, then the variance ratio should be close to 1. If it is greater than 1, the sequence has positive serial correlation, and if it is less than 1, the sequence is mean reverting.

All of the variance ratios shown in **Figure 1** are greater than 1. As the observation period is extended, the variance ratios increase. The ratios exceeding the horizontal line shown in Figure 1 are significant at the 5 percent level. The ratios peak at observation periods of between two and three years, which indicates that the trends last between two and three years.

Table 2 contrasts the *t*-statistics of these currency tests with the *t*-statistics from the same tests for the same measurement period applied to the difference between stock and bond returns. For stocks and bonds, the *t*-statistics are all near zero, indicating that the risk premium has been random. In comparison, the *t*-statistics for the currency return tests are very high.

Another positively correlated time series is the difference between large- and small-capitalization returns. Historically, S&P 500 Index returns have

Table 1. Evidence of Nonrandomness: Runs Test, 1977–88

Currency	Expected Number of Runs	Actual Number of Runs	t-statistic
British pound	73	50	–3.84
German mark	72	57	–2.59
Japanese yen	73	66	–1.15
Swiss franc	73	57	–2.63
French franc	73	54	–2.93

Source: Windham Capital Management.

been close to random, as have been the returns of small-capitalization stocks, although they have not been as close to random as S&P 500 returns. The difference between these two series is highly nonrandom, however. When small-cap stocks have done well relative to large-cap stocks, this performance has occurred for a long time, and when they performed poorly relative to large-cap stocks, they did so for a long time. This relationship is not easy to exploit, however, because of the significant transaction costs incurred when moving between large-cap and small-cap stocks. In contrast, the transaction costs of trading currencies are small.

Strategies to Exploit Nonrandomness

One way to exploit the nonrandomness of currency returns is to follow a trading strategy that generates a convex payoff function, as illustrated in

Figure 1. Evidence of Nonrandomness: Variance Ratio Test, 1977–88

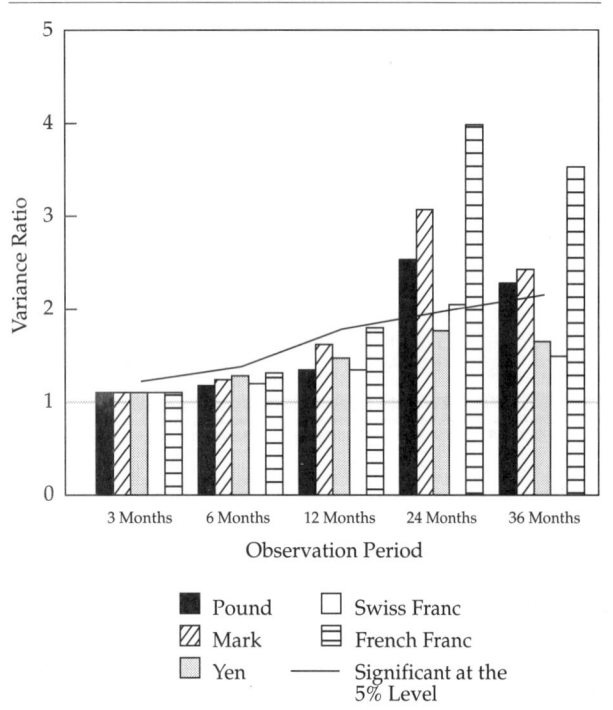

Source: Windham Capital Management.

Table 2. Evidence of Nonrandomness: Currencies versus Risk Premiums, 1977–88
(t-statistics)

Test Type	Currencies	Risk Premiums (Stocks – Bonds)[a]
Runs test	–2.63	–0.76
Variance-ratio test:		
12 months	1.63	0.02
24 months	3.65	0.00
36 months	2.34	–0.20

Source: Windham Capital Management.

Note: A t-statistic equal to 2 (absolute value) indicates with 95 percent confidence that the difference from expectations is not attributable to chance.

[a] S&P 500 Index monthly return less long-term bond monthly return.

Figure 2. The straight line represents the return from a buy-and-hold currency exposure. In this case, the buy-and-hold strategy line has a slope of one-half, which means the investor is half exposed to the currency. Hence, the return is half of whatever movement takes place in the exchange rate. A strategy that buys currencies as they appreciate and sells currencies as they depreciate generates the convex payoff function.

Figure 2. Convex Strategy to Exploit Nonrandomness

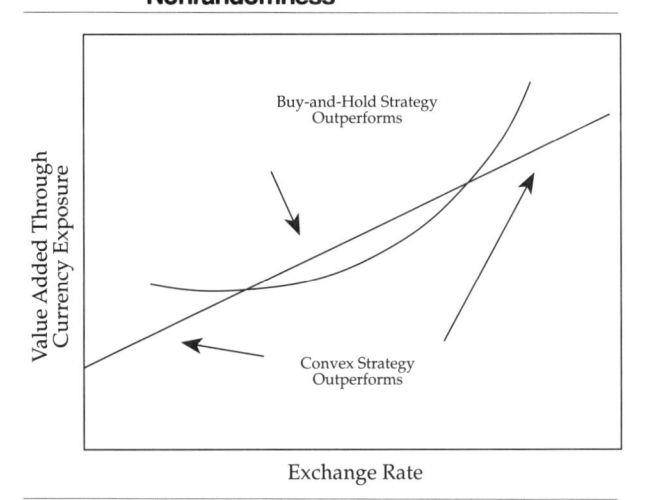

Source: Windham Capital Management.

If currencies trend, the exchange rate is more likely to move to one extreme or the other than to fluctuate around the middle. In trending markets, the convex payoff function will add value beyond a buy-and-hold strategy. If the exchange rate reverts to the mean, the buy-and-hold strategy will add value beyond the convex payoff function.

Table 3 presents a numerical example. The underlying assumptions are that (1) the currency depreciates 1 percent a month for the next two years and then appreciates 1 percent a month for the next two years and (2) the investor has an underlying portfolio of T-bills yielding 50 basis points and buys and sells currencies as an overlay. The convex strategy sells the currency as it depreciates and acquires it as it appreciates. The table compares the cumulative wealth generated (based on an initial $100) by the convex strategy, a fully exposed strategy, and a fully hedged strategy. Over the full cycle, the degree of currency exposure does not make much difference, but the convex strategy adds value to both unhedged and hedged strategies.

Table 3. Convex Strategy Results Compared with Hedging Strategies' Returns
(quarterly cumulative wealth)

Hypothetical Convex Exposure[a]	Convex	Fully Exposed	Fully Hedged
–15%	$101.66	$98.51	$101.51
–30	103.81	97.04	103.04
–45	106.48	95.59	104.59
–50	109.65	94.16	106.17
–50	112.97	92.76	107.77
–50	116.40	91.37	109.39
–50	119.92	90.01	111.04
–50	123.56	88.67	112.72
–35	123.74	92.72	114.42
–20	124.49	96.95	116.14
–51	25.80	101.38	117.89
10	127.69	106.0	1119.67
25	130.20	110.85	121.47
40	133.35	115.92	123.30
50	137.19	121.21	125.16
50	141.34	126.75	127.05
Annualized return	9.04%	6.11%	6.17%

Source: Windham Capital Management.

[a]Exposure to a foreign currency at the end of each quarter.

If an investor follows a simple strategy of purchasing the currency as it appreciates, starting to sell it when it reaches its peak, and then starting to purchase it again when it reaches its trough, all of the money the investor makes on the way up will be given back on the way down. The investor needs to impose a ceiling and floor on the currency exposure.

With a ceiling and floor, currency is purchased as it appreciates until the ceiling is reached, which should be relatively early in the trend. The currency continues to appreciate and to generate profits as the currency continues to rise. When the currency hits its peak and begins to decline, the investor starts selling and gets back to neutral without forgoing all the profits. The same approach is applied with respect to the floor. As long as the investor gets fully exposed early in a trend and then stops buying or selling when the ceiling or floor is reached, most of the profits will be preserved through turning points.

Table 4 shows the value added by this strategy to a T-bill portfolio, using the British pound, Japanese yen, German mark, Swiss franc, Canadian dollar, and Australian dollar. This strategy added almost 3 percent a year with a standard deviation of about 3.8 percent.

Table 4. Value Added from Nonrandomness: International T-Bill Portfolio, 1977–93

Year	Value Added
1977	3.92%
1978	3.42
1979	2.27
1980	–0.40
1981	3.56
1982	4.78
1983	3.57
1984	6.75
1985	4.21
1986	6.55
1987	11.07
1988	–5.30
1989	1.71
1990	5.41
1991	–3.47
1992	–0.51
1993[a]	0.42
1977–93[a]	2.91

Source: Windham Capital Management.

[a]Through February 4, 1993.

Sources of Nonrandomness

My conjecture about why this nonrandomness exists relates to central bank intervention. Central banks prefer stable exchange rates. When a currency increases abruptly, they sell the currency. If a currency decreases abruptly, they purchase the currency. This strategy is similar to that used by companies in managing their dividends. With a sharp rise in earnings, management usually lowers the payout ratio, and vice versa. The dividend stream through time is much less volatile than the underlying earnings stream. The dividend stream behaves like a moving average of the underlying earnings streams, and moving averages are positively serially correlated. Central banks induce this positive serial correlation by promoting stability in the currency markets.

Forward-Rate Bias

Currency markets also exhibit forward-rate bias, as illustrated in the following example. Suppose interest rates in the United States are 5 percent, and in

Europe, they are 10 percent. In this situation, some U.S. investors might consider converting U.S. dollars into a foreign (European) currency, lending at 10 percent and accepting the risk that the foreign currency might depreciate, because they can lose 5 percent before their return equals the riskless return in the United States. Few investors in Europe, however, would want to convert their currency to U.S. dollars, lend in the United States at 5 percent, and depend on the U.S. dollar increasing 5 percent just to break even with what they can earn risklessly in their own countries.

Think about the flow of funds that results because of this asymmetry in preferences. Investors sell U.S. dollars and buy the currency of the high-interest-rate country. Money flows from the United States, which supports the foreign currency and prevents it from declining as the forward rate predicts. At the same time, the supply of loanable funds in the United States is reduced, which places upward pressure on interest rates. The supply of loanable funds in the high-interest-rate country increases, which places downward pressure on interest rates there. Thus, the interest rates converge without the currency depreciating.

To address forward-rate bias, we need to distinguish covered interest rate parity from uncovered interest rate parity. Covered interest rate parity describes the relationship between the spot rate and the forward rate:

$$\text{Foward rate} = \text{Spot rate} \times \frac{(1 + \text{Domestic rate})}{(1 + \text{Foreign rate})},$$

in which the domestic and foreign rates are the nominally riskless rates with the same maturity as the forward contract. Covered interest rate parity states that investors cannot borrow money at 5 percent in the United States, convert it to the foreign currency, lend it at 10 percent in Europe, and sell a forward contract to hedge away the currency risk and make money.

Uncovered interest rate parity assumes that the forward rate is an unbiased estimate of the future spot rate. Therefore, the expected return of a forward contract is zero percent. That is, investors should not be able to make any money by borrowing money in the United States at 5 percent, converting it to the foreign currency, lending it at 10 percent, and not hedging. The reason is that the foreign currency should depreciate, on average, just enough to offset the interest rate differential.

Whereas covered interest rate parity must hold, because it is an arbitrage condition, uncovered interest rate parity has not held so far. The forward rate has systematically and significantly overestimated subsequent changes in the spot rate. **Table 5** shows the percentage of times the forward rate overestimated the decline in the spot rate between July 1973 and December 1991 and the annualized average error. Consider the case of the U.S. dollar and the pound. If the forward rate sold at a discount to the spot rate, I looked at the predicted decline in the pound. On the other hand, if the forward rate sold at a premium, I looked at the predicted decline in the U.S. dollar. By shifting the base currency, I eliminated the problem that overestimated increases might cancel out overestimated decreases and obscure the bias.

Table 5. Forward-Rate Bias, July 1973–December 1991

Currency	Percentage of Times Forward Rate Overestimated Decline in Spot Rate	Average Gain or Loss (annualized)
Dollar/pound	60%	8.07%
Dollar/mark	54	2.59
Dollar/Swiss franc	55	4.49
Dollar/yen	58	2.97
Pound/mark	54	3.33
Pound/Swiss franc	55	3.00
Pound/yen	51	0.44
Mark/Swiss franc	58	3.55
Mark/yen	61	8.17
Swiss franc/yen	60	8.96

Source: Windham Capital Management.

The average cost of hedging when domestic rates are low or the profit when domestic rates are high is 4.6 percent a year. Roughly interpreted, the cost of hedging from a low-interest-rate country was about 4.6 percent a year on average and the gain from hedging from a high-interest-rate country was about 4.6 percent a year on average. This is a big number.

There are some obvious strategies for exploiting the forward-rate bias to generate profits: One can buy currencies of high-interest-rate countries and sell currencies of low-interest-rate countries. To pursue this strategy without incurring too much risk, one should neutralize the U.S. dollar exposure and only arbitrage the cross-rates. Otherwise, because of the big swings in the U.S. dollar, the strategy might lose a lot of money in some years and make a lot of money in others. By eliminating the U.S. dollar risk, this anomaly can be exploited with significantly less risk.

Hedging with Biased Forward Rates

Currency hedging is controversial, and the fact that forward rates appear to be biased complicates the matter even further. Theoretically, the best approach for determining the optimal currency hedge ratio is to break out currency forward contracts as a separate asset class and then to choose the optimal portfolio simultaneously with the currency exposure. In practice, however, most investors consider hedging independently of the choice of the underlying portfolio.

If the expected return of a forward contract is assumed to be zero percent, the hedging problem becomes one of minimizing risk as a function of exposure to forward contracts. If forward contracts are biased, however, the problem is not simply one of minimizing risk; it is one of maximizing expected utility. Assuming that history will repeat itself, and that forward contracts are biased—that is, the expected return is nonzero and reasonably predictable—the optimal hedging policy should be tied to the expected return of those contracts.

The process for determining the optimal currency hedging policy involves determining the investor's risk aversion, identifying constraints, and estimating forward contract expected returns and their variances and covariances. Then one simply determines the exposure to currency forward contracts that maximizes expected utility. Two typical constraints are (1) the asset weights of the underlying portfolio and (2) the exposure limits to the currency forward contracts. This approach yields a currency hedging policy that matches the risk–return trade-off of the underlying portfolio.

Think about it this way. When a manager tries to determine what a client's exposure should be to stocks, bonds, and foreign assets, the manager asks how many units of expected return the client is willing to relinquish in order to lower portfolio risk by one unit. The object is to arrive at an asset mix with a comfortable risk–return trade-off. When hedging currencies, the question is the same: How many units of expected return is the client willing to relinquish or what hedging cost is the client willing to incur in order to lower portfolio risk by one unit? A rational client should give the same answer to these questions. It would not make sense to have one trade-off associated with the underlying portfolio and a completely different trade-off associated with the hedging policy.

Let me illustrate the mathematics of a simple case: We wish to maximize

$$\Phi = R_P + R_F W - \lambda(S_P^2 + S_P^2 W^2 + 2rS_P S_F W),$$

where
- Φ = expected utility,
- R_P = expected return of the underlying portfolio,
- R_F = expected return of the currency forward contract,
- W = weighting of the currency forward contract,
- λ = risk aversion,
- S_P = standard deviation of the underlying portfolio,
- S_F = standard deviation of the currency forward contract, and
- r = correlation of the portfolio with the currency forward contract.

Then we take the partial derivative with respect to W and set it equal to zero:

$$\frac{\delta \Phi}{\delta W} = R_F - \lambda\left(2S_F^2 W + 2rS_P S_F\right) = 0.$$

Simple algebra gives the solution:

$$W = \frac{R_F}{2\lambda S_F^2} - \frac{rS_P}{S_F}.$$

The object is to maximize expected utility. We assume this portfolio includes only one foreign asset. We want to take this expected utility's derivative with respect to the weighting of the currency forward contracts, set it equal to zero, and solve for W. If the expected return of the forward contract is zero percent, the optimal hedge ratio equals the portfolio's beta with respect to the currency. Once we assume that the forward rate is biased and its expected return is nonzero, then we must look at the risk–return trade-off.

The risk–return trade-off can be determined by backing out the investor's risk aversion. Assume a client has selected a portfolio. To select this portfolio, the client considered the expected return of the alternative assets, the volatility of those assets, and their correlations. The slope of the line tangent to the chosen portfolio along the efficient frontier is the client's risk aversion. This level of risk aversion is used to determine the hedging policy. The process is illustrated in **Figure 3**.

The optimal hedging policy changes as a function of the forward-rate bias. **Table 6** illustrates the optimal solution with one foreign asset for three levels of expected return. Assuming the forward contract has an expected return of zero percent, the optimal amount of the currency contract to sell short as a function of the underlying portfolio is 50 percent. If, instead, the contract has an expected return of 2 percent, the optimal exposure is only 15 percent, which means the investor would expect to lose money by hedging. This is the expected cost. If the forward contract has an expected return of –2 percent, 85 percent should be hedged. These calculations illustrate the sensitivity of the hedging policy to the forward-rate bias.

The simulated results of implementing this strategy are shown in **Table 7**. The underlying portfolio consists of 35 percent U.S. stocks, 30 percent U.S.

Figure 3. Risk Aversion

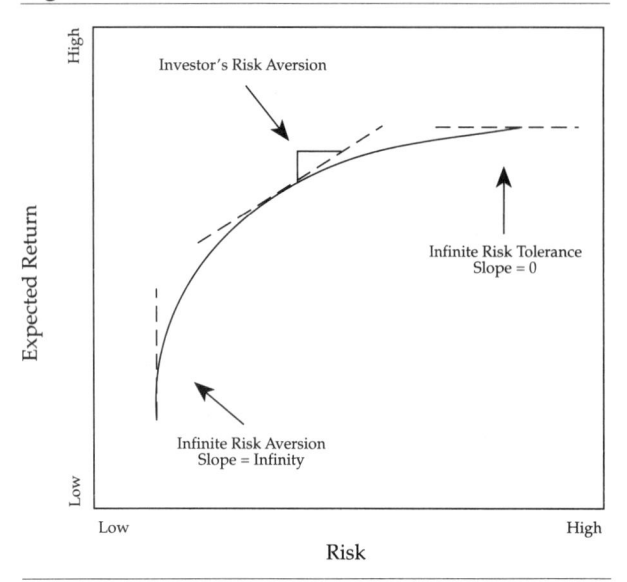

Source: Windham Capital Management.

bonds, 5 percent French equities, 15 percent German equities, 15 percent Japanese equities, and 10 percent U.K. equities. The model is based on the assumptions that the forward contract expected return equals the prior month's ending spot rate divided by the prior month's ending forward rate minus 1, annualized; that the covariance matrix is updated monthly based on the prior 12 monthly forward contract returns; and that the risk-aversion coefficient equals 1. The simulation starts in July 1974

Table 6. The Optimal Solution with One Foreign Asset

Exposure	Expected Return	Risk Aversion	Variance	Expected Utility
Forward contract expected return: 0%				
0%	0.1000	2	0.0225	0.0550
−50	0.1000	2	0.0189	0.0622
−100	0.1000	2	0.0225	0.0550
Forward contract expected return: 2%				
0%	0.1000	2	0.0225	0.0550
−15	0.0969	2	0.0206	0.0557
−100	0.0800	2	0.0220	0.0350
Forward contract expected return: −2%				
0%	0.1000	2	0.0225	0.0550
−85	0.1169	2	0.0206	0.0757
−100	0.1200	2	0.0225	0.0750

Source: Windham Capital Management.

Note: The table is based on the following assumptions:
    Portfolio expected return = 10 percent
    Portfolio standard deviation = 15 percent
    Forward contract standard deviation = 12 percent
    Correlation = 40 percent.

Table 7. Results of Alternative Currency Hedging Policies (Simulated), July 1974–December 1991

Hedging Policy	Portfolio Return	Portfolio Standard Deviation
Unhedged	14.92%	12.38%
Fully hedged	14.11	11.66
Optimally hedged	15.18	11.86

Source: Windham Capital Management.

because one year's worth of observations were needed to get estimates of the standard deviations and correlations, and it goes through December 1991.

The results illustrate the negative cost to hedging, because on average, the investor gains from the forward-rate bias. The optimally hedged portfolio has significantly lower risk than the unhedged portfolio and marginally higher risk than a fully hedged portfolio. The returns of the unhedged and fully hedged portfolios should be the same, but they are different because the returns are period specific. The optimally hedged return should be compared with the average for the fully hedged and unhedged portfolios to obtain an estimate of what to expect in the future. The realized risk is the more realistic estimate of what to expect in the future. A strategy that calls for changing the hedge ratio monthly based on historical covariances and forward-rate bias raises a portfolio's return and lowers its risk.

More on the Optimal Hedging Policy

One of the debates in the investment industry is whether to hedge currency exposure. Many investors believe that one should consider hedging only as one acquires foreign assets. Currency returns have historically been positively correlated with domestic assets, which suggests that the minimum-risk hedge ratio should increase as foreign asset exposure decreases. In reality, the optimal hedge ratio has been found to be higher for lower levels of overseas investment. This result is controversial.

A corollary belief is that, even if investors do not have any foreign assets, they should still sell currency forward contracts, because domestic assets have currency risk. For example, suppose an investor has a currency forward contract for the purpose of minimizing risk, and its expected return is zero percent over the long run. The currency has a positive correlation with the underlying portfolio. By selling the currency short, the investor creates an asset with negative correlation and no return. The investor does not have to give up any expected return by selling portfolio assets in order to take this position. The investor has lowered the portfolio's risk without changing its expected return. So if currency returns are positively correlated with U.S. assets, the minimum-risk hedge ratio increases as the investor reduces exposure to foreign assets. When foreign assets are present, one should still hedge.

Based on historical data, the volatility of the typical major currency is about 10 percent. The historical correlation of the major currencies with a 50/50 stock/bond portfolio has been about 13 percent. The implication is that the minimum-risk portfolio of U.S. stocks and bonds with no foreign assets includes a −16 percent weighting in foreign currencies.

Conclusion

Two anomalies have characterized currency returns. One is that they are nonrandom; they follow trends. This anomaly can be exploited by purchasing currencies as they appreciate and selling them as they depreciate. Historically, this strategy has added almost 3 percent to return with about 4 percent risk. The other anomaly is that the forward rate has systematically overestimated subsequent changes in the spot rate. An investor with currency exposure can implement a hedging policy to maximize the expected utility as a function of exposure to currency forward contracts and condition the expected return of the forward contracts on the forward-rate bias. Historically, this strategy has produced a higher return than either a fully hedged or an unhedged strategy and incurred less risk than an unhedged portfolio.

Question and Answer Session

Mark P. Kritzman, CFA

Question: Is there any fundamental explanation for nonrandomness in currencies that would give credibility to an expectation of future serial correlation rather than just relying on the historical statistical observation? That is, why should we expect nonrandomness in currencies to persist? Should we expect forward-rate bias to persist?

Kritzman: Central banks manage exchange rates, and whenever such a large player is interfering with arbitrage, the result is nonrandomness. Central banks are trying to stabilize exchange rates. Suppose exchange rates are in equilibrium and then some news causes a currency to depreciate significantly. The central banks will then support that currency. The central banks are not necessarily preventing the currency from eventually depreciating to its new equilibrium value, but they are making it get there gradually rather than abruptly. This situation induces serial correlation. Any friction that gets in the way of capital moving back and forth also leads to serial correlation.

Question: Have you found evidence of nonrandomness in the major cross-rates?

Kritzman: A few years ago, I discussed my findings with an audience in England. They had already seen the results with the United States, so they asked me to replicate them, using pound-denominated exchange rates. I did find some nonrandomness but not as much as in dollar-denominated exchange rates. That finding lends credence to the idea that nonrandomness is largely a central bank phenomenon, because the central banks during the period I measured managed the U.S. dollar. Eighty percent of world trade is done in the dollar, and that is of interest to central banks.

Question: If central banks are the major influence behind trends, do they, as the major counterparties to currency traders, absorb the currency losses?

Kritzman: I don't know. I suggest that they do not mind losing money. They can always print more. They just consider it the cost of providing stability. I don't know that central banks lose money on average. I suspect that hedgers probably lose money. They are transferring risk. People taking speculative positions are extracting the risk premium from hedgers.

Question: What considerations could cause a structural change in central banks' currency strategies that would lead to serial correlation no longer holding?

Kritzman: Central banks, for political motives, might choose not to cooperate with each other.

Question: In the past six years, the average returns, the individual-year returns, and the cumulative returns of the strategy are barely positive. Do you foresee some elimination of that bias from which you could profit?

Kritzman: Prior to 1989, the average return was about 3.5 percent; since 1989, it has been about 1 percent. I do not know whether this phenomenon is period specific (related to the coup in Russia and the problems associated with the Maastrict Treaty) or whether it indicates a structural change. So far in 1993, currencies have trended, and the consensus suggests that this pattern will continue. Consensus is strong that the U.S. dollar will appreciate against the European currencies. A strong trend might be underway right now.

Question: The data you used in your tests were monthly data. Have you tested other period lengths?

Kritzman: No, but Engel and Hamilton, and Weigel have published studies using other data.[1]

---
[1] Engel and Hamilton 1990 and Weigel 1991.

International Fixed-Income and Currency Strategies

Vilas Gadkari
Director of Asset Management
Salomon Brothers International, Ltd.

> In the long run, risk reduction through currency hedging appears to be substantial, regardless of the level of currency-hedged bond returns. In the medium term, the clash between political and economic objectives creates investment opportunities. In the short term, market expectations can point out inefficiencies, although this judgment may be highly subjective.

The CAPM, although typically thought of as a tool for equity portfolio management can also be used for international fixed-income and currency portfolios. I will discuss three types of fixed-income and currency strategies:

- currency-hedged international bond investments as long-term strategies;
- high-yielding bond-market investments as medium-term strategies; and
- strategies based on market inefficiencies from a short-term perspective.

Currency-Hedged Bonds

One long-term strategy for investing in international fixed-income markets is to purchase foreign bonds while hedging their currency exposure. The effects of currency exposure on risk–return profiles is illustrated in **Figure 1**, which shows unhedged as well as currency-hedged returns in U.S. dollar terms on Japanese, British, German, and Swiss government bonds. In all cases, risk is reduced substantially as currency is hedged. Although most of the unhedged positions have higher returns, high returns from currencies could imply a weak-dollar period from 1978 to 1993. Notice that the Swiss franc has a slightly higher return with currency hedging than without. Thus, even in this period, hedging did not always reduce returns, although it clearly reduced risk.

Figure 2 illustrates 36-month moving bond-market volatilities in U.S. dollars from 1978 through 1992. The unhedged non-U.S. bond index includes both bond returns and currency returns. The U.S. bond series shows a substantial reduction in volatility in the latter half of this period. The currency-hedged non-U.S. bonds had consistently lower volatility than the other two series.

Given the risk reduction indicated by hedging, the next question is whether improved diversification is worth taking currency risk. **Figure 3** shows correlations of returns on hedged and unhedged non-U.S. bonds with the U.S. bond market. With the currency component hedged, the correlation shown is between global interest rates. This correlation appears to be positive and reasonably high during the entire 1981–92 period. Inflation is globally positively linked, and interest rates are also positively linked. The correlation between U.S. and unhedged non-U.S. bonds is lower than the correlation between U.S. and hedged non-U.S. bonds. The difference between the two, which shows how much diversification the currency adds, is not substantial.

In addition, because the major currencies all move generally together against the dollar, a dollar-based investor does not get much diversification by being in the Japanese yen, German mark, or British pound. All the exchange rate indexes rose until about 1984 (**Figure 4**), because that was a strong-dollar period. In the second half of the 1980s, all the currencies were stronger against the U.S. dollar. **Figure 5** shows correlations between three exchange rate pairs: the U.S. dollar/pound and dollar/mark rates, the dollar/yen and dollar/mark rates, and the dollar/yen and dollar/pound rates. Again, these correlations are all fairly high and positive, which supports the point that, for U.S. dollar-based investors,

Figure 1. Effects of Currency Exposure on the Risk–Return Profiles of Government Bonds, in U.S. Dollars

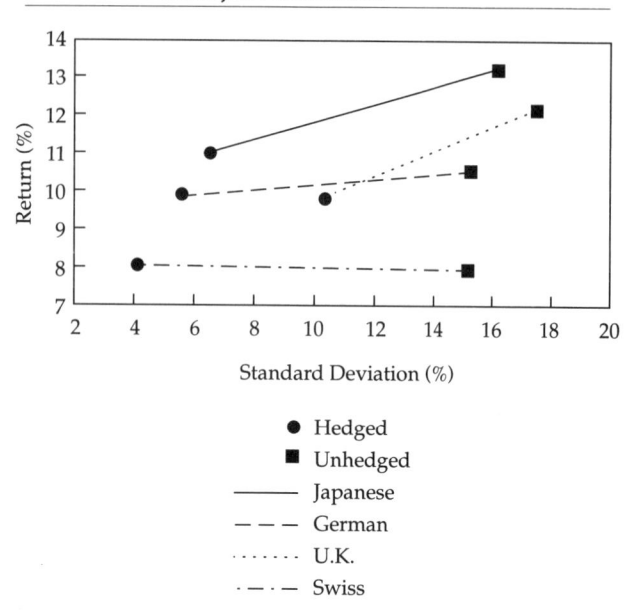

● Hedged
■ Unhedged
— Japanese
– – – German
······ U.K.
–·–·– Swiss

Source: Salomon Brothers.

different currencies do not give substantial diversification benefits.

Although currencies provide only small diversification benefits for dollar-based investors, a non-dollar-based investor could achieve substantial diversification by investing in U.S. markets and accepting currency exposure. The top line in **Figure 6** shows the correlation between a U.S. investment in non-U.S. bonds and the U.S. dollar/foreign exchange

Figure 2. Bond-Market Volatilities: 36-Month Moving Data, in U.S. Dollars

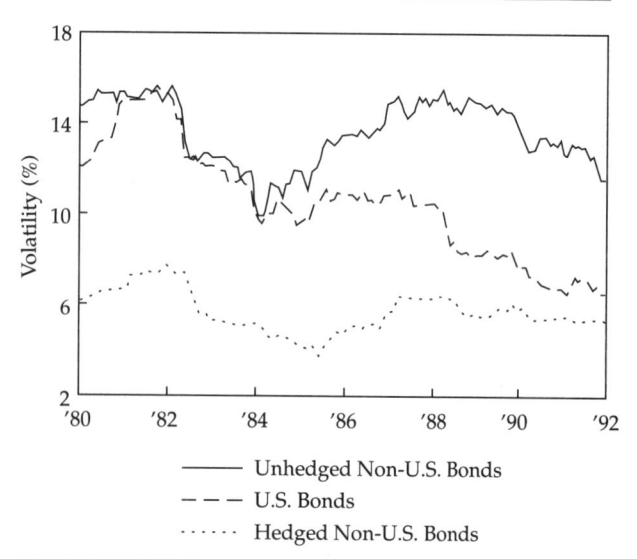

— Unhedged Non-U.S. Bonds
– – – U.S. Bonds
······ Hedged Non-U.S. Bonds

Source: Salomon Brothers.

Figure 3. Correlation of Returns on Hedged and Unhedged Non-U.S. Bonds with U.S. Bonds: 36-Month Moving Data, in U.S. Dollars

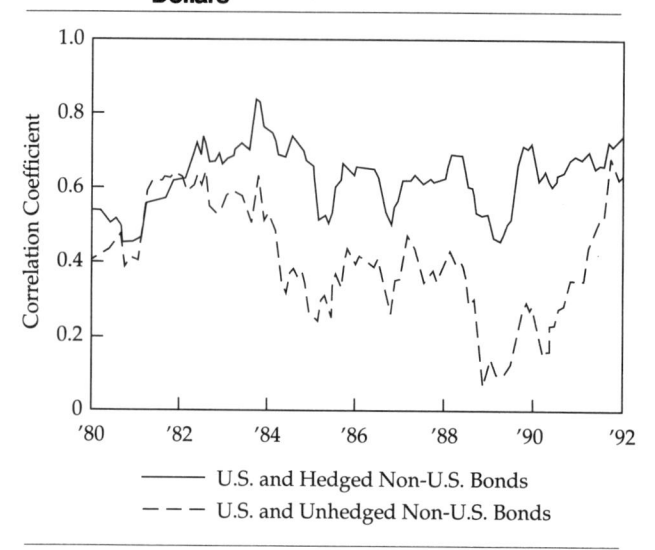

— U.S. and Hedged Non-U.S. Bonds
– – – U.S. and Unhedged Non-U.S. Bonds

Source: Salomon Brothers.

(FX) rate. The correlations are always positive. The lower line traces the converse correlation from a non-U.S. perspective—that is, an investment in U.S. bonds and the foreign exchange/U.S. dollar rate. For the most part, these correlations are negative, indicating substantial diversification benefits.

The reason for this difference in diversification benefits of currencies is related to the dominance of the U.S. economy and the U.S. Federal Reserve Board on foreign exchange markets. In general, when the Federal Reserve is tightening monetary policy, short

Figure 4. Pound, Mark, and Yen Exchange Rates against the U.S. Dollar

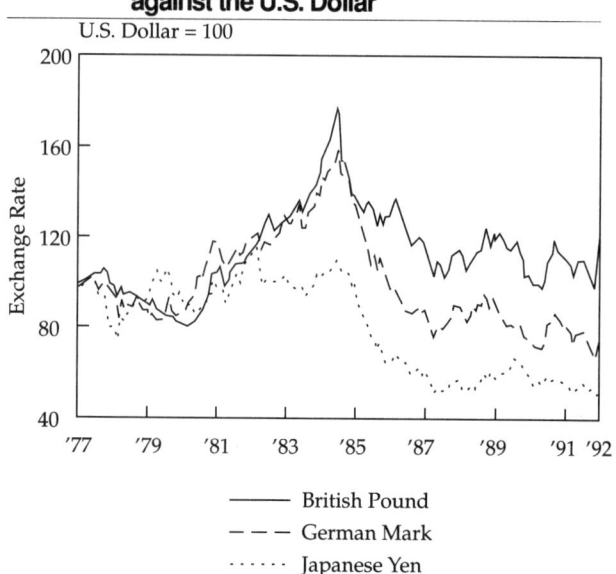

U.S. Dollar = 100

— British Pound
– – – German Mark
······ Japanese Yen

Source: Salomon Brothers.

Figure 5. Correlations between the Pound, Mark, and Yen Exchange Rates versus the U.S. Dollar: 36-Month Moving Data

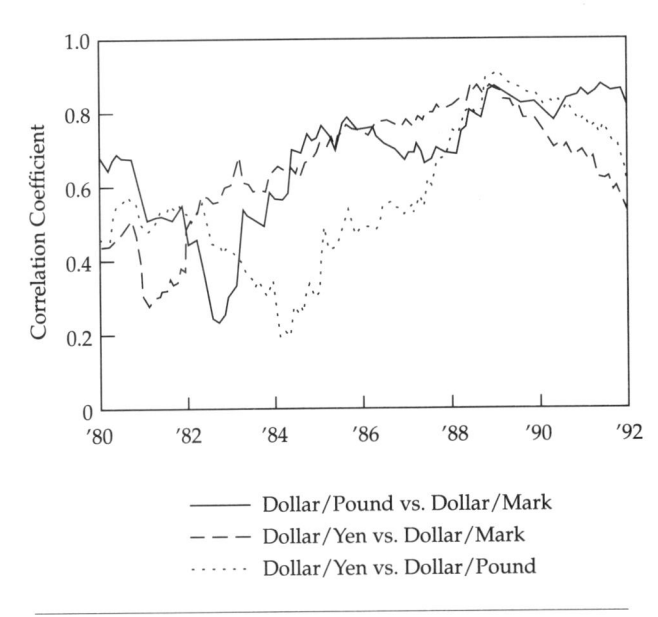

——— Dollar/Pound vs. Dollar/Mark
– – – Dollar/Yen vs. Dollar/Mark
······ Dollar/Yen vs. Dollar/Pound

Source: Salomon Brothers.

rates rise. There is a positive correlation between short and long rates along the yield curve. Therefore, bond yields rise and bond prices fall. Another common consequence of a tightening monetary policy is a strengthening dollar and, by definition, weakening foreign currencies. If non-U.S. investors are investing in the U.S. market, the bonds are going down but the dollar is going up. The correlation between the U.S. market and the U.S. currency in which they are investing is negative.

The U.S. investor investing abroad faces a positive correlation in global interest rates. That is, on average, if U.S. bonds are going down, foreign bonds are also going down. If the U.S. dollar is going up, however, foreign currencies are going down. The bond–currency correlation is positive. The same relationship holds if the policy is reversed and the Fed is easing monetary policy. The U.S. dollar is weaker, and foreign currencies are stronger. U.S. bonds are going up, but so are foreign bonds. Therefore, U.S. investors see a positive correlation when they enter the international marketplace. Positive correlations imply lower diversification benefits than negative correlations.

The role of the U.S. dollar as a world reserve currency could be the cause of such an inefficiency in the global fixed-income and currency markets. When the exchange rate mechanism in Europe was strengthening and Europe began moving toward a single currency, some people believed that Europe would form its own reserve currency. In the Far East, the Japanese yen may become a dominant currency and take some of the burden off the U.S. dollar in the future. These developments would have strong implications for the U.S. dollar-based investor, as they will reduce the asymmetry that is currently observed between correlation structures for U.S. investors on one side and all the major non-U.S. investors on the other side. U.S. investors would do well to consider currency-hedged benchmarks or currency-hedged long-term positions.

Figure 6. Correlation of Bonds and Currencies: 36-Month Moving Data

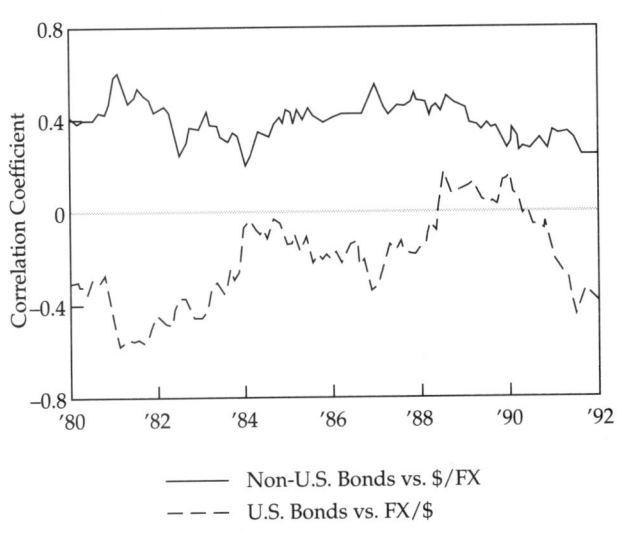

——— Non-U.S. Bonds vs. $/FX
– – – U.S. Bonds vs. FX/$

Source: Salomon Brothers.

Note: FX corresponds to the Salomon Brothers World Government Bond Index currency basket.

High-Yielding Markets

An attractive medium-term international fixed-income strategy involves investing in the higher yielding non-U.S. markets. A comparison of total rates of return on these markets versus U.S. cash and bond markets is presented in **Table 1**. In the cash market, higher yielding cash has had a 4-percentage-point higher return for less than 1 percent higher risk than the non-U.S. cash, unhedged, of the major currencies (Germany, Japan, etc.) since the early 1980s. The five highest yielding cash markets returned almost 6 percentage points more than the U.S. T-bill market.

In the bond markets, non-U.S. bonds had a higher return during this period and much higher volatility than U.S. T-bonds. Currency-hedged non-U.S. bonds had lower returns and substantially lower risk. The five highest yielding bonds had substantially higher returns at lower volatility than the unhedged non-U.S. bonds.

The attractiveness of the high-yielding markets

Table 1. Total Rates of Return on Various Markets

Instrument	Return	Risk
U.S. T-bills (March 1980 through 1992)	8.3	0.9
Unhedged non-U.S. cash	10.0	9.9
High-yielding cash (five highest yielding markets)	14.0	10.7
U.S. T-bonds (January 1986 to December 1992)	9.6	5.3
Non-U.S. bonds	13.7	12.6
Hedged non-U.S. bonds	7.8	4.0
High-yielding bonds (five highest yielding bonds)	16.1	10.5

Sources: Salomon Brothers and J.P. Morgan.

is obvious from this table, but investors should be cautious for the following reasons. First, the observation period may not have been long enough to ensure that these results will always be true. Second, the results for high-yielding markets may not have general application; that is, investors should not pick bonds solely on the basis of yield. Other factors may be important. In the 1980s, for example, a factor boosting these returns was very tight monetary policies around the world. Also, investors in these higher yielding bond markets were demanding extremely high risk premiums because of the high rates of inflation in the 1970s.

Inefficiencies in international capital markets exist because of several factors. Sometimes, the economic policies that authorities in various parts of the world pursue vary widely as a result of varied historical or cultural backgrounds, and the diversity in policies affects the international capital markets. For example, compare policies in the United States and in Germany. Because of the Great Depression, the United States has a policy bias toward accepting an inflationary cycle in order to avoid a recessionary cycle. In Germany, because of hyperinflation in the 1920s, the authorities have a bias toward accepting a recessionary cycle to avoid an inflationary cycle. Such policy differences exist in varying degrees among most countries.

Another factor is the pricing of market expectations, which is not yet efficient in the international markets, partly because the process of internationalization and deregulation is not finished. The global market is still highly segmented. Market expectations in the money markets, for example, could be somewhat different from those in the bond markets, which would create certain inefficiencies.

Liquidity considerations lead to market segmentation. For example, the Spanish market in 1992 had 80 percent of the 10-year bonds held by international investors. In September and October 1992, when international investors did not think the relative value in the Spanish market was very attractive, tremendous liquidity problems developed and certain parts of the market suffered.

The availability and analysis of information for global investors is not uniform and standardized, which also leads to inefficiencies. For example, data on inflation rates are often used for bond-market valuation. Inflation rates, however, are not defined consistently among these countries.

What we in the United States consider standardized market indicators are not necessarily standardized in the rest of the world. The U.K. retail price index (RPI), for example, includes mortgage payments, which have a strong link to short-term interest rates. Thus, as short-term interest rates rise, the RPI in the United Kingdom rises. This effect may or may not be a good reflection of underlying inflation. **Figure 7** illustrates inflation rates in the United Kingdom, Italy, France, and Germany from January 1971 through January 1993.

The high-yielding markets gave a very good re-

Figure 7. European Consumer Price Inflation, 1971–92, Monthly Data

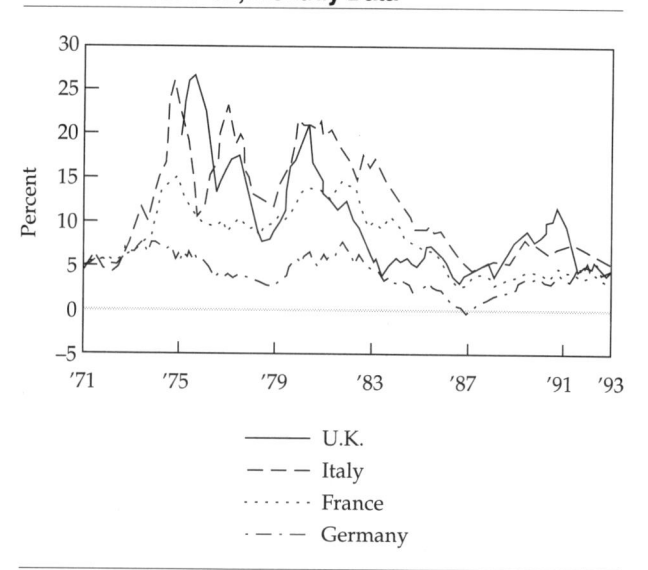

Source: Salomon Brothers.

turn in the 1980s. In the 1970s, inflation rates were so high in these countries that, in the early 1980s, the market demanded very high risk premiums. The market was not necessarily wrong to ask for those risk premiums, but *ex post*, the inflation rates have converged to a great extent, and the tight monetary policies were kept in place long enough for inflation to decline.

Figure 8 illustrates expectations about the manufacturing sectors' productivity in the near future in

Figure 8. Comparison of Estimated Production Prospects in France, Italy, Spain, and Belgium

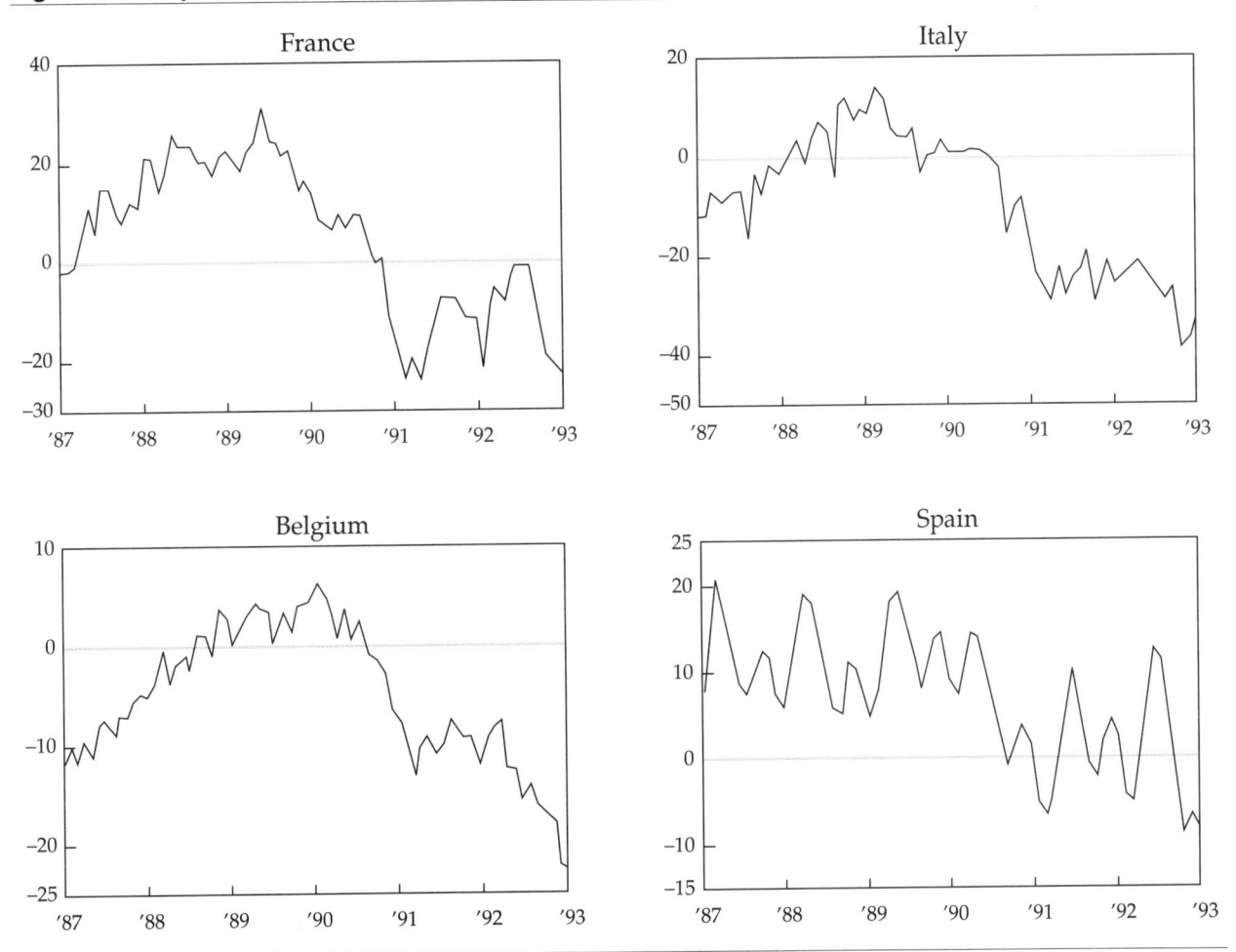

Source: Salomon Brothers.

continental Europe. Surveys that collected consistent, standardized information across markets were not available for this study, so Figure 8 is based on French production prospects, Italian manufacturing sentiment, Spanish production prospects, and leading indicators in Belgium. Sometimes the surveys of sentiment in different countries do not ask the same questions. Nevertheless, international investors will use the answers to form expectations about the countries' performances. If an investment manager could obtain pertinent information about these markets and analyze it, that ability would add value in these markets.

Real bond yields are another possible explanation for the performance of high-yielding markets. Real bond yields have varied considerably in Europe. Real yields in Germany have been relatively stable, even though Figure 7 showed some fluctuation in inflation rates. Real yields can be estimated by subtracting the year-to-year change in the consumer price index from the ten-year yield, but this method does not always work.

Italy, France, and the United Kingdom had much higher short-term rates in the late 1970s and early 1980s than at present, but the rates converged during the late 1980s. Substantial turmoil has characterized the European markets since the middle of 1992. Short-term rates spiked in Italy, for example, in a reflection of political and fiscal problems that created nervousness in that market. Even though France has had a good inflation record, the current exchange rate mechanism (ERM) problems are creating pressures. In the early 1980s, rates in Germany again were well below those in other countries, which suggests that markets were demanding a much higher risk premium from the non-German markets.

France, the United Kingdom, and Italy represent slightly different policy mixes. French policies in the past several years have helped the inflation convergence against Germany. France is still holding on to the ERM, thus short-term interest rates are somewhat higher there than in the United Kingdom, which has recently broken away from the ERM. Italy stands out because its policy moves have not succeeded in containing inflation, and its fiscal problems remain substantial.

The information on higher yielding securities can be used in forming investment strategies in international currency markets. For example, **Figure 9** illustrates how purchasing power parity (PPP) and exchange rate expectations can be used to find value in French bond markets. The PPP is a measure using relative consumer prices. This series starts in 1987, when the last realignment occurred. Assuming the realignment was successful, we should now be looking at the differences between the exchange rate movement and what the PPP suggests since 1987.

The example uses the French franc/German mark (FFr/DM) exchange rate and the FFr/DM PPP. The projection for 1993 through 1997 is that expectations will be the same for the next four years. French francs should be strengthening during the next four years because inflation forecasts for France are lower than those for Germany, although the five-year bond yields suggest that francs will depreciate. The prospect is for fairly substantial cushions in these markets. The medium-term strategy would then favor five-year French bonds versus German bonds. This strategy does not take into account near-term currency risks associated with ERM pressures. The French franc can depreciate by 9.8 percent before the strategy underperforms German bonds.

Figure 10 shows a similar analysis for Italy, which has had major fiscal problems accompanied by substantial currency depreciation. After 1987, the exchange rate moved toward the lower half of what used to be its ERM band and stayed there until September 1992, when it was forced out of the system. By using the inflation forecast most economists are publishing, the PPP again forms the upward band. The exchange rate offers a 22 percent cushion. Some would argue that this cushion is the risk premium the market is demanding above the inflation rate differential. Investors should try to determine whether 22 percent over the next five years is sufficient.

Identifying Inefficiencies

Short-term fixed-income strategies involve identifying inefficiencies in bond markets. These inefficiencies in international bond markets occur because of conflicts created by long-term policy goals versus short-term political objectives and because of central bank independence.

Figure 9. Value in the French Bond Market, 1987–92 and Projections for 1993–97, Monthly Data

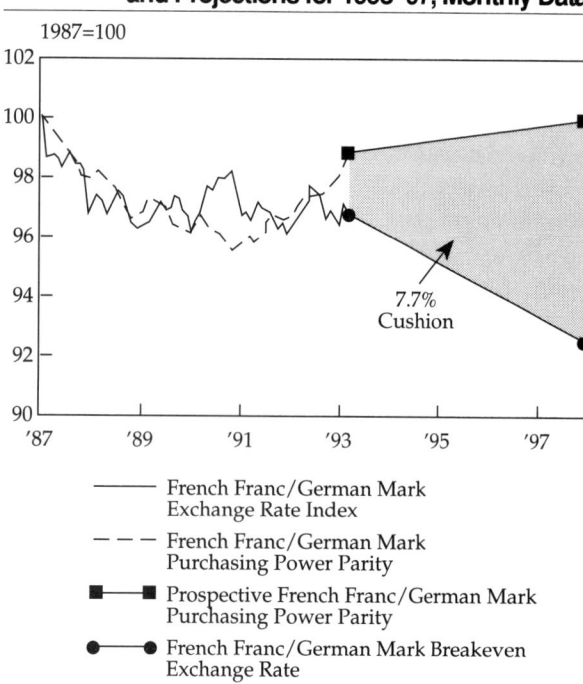

Source: Salomon Brothers.

Notes: PPP is measured using relative consumer prices. Prospective PPP is extrapolated using 1993 CPI forecasts. The breakeven exchange rate is for holding a five-year government bond to maturity.

Figure 10. Value in the Italian Bond Market, 1987–92 and Projections for 1993–97, Monthly Data

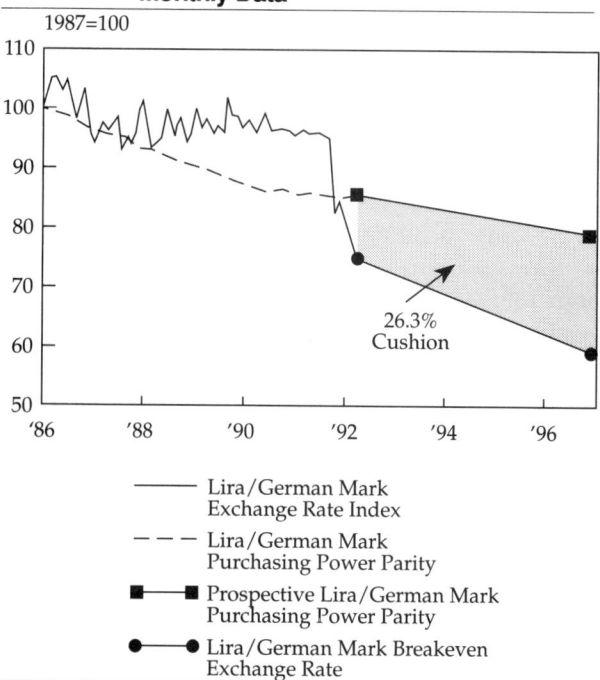

Source: Salomon Brothers.

Notes: PPP is measured using relative consumer prices. Prospective PPP is extrapolated using 1993 CPI forecast. The breakeven exchange rate is for holding a five-year government bond to maturity.

Most countries have low inflation and low unemployment as long-term goals. In line with those goals, most central banks pursue monetary policies designed to keep inflation rates low from a long-term perspective. At times, however, politicians have short-term political goals. These two sets of goals do not always come together. Conflicts are apparent today in Europe, Japan, and the United States as authorities try to balance these ends. The efforts to balance exchange rate policy, monetary policy, and fiscal policy provide an interesting mix of policies among countries and a host of opportunities, particularly in currency markets.

Central bank independence is another interesting issue. Some studies have been done on long-term inflation and central bank independence. In countries such as Germany, where the central bank is very independent, the rate of inflation is low. In countries where central banks are not independent, inflation rates, on average, have been higher.

The European Community illustrates the complexity. **Figure 11** shows that in 1990, inflation was about 10 percent and unemployment was about 5 percent in Sweden. Today, Sweden has an inflation rate of less than 4 percent. The cost of getting that inflation rate down has been unemployment of about 6 percent and rising. The United Kingdom has much higher inflation, which has come down sharply at a much higher price in unemployment. Since mid-1992, these two countries have broken their relationship with the ERM.

The unemployment problems are much more severe than the ones on the inflation front. Only in Germany would the arrow go the other way. Since 1990, both inflation and unemployment have risen. In 1990, the German budget had a surplus, but real rates were very high. Today, the budget deficit is very high and real short-term interest rates have come down. Figure 11 captures the movement of real short-term interest rates during the past six months, which explains the sharp drop in interest rates; the budget deficit is shown for a longer period, from 1990 to 1993.

The three countries that have broken out of the ERM—the United Kingdom, Italy, and Sweden—have declining interest rates. France, Spain, and Denmark are still holding on within the ERM and are suffering high interest rates and high budget deficits. In all cases, as **Figure 12** shows, budget deficits have increased in these European economies.

Yield-Curve Analysis and Short-Term Strategies

Yield curves can be indicators of market expectations. **Table 2** contains a consensus outlook on the U.K. economy. Growth rates have increased slightly, consumer prices decreased from about 6 percent in 1991 to about 3 percent in 1993, but unemployment rose substantially. **Figure 13** illustrates market expectations by using data available through the futures market. These are three-month British pound and German mark interest rates implied by the futures market. The market expects U.K. short rates to

Figure 11. Unemployment and Inflation in Selected European Economies, 1990 and 1993

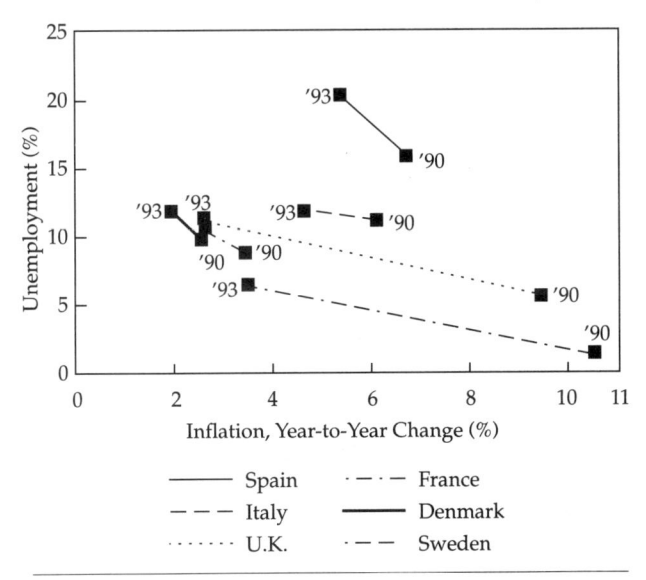

Source: Salomon Brothers.

Figure 12. Budget Deficits and Real Short-Term Interest Rates in Selected European Economies, 1990 and 1993

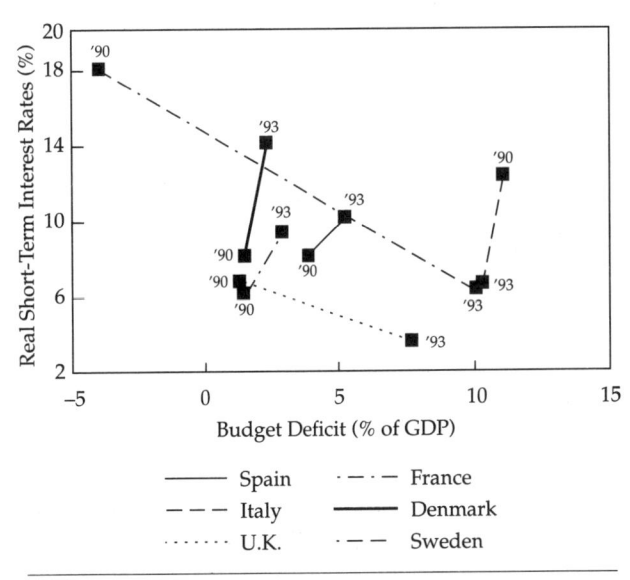

Source: Salomon Brothers.

Notes: Interest rates based on monthly data, September 1992 to March 1993; budget deficits based on annual data, 1990 and 1993.

Table 2. United Kingdom Economic Outlook, 1991–93

Indicator	1991	1992	1993
GDP	−2.4%	−0.9%	1.0 %
Private consumption	−2.1	−0.3	0.9
Investment	−9.9	−3.1	−0.1
Consumer prices	5.9	3.8	2.8
Current account (billions of pounds sterling)	−6.3	−12.2	−14.7
Unemployment rate (level)	8.1%	9.9%	10.9%

Source: Salomon Brothers.

Note: Data are year-to-year percentage changes, except where specified.

drop in the near future but then to start rising very quickly, which suggests that the market is concerned about inflation rates. The German mark rates are used here to exemplify the European environment, in which the marketplace is expecting substantial cuts in rates. Indeed, it is difficult to visualize a situation in which the U.K. authorities would start raising rates when unemployment is still rising rapidly. A base rate cut in the United Kingdom not long after January 14 brought the whole curve down. Using a figure, such as Figure 13, is one way to compare market expectations with one's own expectations based on the economic outlook.

Figure 14 shows the discount and Lombard rates (both short-term rates) in Germany going back to 1967. In each cycle, the discount rate decreased to about 3 percent, but the market's current expectations about the discount rate show short rates bottoming out through 1993 at about 6 percent. The market is expecting rates to flatten out and then start to rise. This pattern of market expectations appears to be at odds with the historical data and may or may not match an individual investor's own expectations based on various economic indicators.

Figure 13. Market Expectations for Three-Month British Pound and German Mark Interest Rates

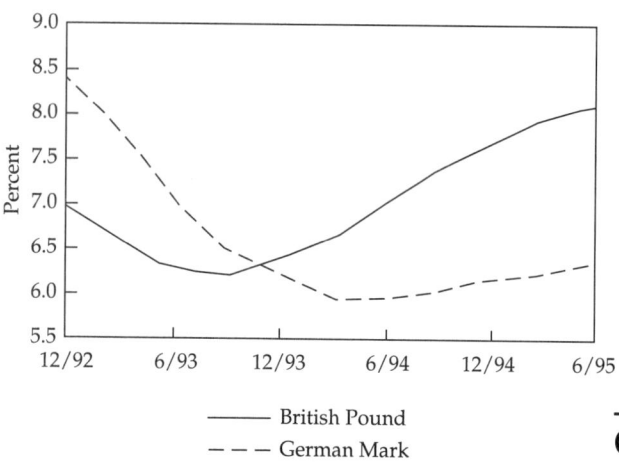

Source: Rates taken from LIFFE contracts as of January 14, 1993.

Figure 14. Three-Month German Mark Rates as Priced in EuroDM Futures Market, 1967–95[a]

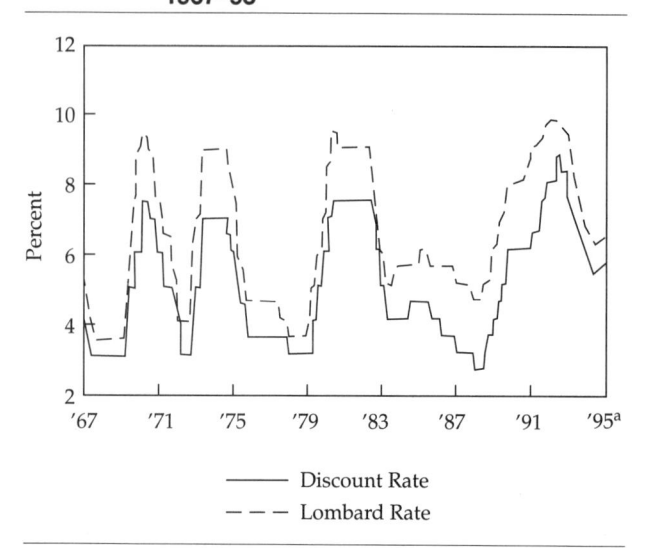

Source: Salomon Brothers.
[a]Estimate.

Figure 15 shows Swedish yield-curve changes (Swedish krona, SKr,) expected between January 1993 and January 1994. The changes implied over the 12-month period by today's yield curve indicate that the entire yield curve in Sweden is going to rise. Rates are expected to rise even though, as shown in **Table 3**, Sweden is in the midst of the worst recession in Europe, unemployment is rising quickly, and the banking system is in deep trouble. The lower line in Figure 15, a benchmark in German marks, suggests that the marketplace in Europe is expecting substantial rate cuts. The expectations in the other European countries suggests, in particular, that market fears are driving expectations in the Swedish market to levels that seem unrealistic or inefficient.

An investor could set up strategies of relatively low risk based on these short-term factors, but they must be subjective strategies based on the investor's own view of the marketplace.

Conclusion

The aim of this presentation has been to focus on what may be considered inefficiencies in the interna-

Figure 15. Swedish Yield Curve Compared with DM Benchmark

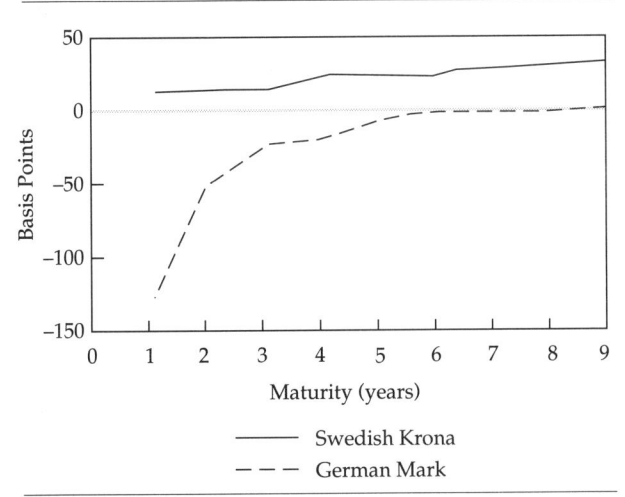

Source: Salomon Brothers.

Note: Yield-curve changes implied over 12-month period beginning January 22, 1993.

Table 3. Swedish Economic Outlook, 1991–93

Indicator	1991	1992	1993
GDP	–1.2%	–1.4%	–1.5%
Private consumption	1.0	–1.5	–2.5
Investment	–8.3	–8.7	–9.0
Consumer prices	9.4	2.3	3.5
Current account (billions of Swedish krona)	–20.2	–20.0	–10.2
Unemployment rate (level)	2.7%	4.8%	6.5%

Source: Salomon Brothers.

Note: Data are year-to-year percentage changes, except where specified.

tional markets and to give a few examples to illustrate the point. First, from a long-term perspective, currency-hedged bond investments seem to offer a better risk–return trade-off for the U.S. investor in foreign markets than unhedged bond instruments. Whether currency-hedged investments will provide higher or lower returns in the long run is not clear, but the risk reduction achieved through currency hedging appears to be substantial. Part of the explanation for this observation may be the role of the U.S. dollar as a world reserve currency, and part the influence of the U.S. economy and the Federal Reserve on foreign exchange markets.

Second, in the medium term, issues related to different policy frameworks in various countries create dislocations. When political priorities and economic realities clash, opportunities are created in international markets.

Finally, from a short-term perspective, yield-curve analysis to extract information about market expectations can point out inefficiencies in international markets. The short-term consideration may at times, however, be highly subjective.

Question and Answer Session

Vilas Gadkari

Question: In your hedged-versus-unhedged examples and your 36-month moving data, how often are you rolling the currency hedges?

Gadkari: The currency hedges are rolled monthly. Each month, we look at the price of the portfolio and the accrued interest and hedge that part but leave the bond price changes unhedged. We have found that the bond price changes are not significant, because from the hedging perspective, the exposure is to the change in exchange rate multiplied by the change in bond price. In other words, if the exchange rate remains unchanged, your position is well hedged. If the bond price does not change, the change in the exchange rate does not matter. The multiplication of those two differences is a small amount, which serves the purpose we are trying to accomplish.

Question: When deciding whether currencies offer a diversification benefit, you looked only at a fixed-income portfolio. If you were to consider the diversifying effect on the total portfolio, would you be more persuaded of the diversification benefit of currencies?

Gadkari: What strikes me most is that exchange rates against U.S. dollars are highly positively correlated. Thus, going into different currencies does not diversify exchange rate risk much. The result is milder for the equity markets, because the correlations between currency and equity markets are very low. Investors would get diversification benefits between currencies and equity markets but not between different currencies.

Prospective Real Yields and Active Global Bond Management

Robert J. Bernstein
Senior Vice President, Director of Fixed Income
Delaware Investment Advisers

Ian G. Sims
Director, Senior Portfolio Manager
Delaware International Advisers, Ltd.

> The prospective-real-yield approach, based on the purchasing power parity concept, appears to have real-world application, with a minimal need for forecasting. Only inflation need be forecast. Both perfect foresight and lagged M2 forecasts appear to produce stable results in the long run.

The prospective-real-yield approach is a simple discipline built on the concept of today's yield minus tomorrow's inflation. Its appeal is that it works without the need to predict short-term interest rates or short-term exchange rate movements; the only variable that needs to be predicted is inflation. Given out-of-sample inflation forecasts that are available from a moment in time with tolerable ranges, this process can add considerable value.

The classic approach to global bond management, as opposed to the prospective-real-yield approach, involves forecasting interest and currency rates within some macroeconomic scenario and then adjusting country allocations according to that scenario. Most managers believe the currency component of return is where applying their efforts will add the greatest value. Unfortunately, most models for forecasting exchange rates and interest rates have proved to be difficult to apply consistently over time. Consequently, global bond managers use a variety of techniques, including econometric modeling, technical analysis, and eclectic reasoning.

We believe that strong excess returns in the world bond market can be achieved by focusing on the highest prospective real yield. We are fairly comfortable that the prospective-real-yield concept has application in the real world, without the need for a lot of data. The theoretical building blocks central to the whole approach are that purchasing power parity (PPP) holds in the long run, that bonds will be redeemed at par on the same date, and that reinvestment rates are negligible.

The PPP concept, one of the oldest economic theories, dates back to 15th century Spain. In words, the theory states that exchange rates between two countries are a function of the price of a basket of goods in one country divided by the price of a basket of goods in the second country. Most foreign exchange observers have found significant deviations from PPP at any given moment, although in the long run, exchange rates do follow price differentials. The reasons for the short-run deviations include major differences in economic cycles and worldwide demand, and current-account differences—all of which create immediate dislocations in the relationship between spot prices and PPP. As a result, the hypothesis that countries with the highest *ex post* long-run prospective real yields provide the highest returns is not merely a function of observations or of data mining but is a tautology, if the inflation forecast is correct.

An example of how long-run prospective real yield works is presented in **Table 1**. Assume today's yields are 6.5 percent in the United States and 7 percent in Germany. Also assume that during the next 10–20 years, the inflation rate will be 2 percent in the United States and 4 percent in Germany. Subtracting the expected inflation rates from today's yields for each country produces the prospective

Table 1. Purchasing Power Parity Example

Country	Yield	Inflation	Currency Return (PPP holds)	Nominal Return in U.S. Dollars	Prospective Real Yield
United States	6.5%	2.0%	0.0%	6.5%	4.5%
Germany	7.0	4.0	−2.0	5.0	3.0

Source: Ian G. Sims.

yields of 4.5 percent and 3 percent, respectively. Assuming PPP holds, the nominal returns in U.S. dollars are 6.5 percent and 5.0 percent, respectively. Thus, both the nominal return in U.S. dollars and the prospective real yield are higher for the United States.

The empirical evidence of this simple framework escapes a great number of practitioners. **Figure 1** illustrates this relationship using countries in the Salomon World Bond Index from 1974 to 1990. The *ex post* prospective real yield at the time of the index's inception is plotted against the annualized returns of a long-term bond purchased on the basis of those prospective real yields. The relationship between returns and the prospective real yields is solid.

Of course, portfolio managers in the real world do not buy and hold securities for 17-year periods, nor can they accurately forecast inflation over 17-year time frames. From a real-world perspective, portfolios will be rebalanced more frequently and two years is probably the time frame in which an inflation forecast has some value. Anything significantly less than two years provides a strong argument that the embodiment of that forecast is in the current rates, and anything significantly longer involves predicting major political changes, which ultimately have a significant impact on inflation rates.

Figure 1. Annualized Returns and Prospective Real Yields: Countries in Salomon World Bond Index, 1974–90

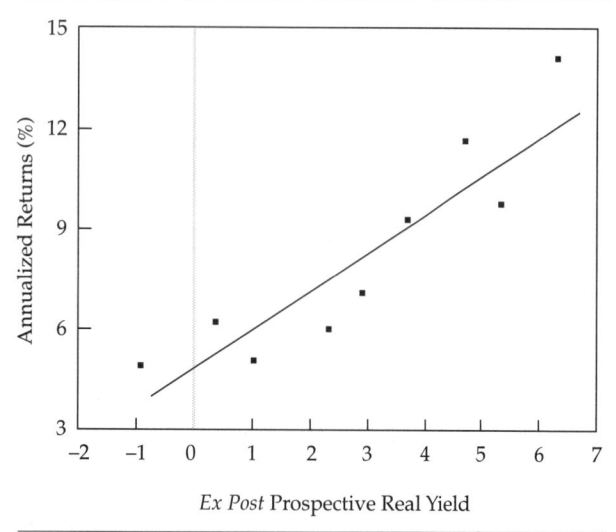

Source: Ian G. Sims.

Tests of Prospective Real Yield

Two tests were performed to evaluate the usefulness of the prospective-real-yield (*PRY*) technique. The first is a statistical test using regression analysis. The second is a simulated investment strategy that constructs portfolios using a mean–variance optimizer.

The Statistical Test

The statistical test is a simple linear regression:

$$RELRET_{j:t+1} = a + b\,PRYDF_{j:t,t+24} + E_{t+1},$$

where

$RELRET_{j:t+1}$ = monthly unhedged total return differential with the U.S. of the *j*th country bond market in U.S. dollars, and

$PRYDF_{j:t,t+24} = PRY_{j:t,t+24} - PRY_{us:t,t+24}.$

In this definition,

$$PRY_{j:t,t+24} = 100\left[\frac{(1+Y_{j:t})/100}{(1+P_{j:t,t+24}/100)} - 1\right]$$

where

$Y_{j:t}$ = yield to maturity of *j*th country benchmark maturity bond at time *t*, and

$P_{j:t,t+24}$ = annualized future two-year (24-month) inflation rate of the *j*th country.

The linear regression represents the relative return of another country's bond market in U.S. dollars less the U.S. bond market return in U.S. dollars as a function of the previous month's prospective-real-yield differential between those two countries. For example, in March 1993, the difference in return (in U.S. dollars) of owning a Japanese bond at the end of that month and a U.S. bond will be a function of the difference in their prospective real yields in February. The prospective real yield is defined as the yield less the next two years' inflation rate.

The data for the analysis are monthly, unhedged

country bond market returns in U.S. dollars. The study used the Salomon World Bond Index, which begins in 1978, and extended it back four years to 1974, the inception of the floating-rate era (although this technique also works well before the beginning of floating rates). The ending time period of the study is 1990. The Salomon index tracks nine countries: the United States, Canada, Australia, Japan, the United Kingdom, Germany, Holland, France, and Switzerland. Data on yields in each country on benchmark bonds of about 10 years in maturity are from the Organization for Economic Cooperation and Development (OECD).

The formulation was tested with three definitions of inflation—two forecasts and the actual outcome. The first inflation forecast for each country was generated from an M2 money supply model based on Friedman's original work (1956, 1970), which proposes that an increase in money supply is followed by a proportional increase in inflation about two years later. This procedure was repeated monthly for each country on an out-of-sample basis, so (9 countries × 17 years × 12 months) 1,836 regressions were performed in total. The two-year lag ensures that these inflation forecasts could have been made with the published data at the time.

The second set of inflation forecasts are those published by the OECD, a large international economic agency based in Paris that has published forecasts for the major 24 industrialized countries for the past 25 years.

The third inflation "forecast" is perfect foresight. This method assumes we know what inflation is. It does not tell us anything we could achieve practically, because no one is capable of making perfectly accurate inflation forecasts, but it does establish a bound on what can be achieved using this model.

The results of the hypothesis-testing regression model using each of the three measures of inflation are presented in **Table 2**. The results suggest that the prospective-real-yield differentials when the M2 model and the OECD forecast are used appear to be good predictors of future monthly return differentials. For the regression using the M2 model to forecast inflation, the average slope across countries is statistically significant at 0.31. The R^2 is 2.9 percent, which may seem low, but these are monthly data

Table 2. Regression Results: Average over Nine Countries

Predictor	Slope	t-statistic	R^2
M2 model	0.311	2.35	0.029
OECD	0.240	1.56	0.016
Perfect foresight	0.394	3.44	0.057

Source: Ian G. Sims.

and, therefore, have a lot of noise; with quarterly, six-month, or one-year data, the R^2 would increase. With the OECD forecast, the slope is 0.24 with a t-statistic of 1.56 and an R^2 of 1.6 percent. Despite the low R^2, this technique achieves a lot of consistency, as will be seen later from the simulations. Finally, the perfect foresight forecast shows a strong positive slope of 0.39 and an R^2 of 5.7 percent.

To strengthen the results, we tested the accuracy of the inflation forecasts. The M2 model, for example, may actually be a poor predictor of inflation, but it may capture some other aspect of currency movements, which would then make it a good predictor of future returns. **Table 3** shows the results of tests of inflation forecast accuracy for the three methods. The M2 model forecast, with a variance of 11.3, has the largest variance between predicted and actual outcome. M2 monetary models worked well in the early 1970s, but because of financial deregulation and liberalization in the 1980s, these models lost much of their explanatory power and fell into some degree of disrepute. The current inflation rate as a predictor of the next two years' rate has a variance of 9.3. The OECD forecasts have the least variance of the three methods.

We also used variance analysis to examine inflation differentials between countries. The usefulness of the prospective-real-yield technique does not depend on the absolute level of inflation but on the differentials between countries. The results are identical to the actual variances for the OECD rate and slightly worse for the current inflation rate forecast. The M2 inflation forecast, however, is significantly better at forecasting differentials between countries' inflation rates than at forecasting the actual level of inflation in each country. The fact that the M2 model is better at forecasting country-differential inflation than the current inflation rate is very promising, because even though analysts may not have a particularly good inflation forecast for a particular country, they can still get good returns if the inflation differentials are being forecast well.

To illustrate this point, **Table 4** is a hypothetical example, using Germany and the United States, of a comparison of inflation forecasts based on differentials and actual levels of inflation. Assume that actual future inflation rates will be 2 percent in the United States and 4 percent in Germany. The U.S./Germany differential is –2. The next two columns compare two inflation forecasts. Forecast X shows 4 percent inflation in the United States and 3 percent in Germany. Forecast Y shows 5 percent in the United States and 6 percent in Germany. Forecast X is closer to the actual rate than forecast Y in both countries. Forecast Y, however, is implicitly fore-

Table 3. Inflation Forecast Accuracy

	Variance		Snedecor's F-Value	
Predictor	Actual	Country Differentials	Actual vs. Differentials	Forecast vs. Current Differentials
M2	11.3	8.4	1.35**	1.24**
OECD	7.5	7.5	1.03	1.42**
Current inflation rate	9.3	9.8	1.05	

Source: Ian G. Sims.

** Significant at the 1 percent level or better.

casting a differential of –1, which is much closer to the –2 outcome than the differential of forecast X, 1, which is closer at the individual country level.

The prospective real yields based on actual inflation are 4.5 percent in the United States and 3.0 percent in Germany, giving a differential of 1.5. With the inflation forecast from forecast X, the prospective real yields are 2.5 percent in the United States and 4.0 percent in Germany, giving a differential of –1.5. For forecast Y, the prospective real yield is 1.5 percent in the United States and 1.0 percent in Germany, giving a differential of 0.5. To the extent that prospective real yield is a good predictor of country return differentials, forecast Y will have better investment success because Y's differential forecast is better than X's.

Of course, many factors that affect world inflation are hard to predict. For example, oil prices have been very volatile over the years, which affects all countries to some extent. The method's dependency on forecasting inflation differentials, rather than absolute inflation levels, strengthens the prospective real yield as a practical investment tool.

Investment Strategy Simulation

Simulation may provide more interesting results than the statistical approach. In this study's simulation, we used mean–variance optimization to create a global bond portfolio each month. The prospective real yield was used as the expected return estimate, and the variance–covariance of returns relative to the Salomon World Bond Index was used as the risk estimate. (Using relative risk is more appropriate than using the absolute level of risk for an active global bond manager because the manager's benchmark is generally the index and it is the responsibility of the client and consultant to monitor and plan the risk of the overall fund.)

Because this test extends over time, several portfolios were created. A consistent point on the efficient frontier must be selected, and we chose three-quarters of the expected excess return. The choice may seem a little aggressive, but in global bond management, most managers outperform the index. No one can afford to fall too far behind competitors, so return is of great importance.

The simulation approach provides strong support for the use of prospective real yields. **Table 5** shows the results of the simulation for each of the three inflation-forecasting methods. With the M2 inflation forecast, the excess return exceeded the benchmark index by 4.6 percent, or 460 basis points. That is top-decile performance. When the OECD inflation forecast and the perfect foresight forecast were used, the excess returns exceeded the benchmark by 2.3 percent and 7.3 percent, respectively. These numbers are net of management fees and transaction costs, so at least 100 basis points have been taken out of these numbers annually.

The cumulative net performance of the prospective-real-yield strategies are shown in **Figure 2**. For the 1974–90 period, perfect foresight, not surprisingly, gives significantly higher returns than the other measures. The performance is extremely stable, with no two-year underperformance periods. Considering how many factors affect currencies, this

Table 4. Inflation Forecasts: Differentials versus Actual

Country	Actual Future Inflation (a)	Inflation Forecast X (b)	Inflation Forecast Y (c)	Bond Yield (d)	Ex Post Prospective Real Yield (d) – (a)	Prospective Real Yield X (d) – (b)	Prospective Real Yield Y (d) – (c)
United States	2	4	5	6.5	4.5	2.5	1.5
Germany	4	3	6	7.0	3.0	4.0	1.0
U.S./Germany differential	–2	1	–1		1.5	–1.5	0.5

Source: Ian G. Sims.

Table 5. Investment Strategy Annualized Net Returns

Predictor	Net Return	Standard Deviation	Currency Contribution	Turnover
M2 model	15.7% (4.6)*	10.0% (1.0)	2.8% (1.6)	170%
OECD	13.2 (2.3)*	10.8 (1.8)	1.0 (−0.2)	205
Perfect foresight	18.7 (7.3)*	11.6 (1.6)	4.4 (3.6)*	144

Source: Ian G. Sims.

* Significant at the 5 percent level or better.

result is quite interesting. During this period, there were oil shocks; the Reagan years of twin (budget and trade) deficits; massive fiscal shocks to the world economy; German unification; large deficits in the late 1980s, particularly on a bilateral basis between Japan and the United States; and some significant changes in monetary policy. Throughout these political and economic changes, the perfect foresight approach generates stable returns. This result stands perhaps in some contrast to the perception that currencies are irrational, speculative, or hard to explain.

The result for the M2 model is surprising because of its consistency. The M2 model gave a 4.6 annualized excess return, but over time—apart from some underperformance in very strong markets in 1985 and 1986, when investors were getting 30–40 percent annual returns on international bonds from a U.S. base—M2 has had a consistent and stable cumulative outperformance pattern. The 1970s are not much of a surprise, because money supply models worked well then. What may be surprising is how well this model worked throughout the 1980s; money supply was not a good predictor of domestic inflation in the 1980s because of financial liberalization and deregulation. Those processes were occurring to a greater or lesser extent in various countries, however. When looking at the differences between those countries' inflation rates, as forecasted by M2, a lot of netting out occurs. The forecast errors are closely correlated in some cases, particularly in the Anglo-Saxon world.

On the whole, the OECD forecasts had a stable outperformance pattern over time, except for 1980 and 1981. In those two years, the OECD forecasts underperformed the M2 forecasts because the OECD did not believe U.S. Federal Reserve Chairman Paul Volker. The OECD analysts forecast that inflation in the United States would continue at high double-digit levels for several years, but they were very benign about the German inflation outlook.

Extensions to the Study

Nothing is free in using the prospective-real-yield technique: If you get inflation wrong, you will suffer. The overall message, however, is that inflation forecasts of sufficient accuracy to enable this technique to be successful do exist.

Because of the sensitivity of the strategy to inflation forecasts, we tested alternative proxies for future inflation. First, we looked at the results for the prospective real yield assuming current inflation rates and zero inflation—that is, the nominal yield. **Figure 3** shows the cumulative net performance relative to an unhedged index of the nominal and real-yield strategies. In both cases, the pattern is quite volatile. In some subperiods, the outperformance of real yield is very strong. For example, it performed well in the late 1970s; its cumulative outperformance reached 130, which would have been 3–4 percent annually. From 1980 onward, however, performance deteriorated.

These results suggest that the current real yield is not a consistently good forecast of future returns. This finding is in contrast to studies that have demonstrated that using the present inflation rate has some benefit in this framework. Those studies do not include Australia, however, and between 1985 and 1986, when Australia had high current real yields but performed very badly, that naive strategy failed.

Figure 2. Cumulative Net Performance Relative to Unhedged Index: Prospective Real-Yield Strategies

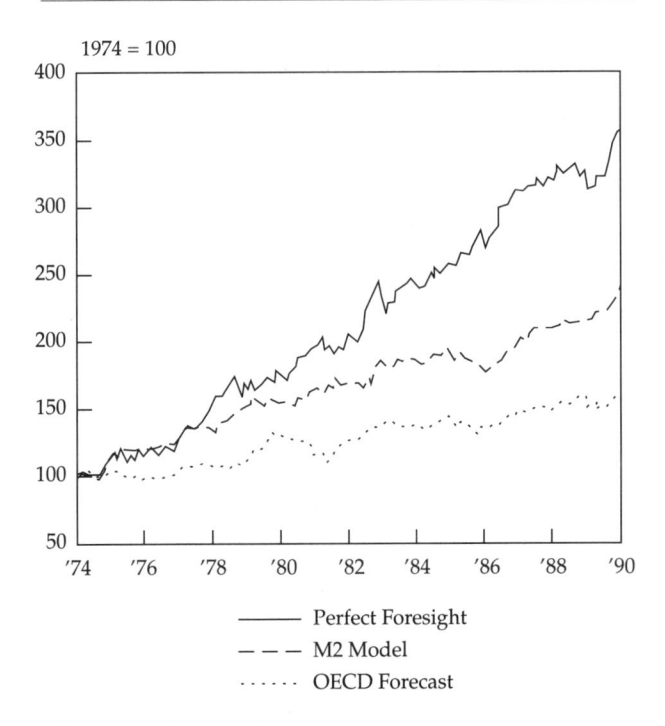

Source: Ian G. Sims.

Figure 3. Cumulative Net Performance Relative to Unhedged Index: Nominal and Real-Yield Strategies

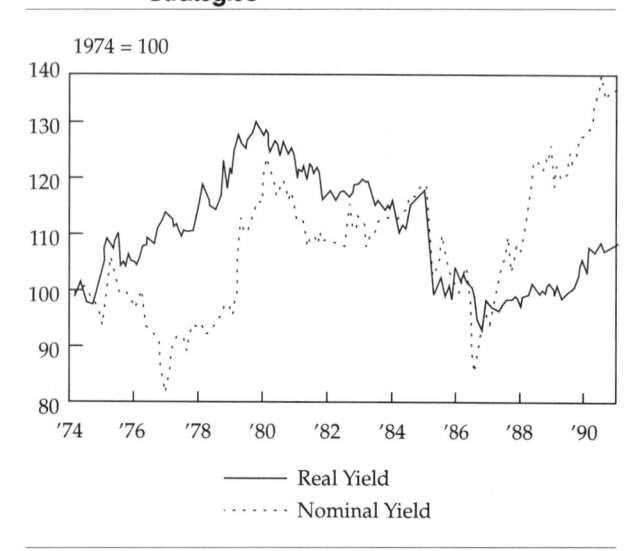

Source: Ian G. Sims.

How about simply investing in high-yielding countries and ignoring inflation? A number of global bond managers operating from a U.S. base are fairly new, and many have merely played the yield game and it worked. It did not work in 1992 because the European exchange rate mechanism (ERM) fell apart. Although simple yield does work at times, it is not a good technique if one is looking for something stable for long periods.

Using short-term interest rates instead of yields provides somewhat better results. **Figure 4** shows the results for the same analysis as applied in Figure 3 but with the nominal and the real short-term rates used. Over time, the absolute performance achieved with nominal short-term rates is close to the prospective real yield using the M2 inflation forecast—about 4.5 percent annualized. The approach has appeared to be reasonably successful in the past, but it has been very volatile. It can work strongly over subperiods, but it fell apart in 1992 similarly to the simple-yield approach because of the ERM's collapse. The strategy of investing in countries with the highest nominal short-term rates is also devoid of theory. Actually, it runs counter to the theory of uncovered interest parity without risk premiums, which states that currency depreciation should offset short-term rate differences. The performance of the real short-term interest rate is uninspiring.

Finally, we considered using inflation forecasts within domestic markets. If an analyst is good at forecasting inflation, then that analyst should be able to make money in the domestic market by taking long- or short-duration positions. We looked at this possibility for a number of countries. For the United States, for example, we constructed a T-bill/T-bond index—half bills or short-rate instruments and half long bonds. The strategy involved investing 100 percent in T-bills if the forecast for the next two years' inflation rose and 100 percent in T-bonds if the forecast for the next two years' inflation fell. The results for each of the three forecasting models are shown in **Figure 5**.

Most people think they could make a lot of money if they had perfect foresight about inflation. As Figure 5 shows, in the United States, perfect fore-

Figure 4. Cumulative Net Performance Relative to Unhedged Index: Nominal and Real Short-Term Rate Strategies

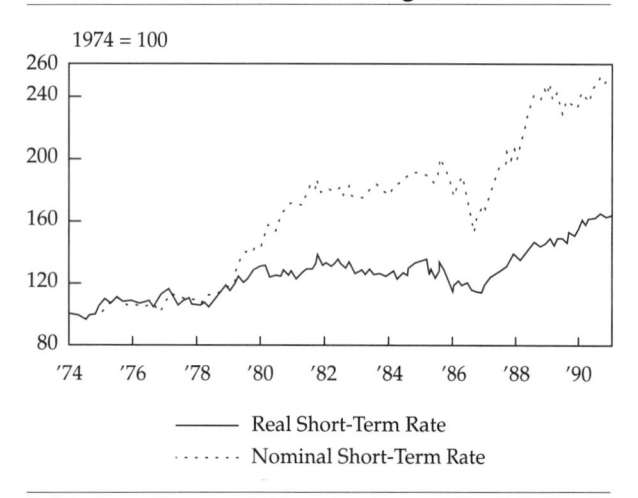

Source: Ian G. Sims.

Figure 5. Cumulative Net Returns versus Bill/Bond Index

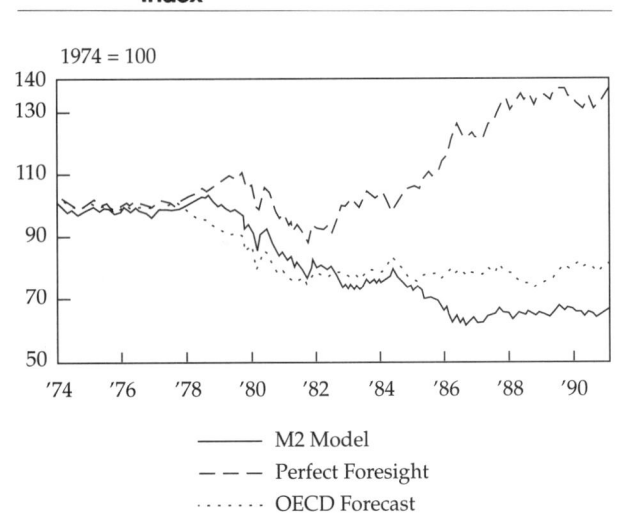

Source: Ian G. Sims.

sight does not provide a consistent advantage. The strategy took a big dive in the early 1980s, and significant underperformance resulted. This outcome suggests that the real-yield effect—the difference between yield and inflation—is both volatile and significant. If an investment manager is managing money domestically on a duration-play basis, the real-yield components of the yield must be forecast; forecasting inflation and adding an average real-yield premium over time is not enough.

The results of the domestic tests are a bit of an enigma, because these same forecasts work extremely well when applied to country allocations in a global bond portfolio. The reason for the result lies in the relationship between currency appreciation or depreciation and the real yield. If the inflation rate declines, the yield will not necessarily follow; it could stay the same or even rise. If yield does not decline, the investor will not make any money in domestic markets but will make money in the currency market because the rise in the real yield will put upward pressure on the currency. Conversely, if inflation rises, yield may not rise; if it stays where it is or falls, the real yield will get significantly squeezed. In this case, the domestic bond will perform all right, but the downward pressure on real yield will put downward pressure on the currency in a global bond portfolio.

Conclusion

When domestic markets during the past 20 years and global markets during the past several years are examined, some observations stand out. The most significant is that forecasting inflation, specifically the differentials, is the necessary link to a prospective-real-yield framework. It is a worthy predictor variable. The stability of the relationship with both perfect foresight, which is the ultimate benchmark, and (more importantly) with the lagged M2 models is significant. The economic rationale is that PPP works in the long run. Both types of forecasts have the benefit or value of literally half a millennium of time behind them, as well as strong empirical evidence from the past 15–17 years. The combination of those two sources of experience provides strong conviction that theory underlies this particular issue.

The prospective-real-yield technique is appealing because it does not depend on forecasting either short-term interest rates or exchange rates. The complexities of budget deficits—the issue of debt to GDP with which forecasters grapple in the markets—create very unstable relationships. For example, Germany recently had 9 percent bond yields with 3 percent inflation rates, but the situation quickly changed to 6.5 percent bond yields with 4.5 percent inflation rates.

Question and Answer Session

Robert J. Bernstein
Ian G. Sims

Question: What is your measure of inflation? What other inflation forecasts might be worth considering?

Sims: We measure inflation by the consumer price index (CPI), but all the different measures of inflation work pretty well. One that does not work well is unit labor costs, but that is not a strict measure of inflation. The OECD data are a good reference point. I do not know of any other body that has gone back and produced consistent inflation forecasts for each country during this period. Different agencies in different countries have similar data—usually expectation-type data rather than people analyzing and forecasting, which is a big distinction.

Question: The presumably better method of forecasting inflation and differentials (i.e., OECD) performs more poorly than M2. Which do you believe more? Has M2's performance deteriorated?

Sims: The difference in the accuracy of the OECD and the M2 model at forecasting inflation differentials is not statistically significant. In terms of the strategy performing better when M2 inflation forecasts are used, the case is one of skewness, because the vast majority of the OECD's failure to match the M2 model's performance when applied in this framework is attributable to one 12-month period. Repeating the simulation several times, using Monte Carlo simulation techniques, for example, would show that the better inflation forecast gives a better actual result in a strategy, on average.

Question: How does the prospective-real-yield method hold up for periods other than between 1974 and 1990—for example, for periods since 1990, between 1981 and 1992, or for rolling five-year periods?

Sims: The simulation works for any such subperiod. For regression models, the results worsen as the subperiods are sliced finer. With the perfect foresight model, if the test is of two subperiods of, say, eight or nine years, it is good for both periods. The M2 model is extremely good in the 1970s but not as good in the 1980s, although the slopes have a good spattering of significant t-statistics. For the OECD, the significance is reduced, but on the whole, it is good at the 10 percent level. From a regression viewpoint, the stability is strong for perfect foresight, so the underlying mechanism is very strong. From a simulation viewpoint, the stability over time can be seen from the cumulative outperformance graph.

Question: Does your model assume that real yield differentials between countries should move toward zero in the long term? In other words, should Italian real yields eventually equal U.S. real yields (i.e., with no risk premiums)?

Sims: The model does not make that assumption. It says take the yield, forecast inflation as far as reasonable (in this case, two years), and overweight those markets with the highest prospective real yields.

Bernstein: The real question is whether government policymakers will take the real yield differentials and motivate the countries in a different direction. There is clearly an income benefit in starting with the high-yielding, developed countries. As those yields decline, the capital gain offsets the currency side.

Question: Global bond management involves making separate decisions about bond markets (interest rates) and currencies. How do you make such decisions with your model?

Sims: The strength of this technique is that you do not know exactly where your returns are coming from. We are not making any judgments about what the future yield will be or about what the level of currency will be commensurate with that future real yield. Sometimes returns come through local bond market appreciation and sometimes through currency. This technique is probably a better way to manage global bond portfolios than to try and separate them *ex ante*.

Question: How does your investment process account for currency overshoot/undershoot? Your model may prove correct from a real yield standpoint, but currencies often deviate significantly from PPP equilibrium levels for extended periods of time.

Sims: We are not using PPP here in the conventional sense, which measures the deviation from its fair value; if the value is under the fair value, go long, and if it is over, go short. The PPP argument from this conventional viewpoint is a long-run rationale. Because we are only forecasting inflation for two years, we cannot claim PPP makes this approach work. We know PPP does not work in such a short period. We have tried to state a long-term rationale and move on to try to apply the approach to the best of our ability—knowing we cannot forecast 17-year inflation but can do a reasonable job on two-year inflation.

Question: Have you looked at the concept of world money supply instead of individual country M2s as another explanatory variable because of the international transmission of inflation?

Sims: I do look at that to improve my inflation forecasting; it makes a lot of sense. You can either model each country individually and accept that the forecast errors are correlated, or you can first try to net out the world money supply effect and then model what is left.

Question: Do you currently manage portfolios based on this approach? Which inflation-forecasting model do you use, and why?

Sims: Yes, we do manage money in this way. I have a bias toward monetary-based models. They have been unjustly discarded, particularly from a country differential-inflation viewpoint. We have some proprietary techniques to get around some of the problems of deregulation and other extraneous factors. I believe this area is of increasing interest to economists. People have said that the simple money figures do not work, but they have not tried to look behind those numbers. There are often some simple reasons why the numbers did what they did, and you can adjust for that.

We do supplement the forecast equations with some subjective analysis. Subjective analysis has not worked well this year, however. A simple M2 model on Japan predicted significant deflation, which put prospective real yield up very high and meant the Japanese bond market or yen would appreciate, which it has done. We missed a lot of that because we did not believe in the 4 percent deflation in Japan that the model was suggesting. In practice, we are not going to put everything on automatic pilot. These models are a very good first step. They provide a substantial part of an investment process, but I do not know anyone who would want to base a decision solely on this quantitative type of analysis.

Question: How does your actual performance compare with the simulated performance?

Sims: It's not as good. The money supply models have worked really well. They helped avoid last year's ERM debacle. For example, Spain had high money supply, and the model certainly would have told you to avoid that market in 1992 and go with France and Japan, which would have been good markets to be in from the summer of last year onward. Canada as well.

Question: Do methods of forecasting two-year inflation work equally well for all nine countries, or might the model be improved by considering other variables?

Sims: The accuracy of inflation forecasts can certainly be improved by considering different variables in different countries. The model we proposed in this study was largely an illustration rather than an attempt to develop an optimal inflation-forecasting model.

Question: Can your studies and results also be applied to stock market returns and allocations? How important are the return expectations of the various stock markets to the results?

Sims: I have done some preliminary work on equity country allocation, and the results are encouraging. The work is in an early stage, however.

Question: The prospective-real-yield model has significant coefficients, but what is the economic significance of a model that explains about 3 percent of variation in relative returns?

Sims: For investment success, all that is necessary is to have consistently better-than-average ability to rank the countries in the correct order of relative returns. If, for example, the model predicts that Germany and Japan will outperform the others by 3 percent and 2 percent, respectively, and the actual outcome is 23 percent and 22 percent, the model will have given you a low R^2 but good portfolio returns.

Question: Given the controversy in the United States over the current validity of M2, because it includes the flow of money into stock and bond mutual funds, do you foresee updating your model?

Sims: Special reasons are always cited why M2 is no longer valid, particularly since the 1970s. What people miss is that the differentials between countries are highly correlated, even in times of severe shocks to the monetary system, such as occurred with financial deregulation.

Question: Does the prospective-real-yield technique using M2 work better with some country differentials than others and with some maturities than others?

Sims: Yes, in the case of country differentials. Regarding maturities, I have looked at different points on the curve and obtained similar results whether I was using ten-year yields or three-month Eurodeposit rates. The prospective real short-term rate is better for currencies than the prospective real yield, but the reverse is true for local bond market returns.

The CAPM and Fixed-Income Markets

David A. Tyson, CFA
Vice President
The Travelers Insurance Company

> In fixed-income markets, changes in the term premium are primarily a function of changes in aggregate risk preferences. Investors must take significant systematic risk to capture additional returns, however, and too few investors are willing to move from their preferred habitats to offset shifts in market supply and demand along the yield curve.

Most people think of the CAPM in conjunction with equity investments. I will discuss the CAPM as it relates to fixed-income markets. I will also review some of the historical evidence on returns in the fixed-income markets, address several theories used to explain the yield curve's behavior and why it is useful, provide the results of my research on the term structure of interest rates, and discuss what the research implies for the different theories.

Historical Evidence

Many theories propose how returns should behave relative to risk. One theory is embodied in the CAPM, which says that an investor gets paid extra for taking extra risks. Risk and return in the CAPM are generally assumed to be measured on a single-period, total return basis. When the model is applied to fixed-income markets, the assumption is that the return on fixed-income assets should increase as total risk increases. Thus, a 30-year bond should have a higher expected return than a six-month bond.

Another theory holds that no increase in return accompanies the taking on of additional risk in fixed-income markets. This theory is based on the pure expectations theory of the yield curve, which argues that the T-bill yield curve is a reflection of what investors expect future rates to be. So, an upward-sloping yield curve means interest rates are expected to rise in the future. A long-maturity asset may produce more income up front, but capital depreciation will make the total return on that asset the same as on a short-maturity asset. Thus, the CAPM and the pure expectations theory have opposing views on return for risk in fixed-income markets.

In the fixed-income area, the yield curve is often used as an indicator of expected returns. **Figure 1** shows the U.S. Treasury yield curve based on zero-coupon rates, which is the pure rate of return for a particular maturity, from March 1951 through December 1992. (Most rates quoted in newspapers are based on coupon-paying Treasuries, but those instruments are complicated to use in research because of the problems associated with the reinvestment of coupons.) The ten-year rate, for example, represents the current value of a payment ten years from now. The slope of the yield curve, as expected, is positive. The ten-year rate from March 1951 through December 1992 averaged 150 basis points above the one-month rate.

The quoted yield going forward is not necessarily the same as expected returns. The actual excess holding-period returns—that is, the average return on a particular maturity of asset in excess of the yield on the one-month T-bill—for this period are also shown in Figure 1. Holding-period returns were calculated by valuing the zero-coupon bond one month later with the next month's interest rate and one month closer to maturity. The excess holding-period returns were calculated by subtracting the one-month zero's return from the holding-period return.

The ten-year excess holding-period returns for this period were much lower than the "advertised" return shown on the yield curve. In fact, the ten-year returns were not that much higher than those of the two-month and three-month returns. The returns are relatively flat from the six-month to the five-year maturities, which is more consistent with the pure expectations hypothesis than with the CAPM; investors are not getting paid any additional return to extend their risk in a total return environment.

One comment often heard about this type of

Figure 1. Zero-Coupon Yield Curve and Excess Holding-Period Returns, March 1951–December 1992

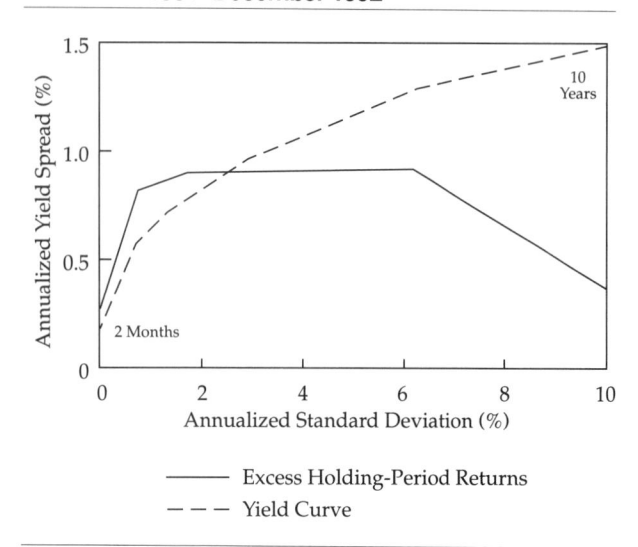

Source: Tyson (1991). Data updated to December 1992 by author.

analysis is that the time period chosen may have influenced the results; inflation and interest rates both increased sharply during the period. This time period was chosen because it includes the years after the Federal Reserve stopped controlling short-term rates. The period also includes the 1970s, when the dollar started floating, which had some major implications for volatility and returns.

Another way to evaluate excess returns is to look at trends in excess returns over time. **Figure 2** shows the performance of a portfolio during the 1951–92 period for which the investor owned a five-year zero-coupon bond and sold short a two-year zero. For most of the period, as interest rates were rising, the return on the five-year asset underperformed the return on the two-year asset. Interest rates peaked in the early 1980s, however, and the relative return

Figure 2. Trends in Excess Returns: Five-Year versus Two-Year Zero-Coupon Bonds, March 1951–December 1992

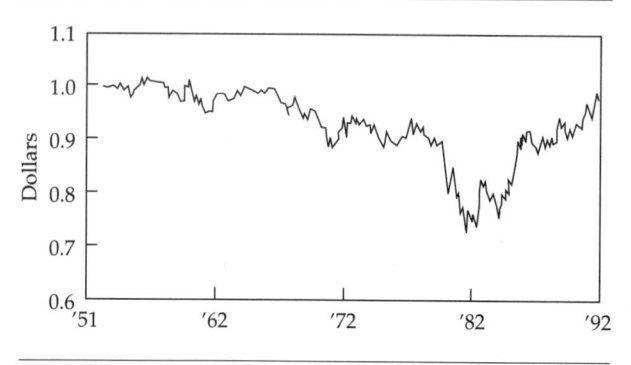

Source: Tyson (1991). Data updated to December 1992 by author.

recovered to nearly $1.

This figure might give the impression that predicting trends in interest rates is easy. Before accepting that notion, however, look at the monthly returns in **Figure 3**. Movements in these returns look like a random walk. For the five-year zero-coupon bond, volatility increased when the Fed started targeting the money supply instead of interest rates in 1979. The monthly variance of this series is about 1.9 percent, which annualizes to about 8.9 percent. The annual return advantage in beginning yields for the one-month zero over the risk-free asset was 140 basis points, but the 9 percent volatility swamped this extra quoted yield. The actual, as opposed to quoted, excess returns were only 74 basis points for the same amount of volatility.

Figure 3. Monthly Excess Returns: Five-Year Zero-Coupon Bonds, March 1951–December 1992

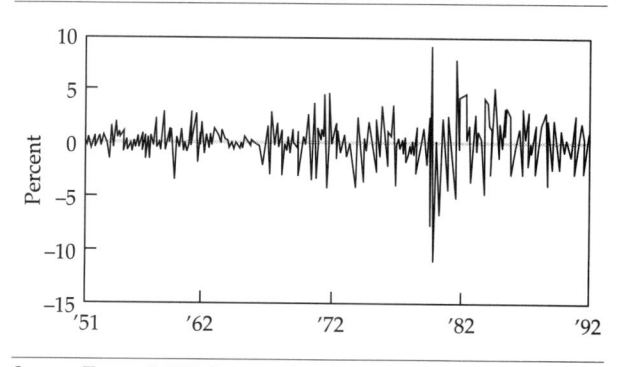

Source: Tyson (1991). Data updated to December 1992 by author.

Term-Structure Theory

Obviously, for fixed-income assets, increasing risk does not necessarily provide the same return as investing in higher beta stocks. Three theories on the term structure of interest rates are dominant:

■ *The pure expectations theory assumes that the yield curve reflects expectations as to future interest rates.* The extreme definition assumes investors are not paid any risk premium for moving out to any maturity along the yield curve.

■ *The liquidity-preference theory assumes that investors expect to be paid extra return to take price risk.* For any risk, they want to be paid additional yield to offset the risk of having to sell an asset at a price loss. Liquidity preference is very much in keeping with the CAPM idea that people have short-term time horizons.

■ *The preferred-habitat, or market-segmentation, theory introduces the idea that investors have different, or preferred, habitats for investment.* Therefore, the risk-free asset is redefined for each investor, and the risk premium is designed to pay them for moving from their preferred maturity to another. This theory also introduces the idea that, for individual investors, the term premium, the extra benefit for increasing the term to maturity, could be negative. If an investor's real preferred asset is a 15-year zero-coupon bond, buying a one-month bond may have a negative term premium for that investor. For example, to save for a child's college education 15 years from now, an investor could buy one-month T-bills and continually roll them over for 15 years, but the investor will not know what the ending dollar amount or return will be in nominal terms. Alternatively, an investor could buy a 15-year zero-coupon bond, lock in the current rate, and be guaranteed a nominal return. In this investor's case, the 15-year bond is preferred to the one-month T-bills.

Expectations Theory

The expectations theory states that long-term interest rates reflect the market's best estimates of future short-term interest rates. This theory implies that investing in any particular maturity along the yield curve has no risk-adjusted return advantage. The expectations theory does not argue that an investor must be paid the same rate at all maturities, but if an investor is paid different rates, the difference reflects the risk premium people require. Mathematically,

$$(1 + YTM_{2yrs})^2 = (1 + YTM_{1yr})(1 + \text{Expected } YTM_{1yr} + \Phi_m),$$

where

$YTM_{x\ yrs}$ = yield to maturity (percent) on a zero-coupon bond of maturity x, and

Φ_m = term premium for maturity M.

The idea is that an investor with a two-year horizon, for example, has the option of investing in a two-year-maturity bond or investing in a one-year-maturity bond and rolling that over into another one-year maturity bond. If the term premium is assumed to be zero as in the pure expectations theory, and given the yield to maturity on a two-year bond, the investor knows exactly what the return will be for that two-year period. If the expectation a year from now is that rates will be higher than the rate on the two-year bond, the investor will invest in a one-year bond and roll it over to earn a higher total return at the end of two years. If the investor thinks rates will be lower, he or she will want to lock in the two-year rate today. The idea of having a zero term premium is that the market will balance the supply and demand of people with differing views on what the rate will be a year from now. People expecting the rate to be higher will buy one-year bonds, and those expecting it to be lower will buy two-year bonds. If the market is in equilibrium, then people should be able to define the expected return.

The three main versions of the expectations theory deal with how the term premium behaves and how to explain it:

■ *Pure expectations theory*. In this version, the term premium is constant at a value of zero.

■ *Constant term premium*. This version assumes that the term premium is constant but not necessarily at a value known in advance. The important point about this version is that any changes in interest rates are the result of changes in expectations about future interest rates; no other factor causes the yield curve to change.

■ *Time-varying term premium*. In this version, the term premium varies over time. Changes in interest rates result from changes in expectations about future rates or from changes in investors' term premiums.

Academic research has rejected the viewpoints of both the pure expectations and constant term premium theories. As Figure 1 shows, excess holding-period returns increase out to a maturity of six months, flatten out, and then decline after about six years. This finding is inconsistent with the pure expectations version of the theory. With a constant term premium, forward rates, which are market-implied expected rates, should be unbiased predictors of future rates. Forward rates predicted by the yield curve have proved to be poor predictors of future rates, however, which contradicts the theory that the term premium is constant.

Some academic research supports the third version of the expectations theory—that the term premium might vary over time. Shiller (1979) performed a variance-bounds test and found that, if the term premium does not vary, then all variation in long-term interest rates should be explained by expected volatility in short-term interest rates. He found that short-term interest rates are not volatile enough on their own to explain the observed volatility in long-term interest rates. Therefore, the volatility of long-term interest rates is a function of volatility in both short-term interest rates and in the term premium. This mathematical finding does not help, from an empirical viewpoint, in forecasting what causes changes in the term premium. Therefore, my research aims for an understanding of why the term premium varies.

Explaining the Term Premium

As the CAPM implies, the term premium, Φ, is a function of investor risk expectations, $E\sigma$. That is,

$$\Phi = f(E\sigma).$$

Changes in the term premium result from changes in that function relating uncertainty to term premium, as well as from changes in uncertainty:

$$d\Phi = df(E\sigma) \times dE\sigma.$$

The two factors behind the variation in the term premium are uncertainty about future interest rates (risk) and how much participants require to be paid for risk (risk preference). These factors relate to the preferred-habitat theory. Changes in how much an investor must be paid for risk can come from two major sources. Market participants in the aggregate may become more risk averse or less risk averse, or risk preference functions may change.

Three major categories of variables were included in the model: measures of interest rate volatility, fundamental economic variables, and data on the yield-curve slope. The hypothesis I originally wanted to test was that, if investors' anticipated volatility increases, their term premiums increase. By testing *ex post* on excess holding-period returns, I hoped to determine whether, in periods with high volatility at the beginning, investors experienced higher expected returns after the fact. Additionally, pursuant to work by Fama and French (1992b) showing some cyclical factors affecting the time-varying term premium, I also wanted to test whether some fundamental economic variables were driving changes in the term premium.

Finally, I wanted to test whether the slope of the yield curve affected the term premium. From an efficient market viewpoint, if information is easily obtained, it should already be reflected in market pricing and, therefore, is not useful in forecasting. Because the yield-curve data were readily available, I did not expect those data to be useful. The results, however, showed I was wrong. I found that the information in the slope of the yield curve was the most powerful piece of information in explaining excess returns.

Two ways of looking at the information in the slope of the yield curve are presented in **Table 1**. The first is forward expectations, which is forecasting the five-year excess holding-period return by looking at the slope of the yield curve beyond five years. The idea is that, if the ten-year rate is higher than the five-year rate, people expect the five-year rate to increase. If it is much higher, then the expected increase is larger. If the five-year rate increases, the excess holding-period returns should be negative. As Table 1 shows, the *t*-statistic was –1.21, which is not statistically significant at the 10 percent significance level. Forward expectations are not, in sum-

Table 1. Ability of the Yield Curve to Predict Five-Year Excess Holding-Period Returns: One-Month Horizon, March 1951–June 1989

Independent Variable	Variable *t*-statistic	Adjusted R^2
Forward expectations	–1.21	0.33
Yield advantage	2.45	3.32

Source: David A. Tyson.

mary, good forecasters of what excess holding-period returns will be.

The second measure is yield advantage, which is the difference in yield between the five-year rate and the one-month rate. If the yield curve stays the same (interest rates do not change), an investor's excess return will be that difference. The results show that the short end of the yield curve contains useful information. The *t*-statistic was 2.45, which is statistically significant.

The information on yield advantage had a slope significantly above 1, which means that not only does a very steep yield curve offer a higher initial yield for longer maturities than the one-month rate but also that, on average, interest rates decline and the investor gains from price appreciation. The converse is the case when the yield curve is flatter than normal.

This finding is contrary to pure expectations theory, in which yield curves reflect only expectations, but it was observed in research by Macauley (1940) in the 1930s and by Kessel (1965) in the 1960s. They noted that, when the yield curve is inverted, rates usually increase; when it is very steep, rates usually decrease.

I also looked at how well different types of volatility measures could predict five-year excess holding-period returns (**Table 2**). Volatility added only slightly to the term premium. Sophisticated volatility measures, such as a Kalman filter-based estimate of volatility, did not add much to simpler measures in predicting volatility. The absolute value of the most recent change in volatility was the most significant single factor in forecasting excess returns. Combining the volatility estimates with the slope characteristic increased the significance of the slope and reduced the significance of the volatility characteristic.

In contrast, as Table 2 shows, fundamental economic data had a significant negative effect on holding-period returns. When industrial production was strong, for example, excess holding-period returns were usually negative; in periods of strong industrial growth, interest rates rise, causing negative term premiums.

When the yield-curve slope and economic vari-

Table 2. Ability of Yield Curve, Volatility, and Fundamental Data to Predict Five-Year Excess Holding-Period Returns: One-Month Horizon, March 1951–June 1989

Independent Variable	Variable t-statistic	Slope t-statistic	Adjusted R^2
Yield curve slope		2.45	3.32
Historical volatility			
Recent change	1.98	—	1.52
With yield-curve slope	1.67	2.33	4.47
Kalman filter	1.44	—	0.76
With yield-curve slope	0.69	2.03	3.39
Fundamental data[a]			
M1	−1.64	—	0.89
With yield-curve slope	−2.63	3.03	6.04
Industrial production	−2.68	—	0.95
With yield-curve slope	−2.83	2.55	4.54

Source: David A. Tyson.

[a]Monthly percentage change.

Table 3. One-Month Excess Holding-Period Returns: Different Economic Environments, March 1951–June 1989

	Maturities			
Environment	Six-Month	Two-Year	Five-Year	Number of Observations
Bust	0.13%	0.25%	0.31%	59
Normal	0.07	0.07	0.06	320
Boom	0.03	−0.06	−0.11	80
Total				459

Source: David A. Tyson.

ables were combined, the significance of the economic variables' t-statistics increased. The combination also enhanced the t-statistic on the slope data. Combining economic data with the yield-curve data enhanced the information.

Segmenting the model into time periods produced valuable information on how holding-period returns behave in different economic environments. The economic environments were determined by taking the ratio of the growth in cumulative industrial production from 1951 to 1989 over its trend growth rate. Observations one standard error above the trend were considered "boom" periods, and observations one standard error below the trend were considered "bust" periods. **Table 3** shows one-month excess holding-period returns for bust, normal, and boom periods for various rates.

In the bust periods, investors were paid extra for taking risk. The six-month rate in a bust period paid investors 13 basis points of excess holding-period return a month, compared with 7 in the normal period and 3 in the boom period. Moving out the duration spectrum, investors were paid 25 basis points for two-year maturities and 31 basis points for five-year maturities. In the boom period, returns declined (and even became negative) because of increased interest rate risk. In the normal period, returns were relatively flat. Investors were paid relatively evenly across the yield curve, which is in keeping with the constant term premium theory's view of the world.

The results of segmenting the data by economic environment are shown in **Table 4**. Clearly, the characteristics of some of these environments help explain the slope of the yield curve's impact on excess holding-period returns. Bust periods tended to have the steepest slope. During bust periods, investors in six-month securities received 80 basis points, on average, over the one-month rate, versus 53 basis points normally and 56 during the boom periods. The slope for the bust periods increased to 164 for the two-year and up to 214 for the five-year maturities. Conversely, in the boom periods, the slope was flat to inverted—that is, when the term premium was negative. The normal periods exhibited the normal positive slope to the yield curve with fairly flat returns across different points on the curve.

Implications for Investors

This research supports the preferred-habitat theory. Variation of the term premium is primarily a function of changes in aggregate risk preferences rather than changes in uncertainty, and changes in aggregate risk preferences can be described using the pre-

Table 4. Annualized Excess Holding-Period Returns (XHPR) Compared with the Average Slope, March 1951–June 1989

Environment	Six-Month	Two-Year	Five-Year
Bust			
XHPR	1.56%	2.96%	3.69%
Slope	0.80	1.64	2.14
Normal			
XHPR	0.81	0.83	0.70
Slope	0.53	0.93	1.24
Boom			
XHPR	0.38	−0.76	−1.28
Slope	0.56	0.53	0.38
All years			
XHPR	0.83	0.83	0.74
Slope	0.57	0.95	1.21

Source: David A. Tyson

ferred-habitat theory.

Take, for example, Federal Reserve policy. In a bust period, when the economy has a lot of slack in it, the Fed, not worrying about inflation, drives short-term interest rates down. During these times, investors actually receive even higher returns than are implied by the yield curve's slope. Many participants in the market, however, because they have liability risks, are not comfortable extending their durations to take advantage of the relatively higher long-term rates. They do not want to move out the curve and take more interest rate risk. So, to encourage more people to invest longer, the Federal Reserve pushes down short-term rates, which drives up the term premium on longer term rates.

The reverse occurs during boom periods. The boom period is when the economy has used up its excess capacity and is close to becoming inflationary; so the Federal Reserve tightens the money supply, which pushes up short-term rates relative to long-term rates. Investors, however, usually do not shift easily from their preferred habitats. Therefore, during these periods, the slope is flat to inverted and the average actual excess return is negative, which indicates that rates are increasing most of the time in that environment.

The normal periods provide support for the constant term premium view. The yield curve usually has a positive slope, similar to the full-period average. The actual returns are relatively flat across the yield curve, however, indicating that beyond six months, investors are not paid much of a term premium. This pattern is somewhat encouraging because it supports much of the view of arbitrage pricing theory that the market is an expectations function. In the normal period, investors are being paid a normal term premium. Although the curve has a positive slope, as the economy goes through its natural expansion, rates usually rise over time. An investor may be paid a higher yield for investing in a longer maturity, but that higher yield is offset by some price depreciation as rates rise. Only when the economic situation deviates from normal does the Federal Reserve, trying to drive investors to a particular maturity, alter the term structure away from pure expectations.

Conclusion

Changes in risk preference can be described in terms of the preferred-habitat theory. The devaluation or revaluation of the term premium is primarily a function of changes in aggregate risk preferences rather than changes in uncertainty about interest rates. This apparent anomaly does not defeat the CAPM. In fact, I would not consider it an anomaly, because investors must take significant systematic risk to capture these additional returns. For someone running a leveraged financial institution, taking a duration mismatch runs a significant risk of ruin because the standard errors, from my results, are still high. Much is required for people to move from their preferred habitats. Those investors who can take a total return view of the world will be able to switch maturities and capture opportunities in various parts of the yield curve. My results indicate that there are not enough of these investors to offset shifts in market supply and demand along the yield curve.

This research also provides support for using pure expectations in forward rates in a normal environment. Many people tend to use the idea that the yield curve is normally positively sloped and that they can get paid for investing long. They believe they can invest longer than their liabilities and get a free lunch from that strategy. More research like the research reported here that can be used to defeat the free lunch viewpoint would be helpful.

Question and Answer Session

David A. Tyson, CFA

Question: Given the steepness of today's yield curve, would you predict that we will have either a reversion to a flatter curve or a steeper curve at lower levels?

Tyson: Rather than the slope of the curve indicating higher returns, it indicates a reversion to a more normal point of the curve. I do not know whether the short end will move up or the long end will move down, but during the next couple of years, the curve will be flatter. We have not seen the last of inverted yield curves. They will be part of the normal course of business, which fits with the viewpoint that Federal Reserve policy is driving changes in term structure. People have become more comfortable taking interest rate risk as they see that they are not being penalized for it. The environment of the past few years fits well with what I expected; people are slightly increasing their risks along the yield curve to take advantage of the high quoted yields. That is precisely what the Fed wants them to do.

My boom/bust measure does not show a bust in this latest period, and it mirrors capacity utilization fairly well. Capacity utilization is nowhere near as low as it was in the early 1980s recession. Capacity utilization and the boom/bust measure are based on industrial production. If more of this recession is attributable to the service economy, I may not have properly identified a bust period. The labor markets and other segments of the economy may have a lot of slack that data on the manufacturing sector may not be picking up.

Question: Does the conventional wisdom that intermediate maturities offer the best blend of return and risk have the potential to alter established behavior?

Tyson: People tend to move out on the curve over time. In a normal environment, even though an investor receives a flat return for taking risk, the spread on intermediate corporate bonds justifies the credit risk taken. The intermediate bonds give them a much better Sharpe ratio than long-term bonds or one-month bills because the spread helps improve the return-to-risk relationship in a normal environment.

Question: In your model, when did you assume industrial production figures are available?

Tyson: I looked at those figures two ways. One way used contemporaneous data. I wanted to explain what was really underlying the term premium. Using this approach, the adjusted R^2s in combination with the other variables were about 18 percent. The other way used lagged data. The R^2s were cut to about 9 percent when used on a lag basis.

I also surveyed the literature for other successful methods of predicting interest rates, but I did not find any. One article found significant results using contemporaneous economic data, but the significance disappeared when time lags and revisions were adjusted (Elliot and Baier 1979).

Question: Why do you regard correlations with such low R^2s to be significant relative to excess holding-period returns?

Tyson: I was looking at almost 500 data points, so a high correlation is not necessary to have statistical significance. On average, the results were strong statistically but the R^2s were low, so there was a lot of residual error. This finding helps explain how people behave in their preferred habitats. People with strong liabilities do not take advantage of opportunities at other points in the term structure. A long-term investor or a total return investor with a long time frame is more able to take advantage of this than is a tight asset/liability manager.

Question: During the 19th century, yield curves were consistently downward sloping. Free-banking advocates suggest that this effect was related to stable prices and no Federal Reserve intervention. What do you think?

Tyson: This issue points out the problem in looking at term structures for different markets. If the theory is a universal truth, one would expect to see it work during other time periods. The problem is that data collection in other time periods is difficult.

In the United States, the 1800s had periods of deflation and inflation. In the 1930s and 1940s, the Federal Reserve controlled interest rates tightly, so that data period would not be good for this type of research. The post–World War II period was more one of inflation than of deflation. Data collection in foreign markets is also difficult. Japan, for example, did not have an active, noncontrolled government bond market until five years ago.

Strategies to Exploit Term Structure and Credit-Spread Anomalies

Jonathan A. Reiss, CFA
Director of Fixed-Income Research
Sanford C. Bernstein & Company, Inc.

> Although the yield curve is a bad predictor of yield changes, it is a good predictor of risk premiums. When the yield curve is steep, managers should bet against the market forecast and take more interest rate risk; they should take less interest rate risk when the curve is inverted.

The yield curve has long been shown to be a bad forecaster of interest rates. This result has generally been interpreted to mean that the yield curve does not reflect interest rate forecasts. This presentation discusses how this fact can be systematically exploited. It also presents evidence that, although the yield curve is a bad forecaster, it does reflect market forecasts.

Term-Structure Anomalies

The shapes of yield curves vary considerably, as **Figure 1** illustrates. On June 30, 1989, the yield curve was almost flat at 8 percent. On June 30, 1992, the yield curve had a steep slope. Two principal theories address what the slope of the yield curve means. One states that the yield curve reflects investors' expectations. Two versions of this theory are the pure expectations hypothesis, which asserts that the yield curve reflects expected future interest rates only, and the constant-risk-premium hypothesis, which states that the yield curve reflects a combination of a risk premium that is constant over time plus investor expectations. Because the risk premium does not vary, any changes in the shape of the yield curve are attributable to changes in expectations.

The second principal theory is that the yield curve reflects market factors. This theory also has two versions: The variable-risk-premium hypothesis states that much of the variation in the shape of the yield curve is the result of market factors, such as supply and demand, rather than of expectations for changes in interest rates; the market-segmentation hypothesis states that investors and issuers are averse to moving from one area of the yield curve to another so the yield curve is not a curve at all but a collection of disjointed markets.

Some background will be useful before a discussion of these theories. Forward rates are the implicit yields on instruments that can be bought today but that produce a yield during some interval in the future. As shown in **Table 1**, the current yield curve on June 30, 1992, went from 4.04 percent at the short end to 6.41 percent at five years. The forward rates show what these rates imply for the yield curve from 1993 to 1996. For example, the difference between the two-year and the one-year rates implies a yield between 1993 and 1994 of 5.65 percent. This is the rate an investor could have locked in on a one-year investment that began June 30, 1993, and matured on June 30, 1994. The investor could have bought that yield either in the futures market or by purchasing a two-year bond, then shorting a one-year bond, and creating a synthetic one-year investment. When the yield curve is somewhat inverted, as in June 1989, the forward curve is slightly below it. Note that the forward rates provide no information about the future that is not already contained in the yield curve.

Pure Expectations Hypothesis

The pure expectations hypothesis states that the expected returns on all Treasuries are equal; thus, the yield curve reflects expected future interest rates. **Table 2** shows how the expected yield curve can be determined according to this hypothesis. For an illustration, consider the one-year bond. On June 30, 1992, the expected return on a one-year bond (its yield) is known to be 4.04 percent. By assumption,

Figure 1. Yield Curves for June 30, 1989, and June 30, 1992

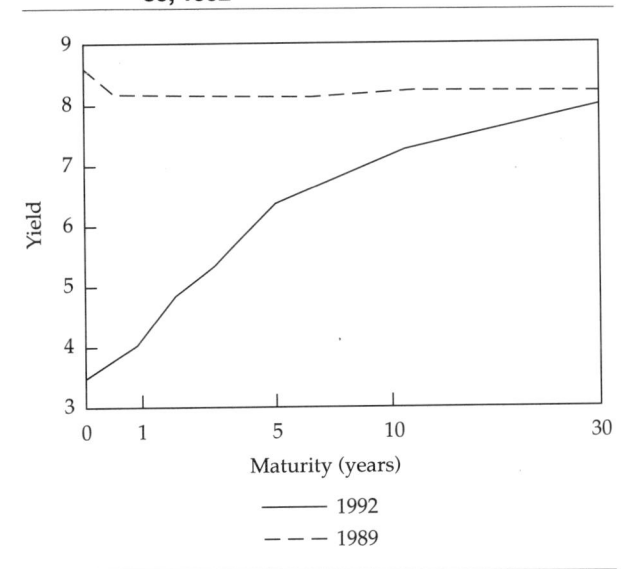

Source: Sanford C. Bernstein & Co.

the expected returns on all bonds are equal, and therefore, all expected returns are 4.04 percent. The expected future interest rate can be computed by using the current yield, the risk premium (assumed to be zero), and the expected return (assumed to be 4.04 percent). With that information, the expected one-year rate one year from now is found to be 5.65 percent. Because the yield today is higher than the expected return, the yield must be expected to increase, creating a capital loss and a total return of 4.04 percent. Similar arithmetic can be done to find the rest of the yield curve.

The expected yield curve calculated in this manner is shown in the lower half of Table 2. The top half shows the same calculation for June 30, 1989.

For the upward-sloping yield curve (June 30, 1992), the forward curve lies well above the current curve. For the slightly inverted yield curve (June 30, 1989), the forward rates are slightly below the current curve. According to the pure expectations hypothesis, those forward rates are equal to the expected future rates.[1]

The pure expectations hypothesis is unsatisfying for two reasons. First, it asserts that taking interest rate risk garners no extra return, which seems somewhat implausible. Second, the yield curve is almost always upward sloping, which implies that people almost always expect interest rates to rise. From 1950 to 1980, that expectation would not have been a bad forecast, but when applied in general, that implication also seems somewhat implausible.

Constant-Risk-Premium Hypothesis

This hypothesis is a modification of the pure expectations hypothesis. The constant-risk-premium hypothesis asserts that longer term securities do carry a risk premium but the premium does not vary over time. (It does increase with maturity.) You can still back out the portion of the slope in the curve that reflects the risk premium and impute the market's expectations. An example of how the expected yield curve is determined is presented in **Table 3**. For the 1989 yield curve, taking the 8.09 percent yield on the one-year bond and adding the risk premium for the two-year bond gives an expected return on the two-year bond of 8.49 percent.[2] To obtain an expected return of 8.49, you must expect 7.59 percent for the yield on that bond a year from now. A decrease in interest rates is what drives the positive return premium that this theory asserts is in the market. A lot of empirical evidence appears to contradict this theory, but I hope to provide it with some credibility.

As shown in **Figure 2** for the upward-sloping yield curve, the forward curve is much above the current curve. **Figure 3** shows the June 30, 1989, yield

---

[1] Because of convexity, this statement is not precisely true, but for the maturities under consideration here, convexity matters little and can be ignored.

[2] These calculations reflect our estimates of the risk premiums, but any constant risk premiums would result in similar conclusions.

Table 1. Spot and Forward Yield Curves

Maturity	June 30, 1989 Spot Rates	June 30, 1989 One-Year-Forward Yield Curve	June 30, 1992 Spot Rates	June 30, 1992 One-Year-Forward Yield Curve
One year	8.09%	7.99%	4.04%	5.65%
Two years	8.04	8.01	4.84	6.00
Three years	8.03	7.98	5.35	6.51
Four years	8.02	7.96	5.89	7.01
Five years	8.01	NA	6.41	NA

Source: Sanford C. Bernstein & Co.

NA = not applicable.

Table 2. Pure Expectations Hypothesis

Maturity	Yield	Risk Premium	Expected Return	Expected Yield Curve
June 30, 1989				
One year	8.09%	0.00%	8.09%	7.99%
Two years	8.04	0.00	8.09	8.01
Three years	8.03	0.00	8.09	7.98
Four years	8.02	0.00	8.09	7.96
Five years	8.01	0.00	8.09	NA
June 30, 1992				
One year	4.04	0.00	4.04	5.65
Two years	4.84	0.00	4.04	6.00
Three years	5.35	0.00	4.04	6.51
Four years	5.89	0.00	4.04	7.01
Five years	6.41	0.00	4.04	NA

Source: Sanford C. Bernstein & Co.

NA = not applicable.

curve with the forward curve somewhat below it and the expected yield curve substantially below it. A flat yield curve implies a forecast of declining interest rates. The difference between the forward curve and the expected yield curve is the imputed risk premium. Figure 3 also illustrates the expected curve for the June 30, 1992, upward-sloping yield curve. In accordance with the constant- and variable-risk-premium hypotheses, the forward curve is far above the current yield curve and the expected curve is again somewhat below the forward curve. If yields move to the forward curve, all securities return the same rate. To earn a positive risk premium, the expected curve must be lower than the forward curve. Both risk-premium theories assert that the yield curve says something about the market's expectations for interest rates.

Table 3. Constant-Risk-Premium Hypothesis

Maturity	Yield	Risk Premium	Expected Return	Expected Yield Curve
June 30, 1989				
One year	8.09%	0.00%	8.09%	7.59%
Two years	8.04	0.40	8.49	7.67
Three years	8.03	0.65	8.74	7.71
Four years	8.02	0.85	8.94	7.75
Five years	8.01	0.95	9.04	NA
June 30, 1992				
One year	4.04	0.00	4.04	5.25
Two years	4.84	0.40	4.44	5.67
Three years	5.35	0.65	4.69	6.22
Four years	5.89	0.85	4.89	6.77
Five years	6.41	0.95	4.99	NA

Source: Sanford C. Bernstein & Co.

NA = not applicable.

Figure 2. Pure Expectations Hypothesis: Yield-Curve Expectations, June 30, 1989, and June 30, 1992

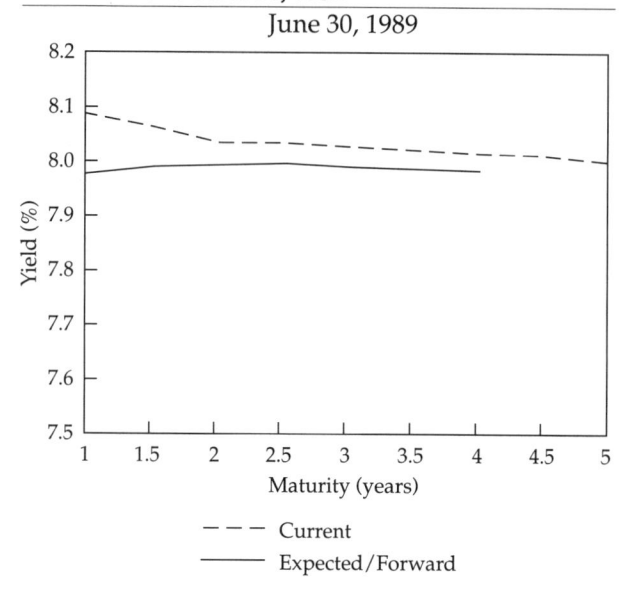

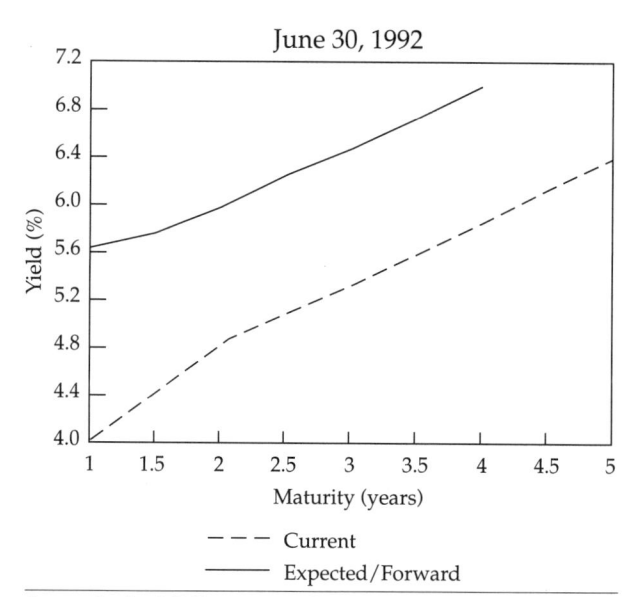

Source: Sanford C. Bernstein & Co.

Variable-Risk-Premium Hypothesis

This hypothesis asserts that a risk premium exists and it varies over time. If this theory holds, one cannot tell whether steep yield curves reflect expectations of rising rates, unusually high risk premiums, or some combination of the two. As I have stated it, this theory does not say anything about how the risk premium varies and, therefore, is useless in determining expectations. Tyson presents evidence for a version of this theory.[3]

---

[3] See Mr. Tyson's presentation, pp. 95–100.

Figure 3. Constant-Risk-Premium Hypothesis: Yield-Curve Expectations, June 30, 1989, and June 30, 1992

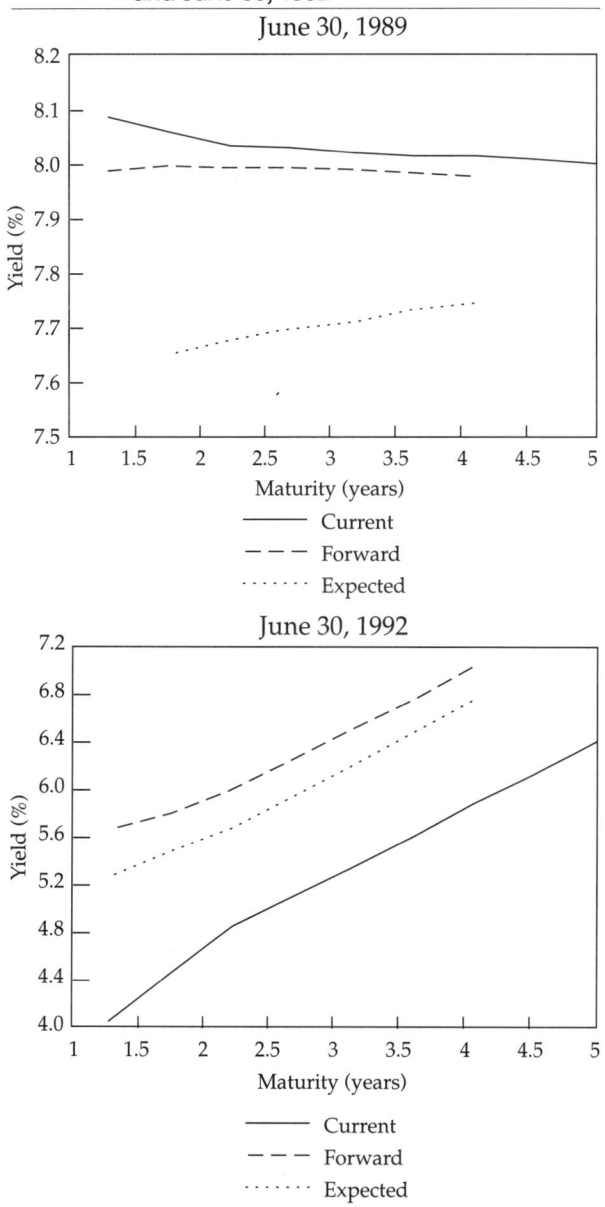

[Chart: June 30, 1989 — Yield (%) vs Maturity (years), showing Current, Forward, and Expected curves]

[Chart: June 30, 1992 — Yield (%) vs Maturity (years), showing Current, Forward, and Expected curves]

Source: Sanford C. Bernstein & Co.

Market-Segmentation Hypothesis

The market-segmentation hypothesis—also known as the preferred-habitat hypothesis—suggests that the markets for short-term bonds, intermediate-term bonds, and long-term bonds are separate. The theory asserts that investors have strong preferences for particular maturities and are thus averse to moving from one market to another. Therefore, separate manifestations of supply and demand form at separate portions of the yield curve, with the effect that bonds at different maturities trade in separate markets.

Proponents of this theory argue that institutional and liability concerns force investors into certain segments of the term structure. Skeptics, such as myself, argue that although rigid investors exist (often for regulatory reasons), the market has enough investors willing to exploit distortions in the yield curve that such distortions do not persist. Both the variable-risk-premium theory and the market-segmentation theory assert that the shape of the yield curve is not primarily a reflection of the market's expectation of interest rates.

Testing the Hypotheses

The first two theories, the pure expectations hypothesis and the constant-risk-premium hypothesis, imply that the shape of the yield curve reflects market expectations. Assuming that the market is efficient, those expectations should be good forecasters of future changes in rates. This proposition is testable.

Because the pure expectations hypothesis is a special case of the constant-risk-premium hypothesis (the case in which the risk premium is zero), I will discuss them together and refer to them as the expectations hypotheses.

The expectations hypotheses assert that the expected change in yield, $E(dY)$, is equal to the difference between the forward rate and the spot rate minus a constant:

$$E(dY) = (\text{Forward} - \text{Spot}) - \text{Constant}.$$

The pure expectations hypothesis suggests that the constant is equal to zero, and the constant-risk-premium hypothesis suggests that the constant is greater than zero.

The following regression equation is used to test these hypotheses:

$$dY = A(F - S) - B + \varepsilon,$$

where dY is the subsequent change in yield, F is the forward rate, S is the spot rate, A and B are parameters to be estimated, and ε is the error term. The hypothesis that A is equal to 1, which is asserted by these theories, can now be tested.

The results of the regression are shown in **Table 4**. Tested on three-month forward rates from 1983 through 1992, the A coefficient, which was expected to be close to 1, is 0.22 with a standard error of 0.29. The standard error suggests that forward rates have no discernible value for predicting interest rates. The naive forecast of no change in interest rates is a better forecaster than the pure expectations theory.

I have run the same regression using other historical periods, time intervals, and maturities with similar or even more negative results (also shown in

Table 4. Results for Other Maturities and Periods

Asset	Time Interval	Historical Period	Coefficient	Standard Error of Coefficient	R^2
Three-month bills	Quarterly	1983–92	0.22	0.29	0.02
Two-year bonds	Quarterly	1969–92	–0.40	0.61	0.00
	Quarterly	1969–78	0.00	0.88	0.00
	Quarterly	1979–82	–0.73	1.89	0.01
	Quarterly	1983–92	–0.35	0.90	0.00
	Annually	1969–92	–0.30	0.69	0.01
Five-year bonds	Annually	1969–92	–0.70	1.14	0.02

Source: Sanford C. Bernstein & Co.

Table 4). This question has also been addressed by a number of other people, who reached the same conclusion. Forward rates have little or no value for predicting changes in interest rates.

These results are negative from a theoretical standpoint but very interesting—and exploitable—from an investment standpoint. The results are interesting because of the connection between expected changes in interest rates and expected return premiums:

$$\text{Expected return} = \text{Yield} \times \text{Time} - \text{Duration} \times E(dY) + \text{Convexity} \times E(dY^2).$$

If you know the expected change in yield on a bond, you know its expected return.[4] Therefore, the apparently dull forecast of no change in yields results in a quite interesting forecast of expected returns.

From the preceding equation, the following (for three-month and six-month bills) can be derived:

$$\text{Annualized risk premium} = 1 \times (\text{Forward} - \text{Spot}) - E(dY).$$

This relationship implies that if the expected change in yield is zero, the expected return premium is equal to the forward rate premium. Variations in the steepness of the curve imply variations in the differences between forward and spot rates, which in turn, imply variations in the realized return premiums.

As Table 4 illustrates, no change in interest rates is a better forecaster than the yield curve itself. This finding suggests that the difference between the forward curve and the spot curve is a good forecaster of risk premiums, because investors will actually earn the forward rate. The regression equation can now be restated in terms of return premiums as follows:

$$RP = M(F - S) + P + \varepsilon,$$

where RP is the annualized return difference be-

---

[4]Convexity is small enough for the maturities I am discussing that it can safely be ignored.

tween the six-month T-bill and the three-month T-bill rates, M is equal to 1 minus α (the coefficient on the interest rate forecast model), P will reflect the market's risk premium, and ε is the error term. An α equal to 0 indicates an ability to forecast returns using the difference between the forward rate and the spot rate.

The empirical results support the hypothesis that the difference between the forward curve and the spot curve is a good forecaster of risk premiums. The coefficient is 0.75, which is close to 1 and significantly different from zero. The results are

$$RP = 0.75(F - S) + 0.25$$

with a standard error of the coefficient of 0.28. The basic conclusion is that forward rates are bad predictors of future interest rates but good predictors of holding-period returns.

Implications

The results discussed here have several implications for fixed-income strategies. When the yield curve is steep, the expected return pick-up from increasing duration is large. When the yield curve is inverted, the expected return pick-up from increasing duration is negative. That is, the slope is a good predictor of excess holding-period returns.

At the short end of the curve, where this strategy works best, the strategy would return 1.3 percent a year in excess returns with a standard deviation of 1.4 percent. The strategy involves taking risk, but not systematic risk. It would average exactly the same duration as its benchmark, with some longer and some shorter values. The results are appreciably weaker for the longer part of the curve, but an investor can still add 30–40 basis points with a standard deviation of 80 using a very similar approach.

The results presented so far appear to contradict the expectations hypotheses, and that is the usual interpretation they are given. Tyson, for instance, would observe that investors have a useful tool (the yield curve) that predicts variations in the risk premium. Surely, therefore, the risk premium does indeed vary.

I believe there is a different explanation. The hypotheses concern expectations, but so far the tests have been of realizations of risk premiums and yield changes. This approach is common, and the rationale is twofold. First, if the market is efficient, the realizations will, on average, reflect expectations. Second, researchers cannot directly observe market expectations, so they have no choice. In this case, a good proxy for expectations can be observed.

I tested whether the spot curve reflects the expectations of economists by using the Blue Chip Financial Forecasts, which are based on the forecasts of 50 respected economists, monthly from 1983 to 1992. I regressed these forecasts against the yield curve using the following equation:

$$\text{Forward} - \text{Spot} = A[E(dY)] + B.$$

where $E(dY)$ is the Blue Chip consensus forecast for the change in three-month T-bill rates from the current quarter to the next one. The forward and spot rates are for three-month T-bills as in the previous test. Theoretically, the coefficient A should equal 1. For the period tested, the coefficient was 0.98 (remarkably close to 1) and significantly different from zero:

$$\text{Forward} - \text{Spot} = 0.98[E(dY)] + 0.51$$

with a standard error of 0.034.

Also worth noting is that the constant term is positive. When the expected change in interest rates is zero, the difference between forward rates and spot rates is positive. Therefore, the yield curve is upward sloping, even when the market does not expect interest rates to go up, which is consistent with a risk premium greater than zero.

Conclusion

The results of this term-structure research suggest the following:
- The market believes economists' forecasts are reflected in the shape of the yield curve.
- The yield curve is a bad predictor of yield changes.
- The yield curve is a good predictor of risk premiums.
- Managers should bet against the implied market forecast and take more interest rate risk when the yield curve is steep and less when the yield curve is inverted.

The latter is a risky but winning strategy.

Question and Answer Session
Jonathan A. Reiss, CFA

Question: From your work, can you tell what the expected risk premium on 30-year bonds is compared with five-year securities? What about ten-year securities versus five-year securities?

Reiss: We believe that the premium is about 60 basis points between five and 30-year bonds and about 20 between five and 10-year bonds. Historical returns contain so much noise that they provide little information. We base our estimates on the normal yield curve.

Question: Is the risk-premium relationship linear?

Reiss: It should be, but we believe it is somewhat concave; that is, you get more for extending from cash to five years than you do for extending from five years to 30 years. The history is so noisy, however, that you cannot be sure one way or the other.

Question: Does the predictability of holding-period returns based on forward rates vary appreciably with either the steepness of the slope of the yield curve or fundamental cyclical variables?

Reiss: When the curve is very abnormal, steep or inverted, you have a stronger prediction. Tyson's research shows some evidence that fundamental cyclical variables help predict holding-period returns.

Question: Can you quantify the steepness of a yield curve? Does the ratio of short to long rates or the size of the spread indicate when to go long or short?

Reiss: We use historical estimates as the indicator for whether a yield curve is steeper or flatter than normal. The estimate of the mean is something of an art, but it is clear when the yield curve is much steeper or much flatter than normal. When the curve is abnormal, you have strong signals.

We believe that the absolute spreads are more meaningful than ratios of yields. The power is most demonstrable at the short end—the slope of the curve between zero and one year—than at the long end of the yield curve. Today, even though the yield curve from front to back is much steeper than usual, the yield curve from zero to one year is somewhat flatter than usual. The indicated strategy is to be somewhat short. The failure in the research reported here to prove anything of interest at the longer part of the curve may be because the longer part of the curve is not volatile enough to allow detection of what is there.

Question: What are the implications for derivatives that are priced off of forwards?

Reiss: To do arbitrage-free pricing, you must embed the forward rates in your model, whether you believe they reflect expectations or not. This is a consistency requirement.

We want a model that correctly prices noncallable bonds, which does not imply that we believe the expectations hypothesis. We use an option model that is consistent with forward rates but generates expected returns that are not.

Question: The 1983–92 period, given the significant decline in rates that occurred during that period, seems to be atypical. Please comment.

Reiss: The 1983–92 period is atypical, but it does not distort the results.

Question: Does increasing convexity of longer term bonds distort the empirical results?

Reiss: No. Although I ignored convexity throughout my presentation, it is so small that it does not matter. The studies I presented looked at T-bills, for which convexity is almost undetectable—less than a basis point a year. If we were looking at 5-, 10-, or 30-year bonds, including convexity in the analysis would be important.

Question: Why did you limit your regression to Blue Chip data on three-month T-bills? Does it work for longer term securities?

Reiss: Yes, it does work on longer term securities, but not quite as well. It is hard to do statistical work on five-year bonds because we have many fewer independent observations than for short-term instruments.

Question: Why is the coefficient M equal to 1 minus A?

Reiss: To give a complete answer, I would need to derive it. However, you can see that it works for two cases: $A = 0$ and A

= 1. If the expected changes in interest rates are zero ($A = 0$), you earn the risk premium ($M = 1$). If the expected changes in interest rates are equal to 1 times the difference between the spot and the forward rates ($A = 1$), you earn the risk-free rate ($M = 0$). That it works out that neatly is a special case, but a direct (and inverse) relationship always exists between the ability of the yield curve to forecast yields and returns. The worse it is at one, the better it is at the other.

What Have We Learned? What Does It Mean? And What Does the Future Hold?

William L. Fouse, CFA
Chairman and CEO
Mellon Capital Management Corporation

> The purposes of the capital asset pricing model and beta are widely misunderstood. They cannot be depended upon to "work" under all circumstances, but that never was their intent. Rather, they were intended to provide a framework for understanding security price formation and changes. In that respect, they are useful concepts.

I thought it would be appropriate to start with a quotation from Sharpe (1970): "To theorize is to abstract. One builds a model—a description of a toy world, one simple enough to be thoroughly understood. . . . The appropriate test of such a model depends on its intended use."

The CAPM is under assault by many who have forgotten, if they ever knew, that it is an expectational model. They make no distinction between expected returns and realized returns. Although Fama and French (1992) use "expected returns" in their title, not a single expected return is to be found in their paper. The reason is that they equilibrate the two; they believe expected and realized returns are the same. Those who practice the trade of investment management know that nothing could be farther from the truth.

The CAPM in Practice

Is beta dead? Is the CAPM valid and useful? Let us examine the process of security price formation. Investors constantly make forecasts, either explicitly or implicitly. Then they must, in some sense, determine what to make of those forecasts. That is where the CAPM enters. If forecasts are made in a primitive manner because the only forecasting methods known are extrapolation, the accuracy of the consensus forecasts will be poor. If, in the context of the CAPM, investors take those forecasts, try to make sense of them, and "price" them to reflect a return for incremental risk bearing, we should not be surprised to have a muddled picture *ex post*.

When clear evidence shows that the price of risk is changing abruptly and the market is moving precipitously, then beta works like magic. In any major market break, the realized returns and betas faithfully line up. During a period without great changes in the way people price risk, there is a sea of underlying instability as investors are surprised by new information, go back to the drawing board and recompute their estimates, and change the expectations they have held near and dear for individual companies. When that happens, the price goes along with the change in one direction or the other.

In the early 1970s, while he was working with my Investment Systems Group at Wells Fargo, Barr Rosenberg developed his fundamental risk model. The well-known BARRA risk factors were originally seen as just that—risk factors. (Ill-advised concepts of expected return to these risk factors came along much later.) If investors are surprised and forced back to the drawing board, there are certain co-relationships across companies and industries. If the numbers are adjusted in one direction, that adjustment, more than likely, has an effect across all similar companies. In fact, Roll (1992) pointed out that this ripple effect seems to go across the whole world with respect to fundamental forecast changes. The world markets react immediately to changes in expectations born of surprises in the fundamentals. Looking over our shoulders, therefore, we can find periods when beta behaved faithfully *ex post* and periods when beta seemed unrelated to realized return.

Critics of the CAPM complain that it is underspecified; it is too simple. That is true. Other factors also affect returns, and systematically so. The apparent systematic pricing of yield was originally described by Litzenberger and Ramaswamy (1979). Working with Sharpe, the Investment Systems Group at Wells Fargo developed the *ex ante* security market plane by adding the current yield portion of expected return orthogonal to beta. The slope to beta in this three-dimensional construct was considerably steeper than the slope in the context of the security market line. Earlier, we had been somewhat confused because our empirical *ex ante* security market lines, when extended, were intersecting above the risk-free rate at zero beta in violation of CAPM. The security market plane, which was publicly introduced September 1, 1978, corrected this problem.

In addition to risk, investors systematically price different levels of market liquidity. They know that, if a security costs a good deal to buy and then sell, they must see a spread that promises to absorb the impact of the cost of their actions (see Fouse 1976).

Tests of Market Efficiency

My interest in the CAPM led me to conduct a study on market efficiency in early 1970. I was curious as to whether I could join the discounted cash flow approach—namely, the dividend discount model— and the idea of systematic pricing of risk—specifically, the security market line. My objectives were to ascertain whether Wall Street forecasts were already embedded in stock prices, to test the validity of the security market line concept, and to determine whether active management can benefit from this perspective on pricing forecasts.

I used macroeconomic inputs to a Gordon–Shapiro model to estimate the discount rate for equities. I then constructed a three-point *ex ante* security market line, estimating the discount rate for below-average, average, and above-average beta stocks. I set up an iterative process to develop dividend streams with present values equal to the prices at appropriate discount rates for what were then the 25 largest holdings in Mellon's trust department. (These were all liquid securities.) After I built the dividend stream, I assumed a pattern of payout ratios that would bring me to an implicit accounting earnings stream and calculated five-year growth rates for those accounting earnings streams. Thus, the forecasts were based on then-current prices. I then set up growth rate ranges for each stock and asked some Wall Street analysts to assign probabilities to them, summing to 100 percent, for each of the stocks in this test. I asked for probabilities across a range of growth rates so I could get as faithful a consensus as possible and avoid any central tendencies. I used a group of blue-ribbon, research-oriented firms with capable analysts who were following these companies; these firms were Auerbach Pollack & Richardson; Baker Weeks; Burnham; Eberstadt; Faulkner, Dawkins, and Sullivan; First Manhattan; Goldman Sachs; Oppenheimer; L.F. Rothschild; Salomon Brothers; and H.C. Wainwright. On average, I was able to get 10 or 12 sets of estimates for each company in the study. The survey was taken during the first quarter of 1970.

The results of the analysis are shown in **Table 1**. The first column shows the five-year growth rates in earnings per share based on the then-current stock prices and my estimated discount rates. The second column lists the means of the distributions from the Wall Street consensus. The overall difference between the two approaches was only a tenth of a percentage point. The R^2 between the forecasts and the forecasts of the forecasts was 0.90. **Figure 1** shows the relationship graphically.

Once I found this close conformance, I immediately extended the experiment. The security analysts at Mellon gave me estimates for the more than 300 companies then on the Mellon trust department's common stock reference list. We classified them into five buckets: high growth, cyclical

Table 1. Results of Growth Rate Analysis, March 1970

Company	Estimate of Required Five-Year Growth Rate in Earnings per Share	Wall Street Consensus
Atlantic Richfield (ARC)	9.6%	10.2%
Avon Products (AVP)	14.9	17.3
Bristol Myers (BMY)	13.7	13.0
Burlington Industries (BVR)	8.1	7.7
Caterpillar (CAT)	7.8	10.7
Control Data (CDA)	15.4	15.5
Eastman Kodak (EK)	13.4	12.2
General Electric (GE)	8.0	8.0
General Motors (GM)	5.1	5.3
Gillette (G)	9.4	9.2
Gulf Oil (GO)	5.4	5.4
IBM	14.0	15.8
IT&T (ITT)	9.6	11.5
Kennecott (KN)	5.8	4.1
Merck & Co. (MRK)	10.4	13.0
3M (MMM)	12.6	11.9
Mobil (MOB)	5.6	5.9
Pfizer (PFE)	11.2	12.4
Polaroid (PRD)	19.3	18.0
Sears (S)	10.1	10.1
Standard Oil (Cal) (SD)	4.7	3.8
TRW	9.3	9.2
Uniroyal (UR)	7.0	6.3
Westinghouse (WX)	10.7	8.4
Xerox (XRX)	18.0	18.1
Average	10.4	10.5

Source: Fouse (1978).

Figure 1. Naive Forecast of Required Five-Year Annual Growth Rates in Earnings per Share versus Wall Street Consensus Forecast

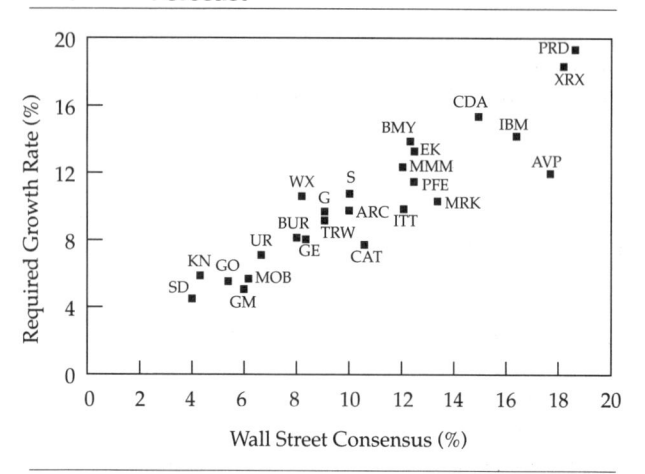

Source: Fouse (1978).

Notes: Company abbreviations are spelled out in Table 1. $R^2 = 0.90$.

growth, noncyclical growth, noncyclical, and cyclical. I calculated what the required growth rates would be and compared those rates with the Mellon analysts' forecasts. As can be seen in **Table 2**, the differential growth rates are subsumed in this discounting process. In contrast to the conventional wisdom at that time, growth companies did not promise higher rates of return. In fact, the growth stocks appear to have been somewhat overpriced, because in the case of two out of three "growth" categories, the forecasts in place were insufficient to support their prices.

We then attacked the problem of security selection by using the dividend discount model in the context of the CAPM to identify overvalued and undervalued stocks.

Several years after this experiment, I was able to compare the expected growth rates with what they actually turned out to be. As shown in **Figure 2**, little

Table 2. Mellon Analysts' Forecasts Substituted for Wall Street Consensus: Common Stock Universe of 313 Companies, March 1970

Stock Groups	Estimates of Required Five-Year Growth Rates in Earnings per Share	Mellon Analysts' Forecasts
High growth	16.7%	15.7%
Cyclical growth	11.2	11.8
Noncyclical growth	11.1	10.8
Noncyclical	5.7	6.9
Cyclical	9.2	9.5
Universe	10.7	10.9

Source: Fouse (1978).

conformance existed between the growth rates the best analysts on the Street expected for these companies and the actual earnings per share that developed. The R^2 was 0.26. The *ex ante* picture was clear, but when looking backward, the picture was muddled, and the forecasts were the problem, not the CAPM.

Figure 2. Wall Street Consensus Forecasts of Five-Year Annual Growth Rates in Earnings per Share versus Actual Experience

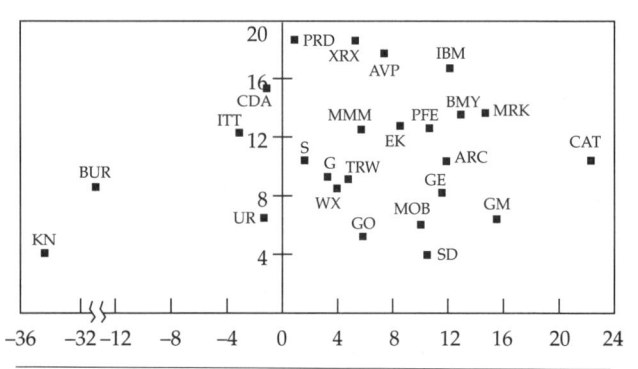

Source: Fouse (1978).

Notes: Company abbreviations are spelled out in Table 1. $R^2 = 0.26$.

Does Beta Work?

When I first arrived at Wells Fargo in late 1970, I was able to conduct an experiment that would not be possible today because analysts today know too much. I asked a group of security analysts who had only heard of beta to weigh and sort the stocks they covered into three risk groups: average, above average, and below average. After the first pass, I asked them to repeat the process of dividing each of the three classes into above-average, average, and below-average risk. No definition of risk was provided. Using Merrill Lynch betas, I demonstrated to the analysts that not a single one of the nine portfolios was out of line as we looked from the lowest to the highest of the groups. There was no material difference between risk as perceived by investors and beta risk. The whole battle in those days was trying to get the traditionalists into the CAPM fold, and this exercise was helpful in that regard.

The fact that beta does not always line up *ex post* is not new. In 1974, I wrote an article with Jahnke and Rosenberg (1974) that attempted to address the problem of differing *ex ante* and *ex post* betas. The concluding paragraph of that article said, "By assessing the predictive power of conventionally estimated betas, going beyond the concept of beta as a mere technical tool to the underlying economics, and showing how systematic changes in either investors' earnings forecasts or risk preferences can produce return realizations which historically have been viewed as beta failure, we hope we have demonstrated the legitimacy of beta. Beta theory is not tangential to the world as traditional investors understand it. Once they view beta as it should be viewed, as an extension of previous knowledge, they can integrate traditional value analysis with the *ex ante*, or expectational, Security Market Line of beta theory. The result is a potentially far richer framework for investment decision-making than traditional value analysis can provide."

In this article, we showed the results of annual returns by beta decile for each year between 1956 and 1973. The conformance between realized return and beta risk worked out almost perfectly in 11 of these 18 years, it was indifferent in a couple of years, and it was just plain wrong in 5.

We also attempted to show how well the betas for 1971, 1972, and 1973 matched the betas that were calculated each January 1 from 1968 through 1973. The differences are not significant. When beta does not work, the reason is simply that beta does not always work; it is not that the betas are "bad" or that the market portfolio is not properly described.

Beta does not work consistently over time, as **Figure 3** illustrates. The *ex ante* security market lines shown in the figure are based on prices and analysts' forecasts. In the first half of 1972, the security market line flattened. Because discount rates were changing more to the right-hand, higher beta end of the line, beta worked like gangbusters in the first half of 1972. In the second half of 1972, a peculiar shift took place in the *ex ante* security market line; it reattained some slope and sent low-risk stocks up and high-risk stocks down. A parallel shift in the rate structure occurred from the beginning of the year to the end of the year, so no beta effect can be found if one is looking over the year as a whole. As pointed out in Fouse, Jahnke, and Rosenberg (1974), occasionally low-beta stocks have outperformed high-beta stocks in an up market in the past. In 1972's second half, faddish popularity of large-capitalization growth stocks was perturbing the stock market's discount rate structure (see Jahnke 1973).

The Small-Stock Anomaly

Betas have not been very reliable in the recent past. **Figure 4** shows annual returns for beta quintiles for 1987 to 1992. For 1987 through 1989, this relationship did not work well, and for 1990 through 1992, it ranged from satisfactory to muddled. In fact, Chan and Lakonishok (1993) said, "If we were to stop the study in 1982, the support for betas would be overwhelming. The last nine years . . . have not been favorable for beta's explanatory role for returns."

The authors proposed a reason: Perhaps the S&P 500 effect is at work. The conventional wisdom is that, because S&P 500 funds have had spectacular growth, the buying impact in those securities has resulted in their being systematically overvalued. That "wisdom" shows how much trouble people can get into when they look only at empirical analyses of past results.

In 1991, I studied whether the S&P 500 was overvalued. I looked at the S&P 500 as though it were a portfolio drawn from a population of some 1,300 stocks to which I had fitted a security market plane. Once adjustments are made for capitalization-size differences, risk, and yield, one can measure an appraisal alpha for each stock. In other words, everything is not exactly on the plane, and to the extent securities are above it, the appraisal alpha is positive.

Figure 3. Security Market Line Shifts, 1972

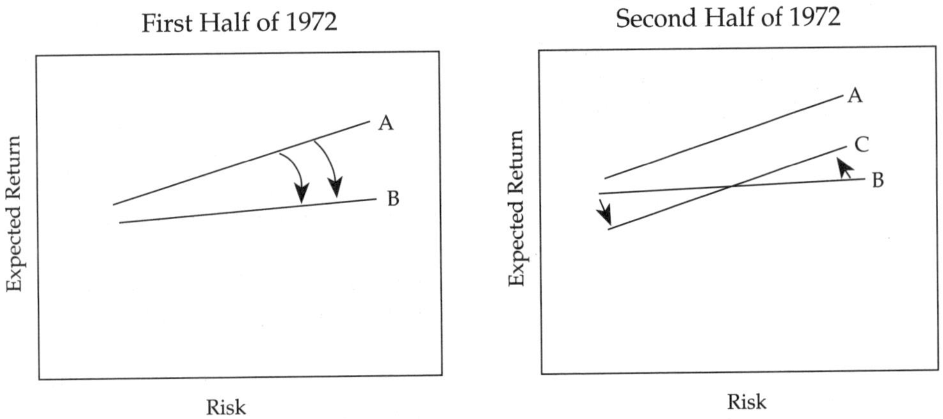

Source: Fouse (1978).

Figure 4. Annual Returns by Beta Quintile: Total Returns Capitalization Weighted for the U.S. Equity Market, Vestek All Shares, 1987–92

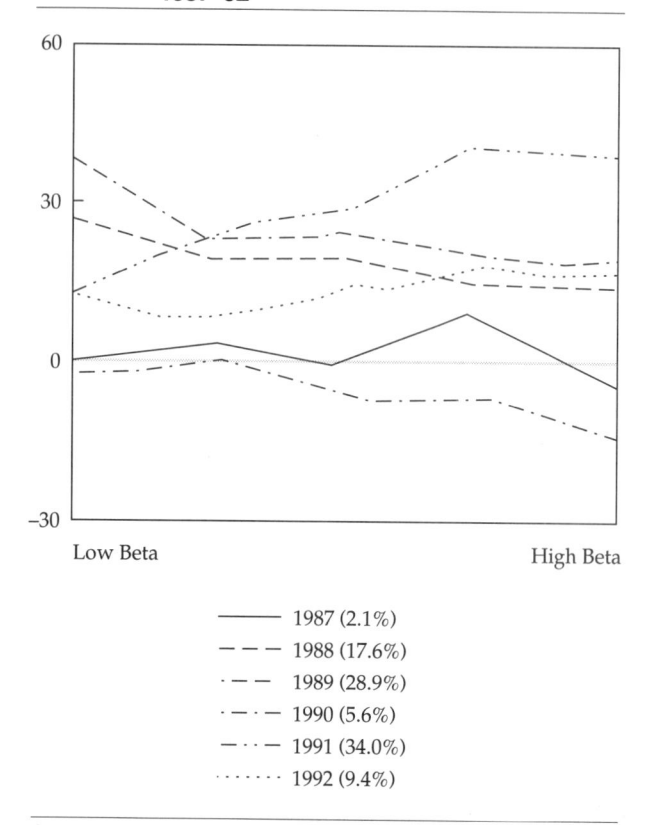

[Chart showing annual returns by beta quintile from Low Beta to High Beta, y-axis from -30 to 60]

——— 1987 (2.1%)
– – – 1988 (17.6%)
– · – 1989 (28.9%)
– · · – 1990 (5.6%)
– · · · – 1991 (34.0%)
· · · · · 1992 (9.4%)

Source: Mellon Capital Management Corporation.

An observation below the plane indicates an overvalued security with a negative appraisal alpha.

I started with the largest capitalized company in the S&P 500 and then added the next largest security, then the next largest, and so on, until I accumulated the appraisal alpha on the S&P 500 stocks capitalization weighted as I incorporated more and more stocks. As I aggregated the securities, the "portfolio" persisted in being slightly undervalued. Not until I got to the last 15 (smallest) securities did I find individual securities that were overvalued in the context of appraisal alphas by capitalization size and their combined weight was insufficient to affect the S&P 500 Index as a whole. My explanation would be that a small stock's S&P membership may do something for its market liquidity. From a portfolio viewpoint, I could not find anything suggesting that the S&P 500 as an index was overvalued.

Managed portfolios, when aggregated, pretty much replicate the market as a whole almost by definition. Moreover, institutional portfolios, in the aggregate, have always had a bias toward larger capitalization companies. In the absence of index funds, much of the institutional buying would nevertheless have been S&P 500 stocks. The same investments that went into index funds would have gone into the same market of securities, although in a much more disruptive fashion than when index funds were used. The least disruptive (to prices) way to "buy" the market is to tap into its natural market liquidity and buy the capitalization-weighted index.

What happened to the overall structure of security prices that tended to obscure the efficacy of beta in the past eight or nine years? We need look no further than small stocks. If you think there is a free lunch in small stocks, you had better stop, look, and listen. No sooner did investors "discover" the small-stock anomaly than it ceased to work well. As can be seen in **Table 3**, for the ten years ending 1992, the S&P 500 has compounded at 16 percent a year and the Russell 2000™ at 12 percent. Small stocks have had a rough time.

Table 3. Small Stocks versus S&P 500 Annual Rates of Return for Periods Ending December 31, 1992

Number of Years	S&P 500	Wilshire 4500	Russell 2000
10	16%	NA	12%
5	16	16%	15
3	11	12	12
2	19	27	32
1	8	12	18

Source: Fouse (1978).

Note: NA = not available.

Capitalization Profile of the Market

Most people are surprised by the capitalization profile of the market and how it changes. **Figure 5** is a profile of the stock market as of December 31, 1992. All the stocks, from the largest to the smallest capitalization—more than 6,000 securities—are lined up on the horizontal axis. The market's value is heavily loaded on the large-cap end. The first 1,000 stocks account for 87 percent of total market value, and the next 2,000 stocks account for another 8 percent. Thus, about 3,000 securities account for only 5 percent of the market's total value. The capitalization size of the 3,000th stock ranges between $10 million and $15 million, which is not large.

There are only two ways to win with a small stock. One is shown in **Figure 6**. It is winning the old-fashioned way—making a superior forecast and recognizing the opportunity before your fellow combatants do. You buy the stock first, the market wises up, and the stock moves from position S_0 to S_1 because its total market value (price times shares) rises. Other things being equal, this stock moved because people did not expect the company to do as well as

Figure 5. Profile of the Stock Market, December 31, 1992

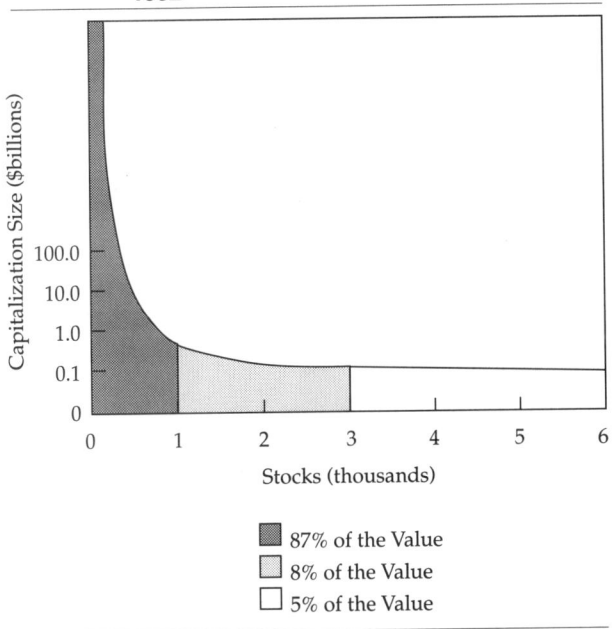

■ 87% of the Value
▨ 8% of the Value
□ 5% of the Value

Source: William L. Fouse.

it did between those two time periods or the longer term expectations for fundamentals were revised in some manner that was positive to the stock's value. Most small-stock managers understand this way of winning very well.

The other way to win with a small stock is shown in **Figure 7**. In this case, I postulate that I won as my stock went from S_0 to S_1 without any change in its capitalization ranking. What happened was that the market profile itself moved in such a way that values went up more for small securities than for large ones. Obviously, that pattern can reverse. M_1 can also

Figure 6. Winning via Earnings Surprise

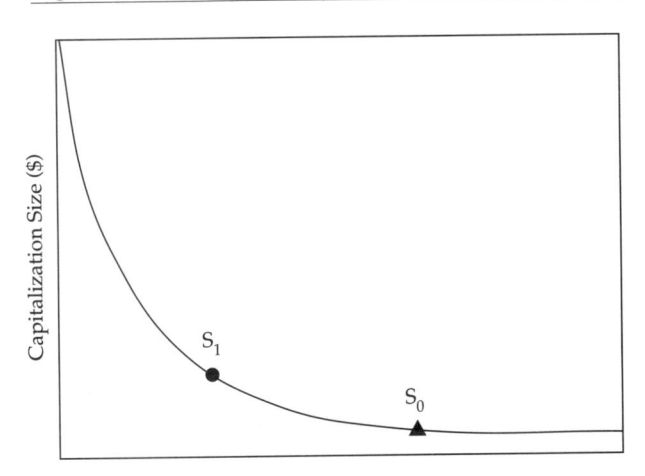

▲ Stock's Market Equity at Beginning of Period (S_0)
● Stock's Market Equity at End of Period (S_1)

Source: William L. Fouse.

Figure 7. Winning via Equity Market Repricing

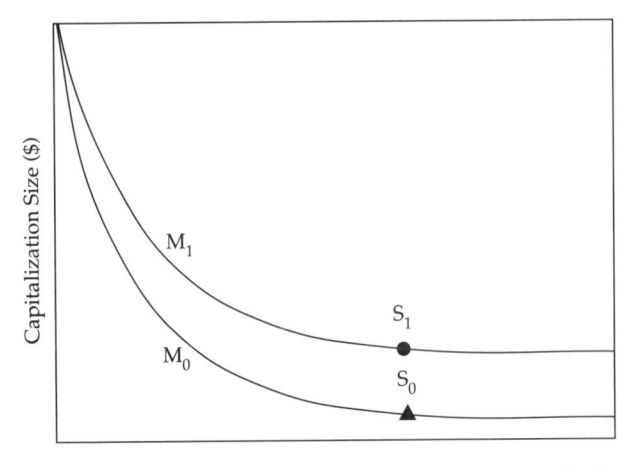

▲ Stock and Market Equity at Beginning of Period (S_0/M_0)
● Stock and Market Equity at End of Period (S_1/M_1)

Source: William L. Fouse.

change course to M_0, and that is how to lose in small stocks without their fundamentals coming into play.

As a test of the performance of a small-cap strategy, I formed a capitalization-weighted portfolio of the smallest quintile of securities in the Compustat universe as of December 31, 1969, and at the end of a five-year period, examined what had happened to the original portfolio of stocks. I then repeated the small-stock portfolio construction and observed what happened over this next five-year period. I approached the analysis this way because the returns calculated by Banz and reported in Ibbotson Associates (1991) were produced in like manner over the 1926–81 period. Banz assumed instantaneous reconstitution of the fifth-quintile portfolio every five years with no transaction costs.

Figure 8 shows what happened to the fifth-quintile portfolio between the end of 1969 and the end of 1974 and from 1974 to the end of 1979. During the first interval, the portfolio "lost" 62 percent of its value. Most of it went out the end of the distribution, because many stocks no longer qualified for the Compustat data base, which had a $10 million capitalization cutoff. Value also disappeared through bankruptcies and acquisitions. Some stocks from the portfolio got all the way up to the fourth decile during that five-year period. Only about 25 percent of the ending portfolio was in the 1969 fifth quintile. The 1974–79 interval was serendipity. One stock got all the way to the second decile, the peak occurs in the seventh, and the original portfolio lost virtually nothing.

Most investors are surprised to see this much flux behind the capitalization profile of the market.

Figure 8. Capitalization Migration of Stocks in Quintile Five, December 1969–74 and December 1974–79

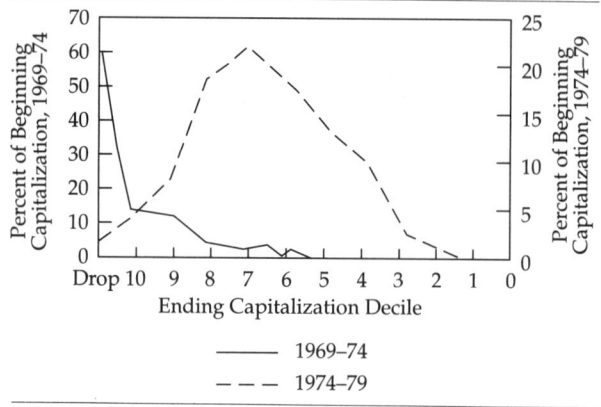

Source: William L. Fouse.

This flux is a joint combination of changes in systematic pricing and changes in forecasts, and it plays havoc with validating an *ex ante* expected returns model with *ex post* realized returns data.

Liquidity Spread

On average, small companies tend to have higher, and large companies lower, betas. Also, there tends to be a liquidity spread at every level of risk. Thus, small, illiquid companies at a given level of beta promise more return *ex ante* than large, liquid companies, as shown in **Figure 9**. Alternatively, Figure 9 could be divided into quadrants with the largest, most liquid names below the security market line and to the left and the smallest, least liquid names to the right and above the line.

When investors change the price of risk, the slope of the security market line changes; or perhaps the market becomes more liquid, so that imposing a large penalty for illiquidity is no longer reasonable. For whatever reason, *ex ante* changes in the slope of the line result in a change in the fit of the securities around that line.

Table 4 presents a historical record of the difference in expected return between a portfolio with all the securities equally weighted and the same securities capitalization weighted. The size of the spread can be read as a litmus test of how risk and liquidity are priced at a point in time. The expected rate of return for the equal-weighted portfolio should always be higher, because it represents more risk and less liquidity, on average, than the capitalization-weighted portfolio.

In 1972, the spread was a mere 60 basis points. In 1974, after the market had tanked, the spread was the largest in modern times—230 basis points. What an opportunity! By the end of 1983, the spread was gone; that was also when the small-stock thesis

Table 4. A Brief History of Spreads, Selected Dates, 1972–93

Date	Expected Return Spread[a] (basis points)
12/31/72	60
12/31/74	230
12/31/83	–5
12/31/87	140
12/31/88	55
12/31/89	95
12/31/90	108
12/31/91	60
1/31/92	34
6/30/92	74
12/31/92	56
1/31/93	56
2/28/93	71

Source: William L. Fouse.

[a] Equally weighted minus capitalization-weighted portfolios.

began to hit the rocks. The spread reopened and fluctuated thereafter, and by the end of February 1993, it stood at 71 basis points.

Table 5 shows the interplay between changes in the spread and differential performance for large-cap and small-cap companies. The interplay will not be totally faithful, because we are talking about price formation, which involves two blades to the scissors: one blade is the discount rate structure, and the other is the fundamental forecast being valued. Also, the beginning of the series is somewhat quirky; because large-cap growth stocks had been overvalued in an overvalued market, they hit with a resounding thud when the market fell and they performed more poorly than might have been expected. Between

Figure 9. Security Market Line and Firm Size

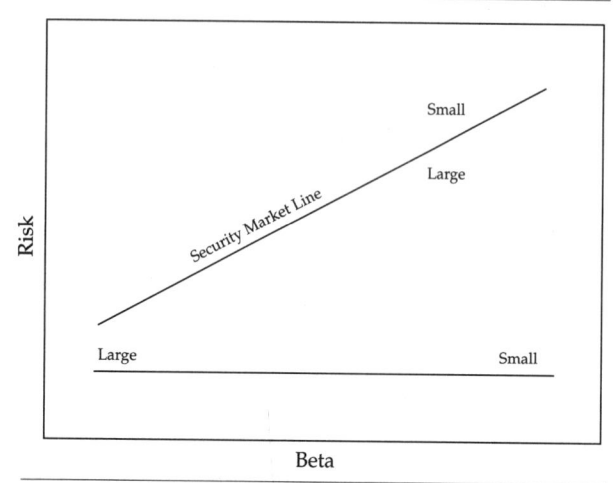

Source: William L. Fouse.

Table 5. Changes in Expected Return Spreads versus Annualized Realized Returns for Small- and Large-Capitalization Indexes, Selected Time Periods

Time Period	Change in Spread (basis points)	Ibbotson Associates Small	Russell 2000	S&P 500
12/31/72 – 12/31/74	170	–26%	NA	–20%
12/31/74 – 12/31/83	–235	35	NA	16
12/31/83 – 12/31/88	60	7	8%	15
12/31/88 – 12/31/90	53	–14	–7	28
12/31/90 – 3/28/91	–43	29	30	15
3/31/91 – 12/30/91	–5	12	13	14
12/31/91 – 1/31/92	–26	NA	8	–2
1/31/92 – 6/30/92	40	NA	–7	1
1/31/92 – 12/31/92	–18	NA	18	8
12/31/92 – 1/31/93	0	NA	3	1
1/31/93 – 2/28/93	15	NA	–2	1
12/31/92 – 2/28/93	15	NA	1	2

Source: William L. Fouse.

Notes: Annual rates of return for periods longer than one year; otherwise, period returns. NA = not available.

1972 and 1974, the rate of return for the S&P 500 was –20 percent a year, and the size of the decline was influenced by the behavior of the large-cap growth stocks.

For the next period, a reduction in the spread benefited small stocks. Size deciles nine and ten were earning 35 percent a year, compared with 16 percent for the S&P 500 over the 1975–83 period. The pattern of good performance for small stocks in the right season and disappointing performance when pricing moves the other way is fairly consistent.

At a spread of 71 basis points and a history that goes from 230 to nothing, are small stocks poised to explode on the upside? My belief is that they are not, unless we have the kind of recovery that benefits small-company fundamentals while leaving the large companies in the dust. That might happen in some fashion, but I do not expect the market mechanism to bail out small-stock buyers with a favorable shift in the discount rate structure.

The poor performance of the small-cap companies in the past nine–ten years has obviously been to the detriment of an orderly *ex post* return to betas. As opposed to having gone through an unusual period for small stocks, a period when they performed more poorly than they should have, we went through a period when small stocks were repriced because they were overvalued at the outset.

Conclusion

Sharpe (1970) suggests that the appropriate text of a model such as CAPM depends on its intended use. The criticism of beta seems to be that it is not a technical signal that works without fail. One might ask, if investors always receive more return from incremental risk bearing, where then is the risk? From my own experience, so-called beta theory has provided a robust framework for understanding security price formation and security price changes. Moreover, one can better capitalize on discounted cash flow, the value of factor analysis, and the insights of arbitrage pricing theory in the context of CAPM than would be possible without it.

Bibliography

Abel, A.B. 1991. "The Equity Premium Puzzle." *Federal Reserve Bank of Philadelphia Business Review*, vol. 3 (September/October):3–14.

Amihud, Yakov, and Haim Mendelson. 1986a. "Asset Pricing and the Bid–Ask Spread." *Journal of Financial Economics*, vol. 17, no. 2 (December):223–49.

———. 1986b. "Liquidity and Stock Returns." *Financial Analysts Journal*, vol. 42, no. 3 (May/June):43–48.

———. 1989. "The Effects of Beta, Bid–Ask Spread, Residual Risk and Size on Stock Returns." *Journal of Finance*, vol. 44, no. 2 (June):479–86.

Amihud, Yakov, Bent Christensen, and Haim Mendelson. 1992. "Further Evidence on the Risk–Return Relationship." Working paper, New York University.

Ariel, R.A. 1987. "A Monthly Effect in Stock Returns." *Journal of Financial Economics*, vol. 18, no. 1 (March):161–74.

Arnott, Robert D., John L. Dorian, and Rosemary Macedo. 1992. "Style Management: The Missing Element in Equity Portfolios," *The Journal of Investing*, vol. 1, no. 1 (Summer):13–21.

Arnott, Robert D., and Roy D. Henriksson. 1989. "A Disciplined Approach to Global Asset Allocation." *Financial Analysts Journal*, vol. 45, no. 2 (March/April):17–28.

Ball, Ray. 1978. "Anomalies in Relationships between Securities' Yields and Yield-Surrogates." *Journal of Financial Economics*, vol. 6, no. 2/3 (June/September):103–26.

Ball, Ray, and P. Brown. 1968. "An Empirical Evaluation of Accounting Income Numbers." *Journal of Accounting Research*, vol. 6, no. 2 (Autumn):159–78.

Banz, Rolf W. 1981. "The Relationship between Return and Market Value of Common Stock." *Journal of Financial Economics*, vol. 9, no. 1 (March):3–18.

Banz, Rolf W., and William J. Breen. 1986. "Sample Dependent Results Using Accounting and Market Data: Some Evidence." *Journal of Finance*, vol. 41, no. 4 (September):779-94.

Barry, Christopher B., and Stephen J. Brown. 1984. "Differential Information and the Small Firm Effect." *Journal of Financial Economics*, vol. 13, no. 2 (June):283–94.

Basu, Sanjoy. 1977. "Investment Performance of Common Stocks in Relation to Their Price/Earnings Ratios: A Test of the Efficient Market Hypothesis." *Journal of Finance*, vol. 32, no. 3 (July):663–82.

———. 1983. "The Relationship between Earnings' Yield, Market Value and Return for NYSE Common Stocks: Further Evidence." *Journal of Financial Economics*, vol. 12, no. 1 (June):129–56.

Berges, Angel, John J. McConnell, and Gary G. Schlarbaum. 1984. "The Turn-of-the-Year in Canada." *Journal of Finance*, vol. 39, no. 1 (March):185–92.

Bernard, V.L., and J.K. Thomas. 1989. "Post-Earnings-Announcement Drift: Delayed Price Response or Risk Premium?" *Journal of Accounting Research*, vol. 27 (Supplement):1–36.

———. 1990. "Evidence That Stock Prices Do Not Fully Reflect the Implications of Current Earnings for Future Earnings." *Journal of Accounting and Economics*, vol. 13, no. 4 (December):305–40.

Bhardwaj, R.K., and L.D. Brooks. 1992. "The January Anomaly: Effects of Low Share Price, Transaction Costs and Bid–Ask Bias." *Journal of Finance*, vol. 47, no. 2 (June):553–75.

Bilson, John F.O. 1981. "The 'Speculative Efficiency' Hypothesis." *Journal of Business*, vol. 54, no. 3 (July):435–52.

Black, Fischer. 1972. "Capital Market Equilibrium with Restricted Borrowing." *Journal of Business*, vol. 45, no. 3 (July):444–55.

———. 1973. "Yes, Virginia, There Is Hope: Tests of the *Value Line* Ranking System." *Financial Analysts Journal*, vol. 29, no. 5 (September/October):10–14.

———. 1980. "The Tax Consequences of Long-Run Pension Policy." *Financial Analysts Journal*, vol. 36, no. 4(July/August):21-28.

———. 1990. "Mean Reversion and Consumption Smoothing." *Review of Financial Studies*, vol. 3, no. 1 (Spring):107–14.

Black, Fischer, and Moray P. Dewhurst. 1981. "A New Investment Strategy for Pension Funds." *Journal of Portfolio Management*, vol. 7, no. 4 (Summer):26-34.

Black, Fischer, Michael Jensen, and Myron Scholes. 1972. "The Capital Asset Pricing Model: Some Empirical Tests." In *Studies in the Theory of Capital Markets*, ed. M. Jensen. New York: Praeger Publishers, 79–121.

Blume, Marshall E. 1971. "On the Assessment of Risk." *Journal of Finance*, vol. 26, no. 1 (March):1–10.

Blume, Marshall E., and Irwin Friend. 1973. "A New Look at the Capital Asset Pricing Model." *Journal of Finance*, vol. 28, no. 1 (March):19–33.

Blume, Marshall E., and Jeremy J. Siegel. 1992. "The Theory of Security Pricing and Market Structure." *Financial Markets, Institutions & Instruments*, vol. 1, no. 3 (February):1–58.

Blume, Marshall E., and Robert F. Stambaugh. 1983. "Biases in Computed Returns: An Application to the Size Effect." *Journal of Financial Economics*, vol. 12, no. 3 (November):387–404.

Breeden, Douglas T., Michael R. Gibbons, and Robert H. Litzenberger. 1989. "Empirical Tests of the Consumption-Oriented CAPM." *Journal of Finance*, vol. 44, no. 2 (June):231–62.

Brown, Phillip, Allan W. Kleidon, and Terry A. Marsh. 1983. "New Evidence on the Nature of Size-Related Anomalies in Stock Prices." *Journal of Financial Economics*, vol. 12, no. 1 (June):33–56.

Campbell, John Y. 1992. "Intertemporal Asset Pricing without Consumption Data." Unpublished paper, Princeton University.

Campbell, John Y., and Robert J. Shiller. 1988. "Stock Prices, Earnings, and Expected Dividends." *Journal of Finance*, vol. 43, no. 3 (July):661–76.

Chan, K.C. 1986. "Can Tax-Loss Selling Explain the January Seasonal in Stock Returns?" *Journal of Finance*, vol. 41, no. 5 (December):1,115–28.

Chan, K.C., and Nai-Fu Chen. 1991. "Structural and Return Characteristics of Small and Large Firms." *Journal of Finance*, vol. 46, no. 4 (September):1467–84.

Chan, Louis K.C., and Josef Lakonishok. 1993. "Are the Reports of Beta's Death Premature?" *Journal of Portfolio Management*, vol. 19, no. 4 (Summer):51–62.

Chan, K.C., Nai-Fu Chen, and David A. Hsieh. 1985. "An Exploratory Investigation of the Firm Size Effect." *Journal of Financial Economics*, vol. 14, no. 3 (September):451–71.

Chang, Eric C., and J. Michael Pinegar. 1986. "Return Seasonality and Tax-Loss Selling in the Market for Long-Term Government and Corporate Bonds." *Journal of Financial Economics*, vol. 17, no. 2 (December):391–416.

———. 1989. "Seasonal Fluctuations in Industrial Production and Stock Market Seasonals." *Journal of Financial and Quantitative Analysis*, vol. 24, no. 4 (March):59–74.

Chen, N. 1983. "Some Empirical Tests of the Theory of Arbitrage Pricing." *Journal of Finance*, vol. 38, no. 5 (December):1393–414.

Chen, N., Richard Roll, and Stephen A. Ross. 1986. "Economic Forces and the Stock Market." *Journal of Business*, vol. 59, no. 3 (July):383–404.

Christie, W. G. 1990. "Dividend Yield and Expected Returns: The Zero-Dividend Puzzle." *Journal of Financial Economics*, vol. 28, no. 1/2 (November/December):95–125.

Connor, Gregory, and Robert A. Korajczyk. Forthcoming 1994. "The Arbitrage Pricing Theory and Multifactor Models of Asset Returns." In *Finance Handbook*, ed. R. Jarrow, V. Maksimovic, and W. Ziemba. Amsterdam: North Holland.

Conrad, J., and G. Kaul. 1988. "Time Variation in Expected Returns." *Journal of Business*, vol. 61, no. 4 (September):409–25.

Constantinides, George M. 1984. "Optimal Stock Trading with Personal Taxes: Implications for Prices and the Abnormal January Returns." *Journal of Financial Economics*, vol. 13, no. 1 (March):65–89.

Cooke, Thomas J., and Michael S. Rozeff. 1984. "Size and Earnings/Price Ratio Anomalies: One Effect or Two?" *Journal of Financial and Quantitative Analysis*, vol. 19, no. 4 (December):449–66.

Cross, F. 1973. "The Behavior of Stock Prices on Fridays and Mondays." *Financial Analysts Journal*, vol. 29, no. 6 (November/December):67–9.

Cutler, D., J. Poterba, and L. Summers. 1989. "What Moves Stock Prices?" *Journal of Portfolio Management*, vol. 15, no. 3 (Spring):4–12.

DeBondt, Werner F.M., and Richard Thaler. 1985. "Does the Stock Market Overreact?" *Journal of Finance*, vol. 40, no. 3 (July):793–805.

Dimson, Elroy. 1979. "Risk Measurement When Shares Are Subject to Infrequent Trading." *Journal of Financial Economics*, vol. 7, no. 2 (June):197–226.

Dyl, Edward A., and Edwin D. Maberly. 1992. "Odd-Lot Transactions around the Turn of the Year and the January Effect." *Journal of Financial and Quantitative Analysis*, vol. 27, no. 4 (December):591–604.

Engel, C., and J. Hamilton. 1990. "Long Swings in the Dollar: Are They in the Data and Do Markets Know It?" *American Economic Review* (September): 689–713.

Fama, Eugene F. 1970. "Efficient Capital Markets: A Review of Theory and Empirical Work." *Journal of Finance*, vol. 25, no. 2 (May):383–417.

———. 1991. "Efficient Capital Markets: II." *Journal of Finance*, vol. 46, no. 5 (December):1,575–617.

Fama, Eugene F., and Kenneth R. French. 1988a. "Permanent and Temporary Components of Stock Prices." *Journal of Political Economy*, vol. 96:246–73.

———. 1988b. "Dividend Yields and Expected Stock Returns." *Journal of Financial Economics*, vol. 22, no. 1 (October):3–26.

———. 1989. "Business Conditions and Expected Returns on Stocks and Bonds." *Journal of Financial Economics*, vol. 25, no. 2 (November):23–50.

———. 1992a. "The Cross-Section of Expected Stock Returns." *Journal of Finance*, vol. 47, no. 2 (June):427–66.

———. 1992b. "Common Risk Factors in the Returns on Bonds and Stocks." Working paper, Graduate School of Business, University of Chicago.

———. 1992c. "The Economic Fundamentals of Size and Book-to-Market Equity." Working paper, Graduate School of Business, University of Chicago.

Fama, Eugene F., and J.D. MacBeth. 1973. "Risk, Return, and Equilibrium: Empirical Tests." *Journal of Political Economy*, vol. 81, no. 3:607–36.

Ferson, W.E., and C.R. Harvey. 1991. "The Variation of Economic Risk Premiums," *Journal of Political Economy*, vol. 99, no. 2:385–415.

Fisher, Lawrence. 1966. "Some New Stock Market Indexes." *Journal of Business*, vol. 39, no. 1, part II (January):191–225.

Fouse, William L. 1976. "Risk, Liquidity, and Common Stock Prices." *Financial Analysts Journal*, vol. 32, no. 3 (May/June):35-45.

———. 1978. "Common Stock Evaluation." In *Proceedings of the Seminar on the Analysis of Security Prices*, vol. 23, no. 2 (November).

Fouse, William L., William W. Jahnke, and Barr Rosenberg. 1974. "Is Beta Phlogiston?" *Financial Analysts Journal*, vol. 30, no. 1 (January/February):70–80.

Freeman, J. 1992. "All Portfolios Are Not Created Equal: But Maybe They Should Be." Unpublished paper, BARRA, Berkeley, Calif.

French, Kenneth. 1980. "Stock Returns and the Weekend Effect." *Journal of Financial Economics*, vol. 8, no. 1:55–69.

Friedman, Milton. 1956. *Studies in the Quantity Theory of Money*. Chicago, Ill.: University of Chicago Press.

———. 1970. "A Theoretical Framework for Monetary Analysis." *Journal of Political Economy*, vol. 64:193–238.

Friend, Irwin, and Marshall E. Blume. 1970. "Measurement of Portfolio Performance under Uncertainty." *American Economic Review*, vol. 60, no. 4 (September):561–75.

Fuller, Russell J., and John L. Kling. 1991. "Forecasting the Return to Size: A Preliminary Investigation." Working paper presented at the October 1991 Q-Group Conference.

———. 1992. "Time-Varying Returns to Size, the Small-Firm Anomaly and Liquidity Premia." Unpublished working paper.

Geweke, J., R. Meese, and W. Dent. 1983. "Comparing Alternative Tests of Causality in Temporal Systems: Analytic Results and Experimental Evidence." *Journal of Econometrics*, vol. 21:161–64.

Gibbons, Michael R., and Patrick Hess. 1981. "Day of the Week Effects and Asset Returns." *Journal of Business*, vol. 54, no. 4 (October):579–96.

Goodman, David A., and John W. Peavy III. 1983. "Industry-Relative Price–Earnings Ratios as Indicators of Investment Returns." *Financial Analysts Journal*, vol. 39, no. 4 (July/August):60–66.

Graham, Benjamin, and David L. Dodd. 1934. *Security Analysis: Principles and Technique*. New York: McGraw-Hill.

Handa, Puneet, S.P. Kothari, and Charles Wasley. 1989. "The Relation between the Return Interval and Betas: Implications for the Size Effect." *Journal of Financial Economics*, vol. 23, no. 1 (June):79-100.

Harris, Lawrence. 1986. "A Transaction Data Study of Weekly and Intradaily Patterns in Stock Returns." *Journal of Financial Economics*, vol. 16, no. 1 (May):99–117.

Haugen, Robert A., and Nardin L. Baker. 1991. "The Efficient Market Inefficiency of Capitalization-Weighted Stock Portfolios." *Journal of Portfolio Management*, vol. 17, no. 3 (Spring):35–40.

Haugen, R., and J. Lakonishok. 1988. *The Incredible January Effect*. Homewood, Ill.:Dow Jones-Irwin.

Hawawini, Gabriel, and Donald Keim. Forthcoming 1994. "On the Predictability of Common Stock Returns." In *The Finance Handbook*. Amsterdam: North Holland.

Hoffman, G.W. 1935. In *The Security Markets*, ed. A. Bernheim and M. Schneider. New York: Twentieth Century Fund.

Huberman, Gur, and Shmuel Kandel. 1987. "Value Line Rank and Firm Size." *Journal of Business*, vol. 60, no. 4 (October):577–89.

———. 1990. "Market Efficiency and Value Line's Record." *Journal of Business*, vol. 63, no. 2 (April):187–216.

Ibbotson Associates. 1991. *Stocks, Bonds, Bills and Inflation: 1991 Yearbook*, Chicago, Ill.

Jaffe, Jeffrey, Donald B. Keim, and Randolph Westerfield. 1989. "Earnings Yields, Market Values, and Stock Returns." *Journal of Finance*, vol. 44 no. 1 (March):135–48.

Jacobs, B., and K. Levy. 1988a. "Disentangling Equity Return Regularities: New Insights and Investment Opportunities." *Financial Analysts Journal*, vol. 44, no. 3 (May/June):18-43.

———. 1988b. "Calendar Anomalies: Abnormal Returns at Calendar Turning Points." *Financial Analysts Journal*, vol. 44, no. 6 (November/December):28-39.

———. 1989a. "Forecasting the Size Effect." *Financial Analysts Journal*, vol. 45, no. 3 (May/June):38–54.

———. 1989b. "The Complexity of the Stock Market." *Journal of Portfolio Management*, vol. 16, no. 1 (Fall):19–27.

Jagannathan, Ravi, and Zhenyu Wang. 1993. "The CAPM Is Alive and Well." Working paper, University of Minnesota (August).

Jahnke, William W. 1973. "The Growth Stock Mania." *Financial Analysts Journal*, vol. 29, no. 3 (May/June):65–68.

Jones, Charles P., Douglas K. Pearce, and Jack K. Wilson. 1987. "Can Tax-Loss Selling Explain the January Effect? A Note." *Journal of Finance*, vol. 42, no. 2 (June):453–61.

Jones, Steven L., Winson Lee, and Rudolf Apenbrink. 1991. "New Evidence on the January Effect before Personal Income Taxes." *Journal of Finance*, vol. 46, no. 5 (December):1909–24.

Kandel, Shmuel, and Robert F. Stambaugh. 1993. "Portfolio Inefficiency and the Cross-Section of Mean Returns." Working paper, University of Pennsylvania (February).

Kato, Kiyoshi, and James S. Schallheim. 1985. "Seasonal and Size Anomalies in the Japanese Stock Market." *Journal of Financial and Quantitative Analysis*, vol. 20, no. 2 (June):243–60.

Keim, Donald B. 1983. "Size-Related Anomalies and Stock Return Seasonality: Further Empirical Evidence." *Journal of Financial Economics*, vol. 12, no. 1 (June):13–32.

———. 1985. "Dividend Yields and Stock Returns: Implications of Abnormal January Returns." *Journal of Financial Economics*, vol. 14, no. 2 (September):473–89.

———. 1986a. "Dividend Yields, Size and the January Effect." *Journal of Portfolio Management*, vol. 12, no. 2 (Winter):54–60.

———. 1986b. "The CAPM and Equity Return Regularities." *Financial Analysts Journal*, vol. 42, no. 3 (May/June):19–34.

———. 1987. "The Daily Returns–Size Connection." *Journal of Portfolio Management*, vol. 13, no. 2 (Winter):41–47.

———. 1989. "Trading Patterns, Bid–Ask Spreads and Estimated Security Returns: The Case of Common Stocks at Calendar Turning Points." *Journal of Financial Economics*, vol. 25, no. 1 (November):75–98.

Keim, Donald, and Robert F. Stambaugh. 1984. "A Further Investigation of the Weekend Effect in Stock Returns." *Journal of Finance*, vol. 39, no. 3 (July):819–35.

———. 1986. "Predicting Returns in the Stock and Bond Markets." *Journal of Financial Economics*, vol. 17, no. 2 (December):357–90.

Kessel, Reuben A. 1965. "The Cyclical Behavior of the Term Structure of Interest Rates." *National Bureau of Economic Research*, New York.

Kleidon, Allan W. 1986. "Variance Bounds Tests and Stock Price Valuation Models." *Journal of Political Economy*, vol. 94, no. 5:953–1001.

Korajczyk, Robert A., and Claude J. Viallet. 1992. "Equity Risk Premia and the Pricing of Foreign Exchange Risk." *Journal of International Economics*, vol. 33 (November):199–219.

Kothari, S.P., and Jay Shanken. 1992. "Stock Return Variation and Expected Dividends: A Time-Series and Cross-Sectional Analysis." *Journal of Financial Economics*, vol. 31, no. 2 (April): 177–210.

Kothari, S.P., Jay Shanken, and Richard G. Sloan. 1992. "Another Look at the Cross-Section of Expected Stock Returns." Working paper, University of Rochester (December).

Kritzman, Mark P. 1989. "Serial Dependence in Currency Returns: Investment Implications." *Journal of Portfolio Management*, vol. 16, no. 1 (Fall):96–102.

Lakonishok, Josef, Andrei Shleifer, and Robert Vishay. 1992. "The Structure and Performance of the Money Management Industry." *Brookings Papers on Economic Activity—Microeconomics*:339–91

———. 1993. "Contrarian Investment, Extrapolation and Risk." Working paper, National Bureau of Economic Research.

Lakonishok, Josef, and Seymour Smidt. 1988. "Are Seasonal Anomalies Real? A Ninety-Year Perspective." *Review of Financial Studies*, vol. 1, no. 4 (Winter):403–25.

Lee, Charles, Andrei Schleifer, and Richard Thaler. 1991. "Investor Sentiment and the Closed-End Fund Puzzle." *Journal of Finance*, vol. 46, no. 1 (March):75–110.

Lehmann, Bruce N. 1990. "Fads, Martingales, and Market Efficiency." *Quarterly Journal of Economics*, vol. 105, no. 1:1–28.

Leroy, S., and R. Porter. 1981. "The Present-Value Relation: Test Based on Implied Variance Bounds." *Econometrica*, vol. 49, no. 3:555–74.

Lintner, John. 1965. "The Valuation of Risky Assets and the Selection of Stock Portfolios and Capital Budgets." *Review of Economics and Statistics* (December):13–37.

Litzenberger, Robert H., and Krishna Ramaswamy. 1979. "The Effect of Personal Taxes and Dividends on Capital Asset Prices: Theory and Empirical Evidence." *Journal of Financial Economics*, vol. 7, no. 2 (June):163-96.

Loeb, Thomas F. 1983. "Trading Costs: The Critical Link between Investment Information and Results." *Financial Analysts Journal*, vol. 39, no. 3 (May/June):39–44.

———. 1991. "Is There a Gift from Small-Stock Investing?" *Financial Analysts Journal*, vol. 47, no. 1 (January/February):39–44.

Lucas, Robert E., Jr. 1978. "Asset Prices in an Exchange Economy." *Econometrica*, vol. 46, no. 6:1429–45.

Macauley, Frederick R. 1940. "Some Theoretical Problems Suggested by the Movements of Interest Rates, Bond Yields, and Stock Prices in the United States since 1856." National Bureau of Economic Research, New York.

Mankiw, N. G., and M. Shapiro. 1986. "Risk and Return: Consumption Beta versus Market Beta." *Review of Economics and Statistics*, vol. 48, no. 3:452–59.

Markowitz, Harry M. 1959. *Portfolio Selection: Efficient Diversification of Investments*. New York: John Wiley & Sons.

Marsh, Terry A., and Robert C. Merton. 1986. "Dividend Variability and Variance Bounds Tests for the Rationality of Stock Market Prices, Aggregate Dividend Behavior and Its Implications for Tests of Stock Market Rationality." American Economic Review, vol. 76, no. 3 (June):-483–98.

Mayers, David. 1972. "Nonmarketable Assets and Capital Market Equilibrium under Uncertainty." In *Studies in the Theory of Capital Markets*, ed. M. C. Jensen. New York: Praeger Publishers.

McCloskey, Donald N. 1985. "The Loss Function Has Been Mislaid: The Rhetoric of Significance Tests." *American Economic Review*, vol. 75, no. 2 (May):201–05.

Merton, Robert C. 1973. "An Intertemporal Capital Asset Pricing Model." *Econometrica*, vol. 41, no. 3 (September):867-87.

Miller, Edward M. 1987. "Bounded Efficient Markets: A New Wrinkle to the EMH." *The Journal of Portfolio Man-

agement, vol. 13, no. 4 (Summer):4–13.

———. 1990. "Divergence of Opinion, Short Selling, and the Role of the Marginal Investor." In *Managing Institutional Assets*, ed. Frank J. Fabozzi. New York: Harper & Row.

Mitchell, Mark L., and Jeffry M. Netter. 1989. "Triggering the 1987 Stock Market Crash: Antitakeover Provisions in the Proposed House Ways and Means Tax Bill." *Journal of Financial Economics*, vol. 24, no.1 (September):37–68.

Mossin, Jan. 1966. "Equilibrium in a Capital Asset Market." *Econometrica*, vol. 34, no. 4 (October):768–83.

Poterba, James M., and Lawrence H. Summers. 1988. "Mean Reversion in Stock Prices: Evidence and Implications." *Journal of Financial Economics*, vol. 22, no. 1 (October):27–60.

Reinganum, Marc R. 1981. "Misspecification of Capital Asset Pricing: Empirical Anomalies Based on Earnings' Yields and Market Values." *Journal of Financial Economics*, vol. 9, no. 1 (March):19–46.

———. 1982. "A Direct Test of Roll's Conjecture on the Firm Size Effect." *Journal of Finance*, vol. 37, no. 1 (March):27–35.

———. 1983. "The Anomalous Stock Market Behavior of Small Firms in January: Empirical Tests for Tax-Loss Selling Effects." *Journal of Financial Economics*, vol. 12, no. 1 (June):89–104.

"Return, Risk and Arbitrage." 1977. In *Risk and Return in Finance*, eds. I. Friend and J. Bicksler. Cambridge, Mass.: Ballinger.

Ritter, Jay R. 1988. "The Buying and Selling Behavior of Individual Investors at the Turn of the Year." *Journal of Finance*, vol. 43, no. 3 (July):701–17.

———. 1991. "The Long-Run Performance of Initial Public Offerings." Journal of Finance, vol. 46, no. 1 (March):3–27.

Ritter, Jay R., and Navin Chopra. 1989. "Portfolio Rebalancing and the Turn-of-the-Year Effect." *Journal of Finance*, vol. 44, no. 1 (March):149–66.

Rogalski, Richard J., and Seha M. Tinic. 1986. "The January Size Effect: Anomaly or Risk Measurement." *Financial Analysts Journal*, vol. 42, no. 6 (November/December):63–70.

Roll, Richard. 1977. "A Critique of the Asset Pricing Theory's Tests, Part I: On Past and Potential Testability of the Theory." *Journal of Financial Economics*, vol. 4, no. 2 (March):129–76.

———. 1981. "A Possible Explanation of the Small Firm Effect." *Journal of Finance*, vol. 36, no. 4 (September):879–88.

———. 1983a. "On Computing Mean Returns and the Small Firm Premium." *Journal of Financial Economics*, vol. 12, no. 3 (November):371–86.

———. 1983b. "Vas Ist Das? The Turn-of-the-Year Effect and the Return Premia of Small Firms." *Journal of Portfolio Management*, vol. 9, no. 2 (Winter):18–28.

———. 1988. "R-Squared." *Journal of Finance*, vol. 43, no. 3 (September):541–66.

———. 1992. "Industrial Structure and the Comparative Behavior of International Stock Market Indexes." *Journal of Finance*, vol. 47, no. 1 (March):3–41.

Roll, Richard, and Stephen A. Ross. 1993. "On the Cross-Sectional Relation between Expected Returns and Betas." Working paper, School of Organization and Management, Yale University (January).

Ross, Stephen A. 1976. "Arbitrage Theory of Capital Asset Pricing." *Journal of Economic Theory*, vol. 13, no. 3 (December):341–60.

Ross, Stephen A., and Richard Roll. 1993. "What Price Risk?" *The Economist*, vol. 327, no. 7797 (1993):81.

Rozeff, Michael S., and William R. Kinney, Jr. 1976. "Capital Market Seasonality: The Case of Stock Returns." *Journal of Financial Economics*, vol. 3, no. 4 (October):379–402.

Samuelson, Paul A. 1967. "General Proof That Diversification Pays." *Journal of Financial and Quantitative Analysis*, vol. 2, no. 1 (March):1–13.

Scholes, Myron, and Joseph T. Williams. 1977. "Estimating Betas from Nonsynchronous Data." *Journal of Financial Economics*, vol. 5, no. 3 (May):309–27.

Schultz, Paul. 1983. "Transaction Costs and the Small Firm Effect: A Comment." *Journal of Financial Economics*, vol. 12, no. 1 (June):81–88.

———. 1985. "Personal Income Taxes and the January Effect: Small Firm Stock Returns before the War Revenue Act of 1917: A Note." *Journal of Finance*, vol. 40, no. 1 (March):333–43.

Schwert, G. William. 1983. "Size and Stock Returns, and Other Empirical Regularities." *Journal of Financial Economics*, vol. 12, no. 1 (June):3–12.

———. 1989. "Why Does Stock Market Volatility Change over Time?" *Journal of Finance*, vol. 44, no. 5 (December):1115–54.

Sharpe, William F. 1964. "Capital Asset Prices: A Theory of Market Equilibrium under Conditions of Risk." *Journal of Finance*, vol. 19, no. 3 (September):425–42.

———. 1970. *Portfolio Theory and Capital Markets*. New York: McGraw-Hill.

———. 1990. "Capital Asset Prices with and without Negative Holdings." In *The Founders of Modern Finance: Their Prize-Winning Concepts and 1990 Nobel Lectures*. Charlottesville, Va.: The Research Foundation of the Institute of Chartered Financial Analysts.

Shefrin, Hersh, and Meir Statman. 1985. "The Disposition to Sell Winners Too Early and Ride Losers Too Long: Theory and Evidence." *Journal of Finance*, vol. 40, no. 3 (July):777–90.

Shiller, Robert J. 1979. "The Volatility of Long-Term Interest Rates and Expectations Models of the Term Structure." *Journal of Political Economy*, vol. 87:1190–1218.

———. 1989. *Market Volatility*. Cambridge, Mass.: Massachusetts Institute of Technology Press.

Shiller, Robert J., and Jeremy J. Siegel. 1977. "The Gibson Paradox and Historical Movements in Real Interest Rates." *Journal of Political Economy*, vol. 85, no. 5:891–907.

Siegel, Jeremy J. 1992. "Equity Risk Premia, Corporate Profit Forecasts, and Investor Sentiment around the Stock Crash of October, 1987." *Journal of Business*, vol. 65, no. 4 (October):557–92.

Sinquefield, Rex A. 1991. "Are Small-Stock Returns Achievable?" *Financial Analysts Journal*, vol. 47, no. 1 (January/February):45–50.

Smirlock, Michael, and Laura Starks. 1986. "Day-of-the-Week and Intraday Effects in Stock Returns." *Journal of Financial Economics*, vol. 17, no. 1 (September):197–210.

Stoll, Hans R., and Robert E. Whaley. 1983. "Transaction Costs and the Small Firm Effect." *Journal of Financial Economics*, vol. 12, no. 1 (June):57–80.

Tobin, James. 1958. "Liquidity Preference as Behavior towards Risk." *Review of Economic Studies*, vol. 25, no. 67:65–86.

Treynor, Jack L. 1963. "Toward a Theory of Market Value of Risky Assets." Unpublished manuscript.

Twentieth Century Fund. 1935. *The Security Markets*. New York: The Twentieth Century Fund.

Tyson, David A. 1991. "An Analysis of the Variation of the Term Premium in the United States Treasury Yield Curve." Doctoral dissertation, Stern School of Business, New York University.

Weigel, E. 1991. "Are There Really Trends in Foreign Exchange Returns?" Russell Research (September).

White, J. 1991. "How Jacobs and Levy Crunch Stocks for Buying—and Selling." *The Wall Street Journal* (March 20):C1.

Williams, T. 1991. "Market Neutral Funds Gain Fans." *Pensions & Investments* (September 16):3.

Self-Evaluation Examination

1. According to Arnott, one reason stock market inefficiencies persist is because:
   a. the investment culture is often contrarian.
   b. investment managers fail to exploit them.
   c. investment managers do not want to invest as market efficiency suggests—passively.
   d. none of the above.

2. Market inefficiencies are difficult to exploit, according to Arnott, because:
   a. market inefficiencies change over time or disappear.
   b. equilibrium relationships change.
   c. risk tolerance is usually lower than expected.
   d. all of the above.

3. According to Arnott's presentation, of the 13 BARRA factors, the largest mean returns are to:
   a. variability in markets.
   b. earnings–price ratios.
   c. size.
   d. success.

4. Current capital market theory includes the possibility that inefficiencies exist.
   a. True.
   b. False.

5. According to Arnott, we will eventually see conclusive proof or disproof of the relationship between beta and return.
   a. True.
   b. False.

6. The P/E anomaly means that a portfolio of:
   a. low-P/E stocks outperforms a portfolio of high-P/E stocks.
   b. high-P/E stocks outperforms a portfolio of low-P/E stocks.
   c. low-P/E stocks is similar to a short portfolio of high-P/E stocks.
   d. low-P/E stocks has more growth potential than a portfolio of high-P/E stocks.

7. Lakonishok's conclusion about beta is that:
   a. the environment in which stock returns are generated improves our ability to reach firm conclusions about the compensation for beta risk.
   b. it is theoretically interesting, but research has proven that it has no practical significance.
   c. behavioral and institutional factors, unrelated to risk, play a major role in generating stock returns, and thereby confound the relationship between risk and return.
   d. 20 years of data is a sufficient time period to determine whether beta is important.

8. Indexation, according to Lakonishok, is an example of an institutional factor that:
   a. weakens the relationship between risk and return.
   b. strengthens the relationship between risk and return.
   c. ignores the relationship between risk and return.
   d. distorts the relationship between risk and return.

9. Fuller says that the small-firm effect seems to be:
   a. correlated with industry effects.
   b. a January effect that results from window dressing.
   c. a spurious statistical quirk.
   d. well documented and understood.

10. The problem with the CAPM, according to Ross, is that:
    a. it applies only to the U.S. stock market.
    b. it has no practical applications.
    c. it cannot be proved or disproved, because it cannot be tested in a practical sense.
    d. it is wrong.

11. On average, small companies have lower betas because they have higher growth.
    a. True.
    b. False.

12. Beta is as applicable to the bond market as to the equities market, according to Karnosky.
    a. True.
    b. False.

13. Using the CAPM in a global context depends upon:
    a. whether you believe that the markets are integrated.
    b. whether you have the data to calculate betas using more than the U.S. stock market.
    c. whether your portfolio includes international securities.
    d. all of the above.

14. The S&P 500 is the most appropriate index to use in estimating beta.
    a. True.
    b. False.

15. According to Weiss, segmented market asset allocation strategy is characterized by:
    a. identifying a key domestic factor in each market, and basing forecasts for performance on one factor.
    b. frequent changes in the main market driver.
    c. no separation of market and currency decisions.
    d. all of the above.

16. Increases in correlations among the world's equity markets are proof of:
    a. increased capital market integration and increased benefit from international diversification.
    b. increased economic and capital market integration resulting in decreased benefit from diversification.
    c. increased economic integration, but not necessarily capital market integration.
    d. increased capital market integration and decreased benefits from international diversification.

17. Variation of the term premium for bonds comes primarily from changes in:
    a. aggregate risk preferences.
    b. uncertainty.
    c. interest rates.
    d. none of the above.

18. The prospective-real-yield concept is based on the premise that:
    a. purchasing power parity holds in the long run.
    b. bonds will be redeemed at par on the same date.
    c. reinvestmewnt rates are negligible.
    d. all of the above.

19. In theory, the slope of the yield curve reflects:
    a. expected changes in future interest rates.
    b. market segmentation among investors and issuers.
    c. supply–demand characteristics of the bond market.
    d. no one is sure.

20. According to Reiss, forward rates are good predictors of:
    a. future interest rates.
    b. returns from investments.

21. A market-neutral portfolio strategy consists of:
    a. holding cash and cash equivalents.
    b. holding equal amounts of stocks, bonds, and cash.
    c. holding equal dollar amounts of longs and shorts.
    d. owning stock and writing covered calls.

22. An equitized strategy consists of holding stocks long and short in equal dollar amounts and an equal portion of stock index futures.
    a. True.
    b. False.

23. Holding equal amounts of stocks long and short, coupled with an amount of stock index futures that depends upon the outlook for the market is called:
    a. a hedge strategy.
    b. a barbell strategy.

24. The CAPM assumes that stocks may be sold short.
    a. True.
    b. False.

25. The currency markets are so efficient, there are no anomalies to be exploited.
    a. True.
    b. False.

Self-Evaluation Answers

1. a. (p. 20, Arnott). The successful investor frequently follows a pattern of paring back recent winners and favoring recently disappointing markets.
2. d. (p. 20, Arnott). Most theorists admit that the market has some inefficiencies. They change over time, however, or take courage to exploit. The returns to the anomaly are highly volatile.
3. b. (p. 18, Arnott).
4. b. (p. 20, Arnott). Current capital market theory rests on market efficiency. Creative investment analysts have used this efficient market theory to find market inefficiencies—stock select, market time, and asset allocate.
5. b. (p. 22, Arnott). Returns are related to beta, but to other factors as well. In addition, using historical data to test an expectational relationship is using flawed logic.
6. a. (p. 33, Jacques).
7. c. (p. 40, Lakonishok).
8. a. (p. 40, Lakonishok). Indexers do not concern themselves with risk and return, only purchasing stocks of a particular universe, or those that mimic the chosen universe.
9. a. (p. 28, Fuller). The small-firm effect appears to have something to do with unequal representation of industries in liquidity sectors and appears to have been overstated.
10. c. (p. 12, Ross). The theory is expectational, and the data are realized. A test of realized data does not show anything about what people expected or whether the expectational model is a reasonable description of how assets are priced.
11. b. (p. 116, Fouse). Small companies tend to have higher betas.
12. a. (p. 57, Karnosky).
13. a. (p. 59, Karnosky). In an integrated market, the risk premium depends upon the price of risk times beta with respect to the reference market times volatility of the reference market. Global investing under the current CAPM assumes equilibrium within markets but disequilibrium across markets.
14. b. (p. 57 Karnosky). The S&P 500 was the index used by U.S. analysts and because computer-readable data existed. In a global environment, the U.S. index is too restricted to use in creating betas.
15. d. (p. 63, Weiss). The characteristics listed are typical factors on which recommendations are made and described.
16. c. (p. 66, Weiss). Although the benefits of diversification may decline, so long as the correlations are imperfect, international diversification is beneficial.
17. a. (p. 99, Tyson). Research supports the preferred habitat theory of changes in risk preference.
18. d. (p. 85, Bernstein and Sims).
19. d. (p. 102, Reiss). Although each of these theories has strong support, the evidence is not clear on which is correct.
20. b. (p. 105, Reiss). Evidence has shown that forward rates are not good predictors of future rates but they do have implications for holding period returns.
21. c. (p. 42, Jacobs and Levy). Holding longs and shorts in balanced equal dollar amounts at all times immunizes the portfolio from changes in market direction. Profits are made from the performance spread between the names held long and those held short, and interest on the proceeds of the short sales.
22. a. (p. 42, Jacobs and Levy). The investor is fully exposed to the equity market, and profits are made from the long/short spread, as well as the rise and fall of the equity market.
23. a. (p. 42, Jacobs and Levy). Hedge strategy profits are made from the long/short spread, and the futures positions.
24. a. (p. 43, Jacobs and Levy). This is true in theory but not in practice. There are restrictions on short selling, such as the uptick rule and portfolio restrictions. This restriction can result in an overvaluation in stock prices since pessimists find it difficult to short, while optimists can hold long positions.
25. b. (p. 67, Kritzman). At least two potential sources of exploitable anomalies are nonrandomness and forward rate bias.

Order Form

Additional copies of *The CAPM Controversy: Policy and Strategy Implications for Investment Management* (and other AIMR publications listed on page 128) are available for purchase. The price is **$20 each in U.S. dollars.** Simply complete this form and return it via mail or fax to:

AIMR
Publications Sales Department
P.O. Box 7947
Charlottesville, Va. 22906
U.S.A.
Telephone: 804/980-3647
Fax: 804/977-0350

Name _____

Company _____

Address _____

_____ Suite/Floor _____

City _____

State _____ ZIP _____ Country _____

Daytime Telephone _____

Title of Publication   Price   Qty.   Total

_____   _____   _____   _____

_____   _____   _____   _____

Shipping/Handling
- ❏ All U.S. orders: Included in price of book
- ❏ Airmail, Canada and Mexico: $5 per book
- ❏ Surface mail, Canada and Mexico: $3 per book
- ❏ Airmail, all other countries: $8 per book
- ❏ Surface mail, all other countries: $6 per book

Discounts
- ❏ Students, professors, university libraries: 25%
- ❏ CFA candidates (ID #_____): 25%
- ❏ Retired members (ID #_____): 25%
- ❏ Volume orders (50+ books of same title): 40%

Discount $-_____

4.5% sales tax
(Virginia residents) $_____

8.25% sales tax
(New York residents) $_____

7% GST
(Canada residents,
#124134602) $_____

Shipping/handling $_____

Total cost of order $_____

❏ Check or money order enclosed payable to **AIMR**   ❏ Bill me

Charge to: ❏ VISA   ❏ MASTERCARD   ❏ AMERICAN EXPRESS

Card Number:_____ ❏ Corporate ❏ Personal

Signature:_____ Expiration date: _____

Selected AIMR Publications*

The Health Care Industry James Balog, *Editor*	$20
Predictable Time-Varying Components of International Asset Returns, 1993 Bruno Solnik	$20
The Oil and Gas Industries, 1993 Thomas A. Petrie, CFA, *Editor*	$20
Execution Techniques, True Trading Costs, and the Microstructure of Markets, 1993 Katrina F. Sherrerd, CFA, *Editor*	$20
Investment Counsel for Private Clients, 1993 John W. Peavy III, CFA, *Editor*	$20
Active Currency Management, 1993 Murali Ramaswami	$20
The Retail Industry—General Merchandisers and Discounters, Specialty Merchandisers, Apparel Specialty, and Food/Drug Retailers, 1993 Charles A. Ingene, *Editor*	$20
Equity Trading Costs, 1993 Hans R. Stoll	$20
Options and Futures: A Tutorial, 1992 Roger G. Clarke	$20
Improving the Investment Decision Process—Better Use of Economic Inputs in Securities Analysis and Portfolio Management, 1992 H. Kent Baker, CFA, *Editor*	$20
Ethics, Fairness, Efficiency, and Financial Markets, 1992 Hersh Shefrin and Meir Statman	$20
Investing Worldwide, 1992, 1991, 1990	$20 each
The Financial Services Industry—Banks, Thrifts, Insurance Companies, and Securities Firms, 1992 Alfred C. Morley, CFA, *Editor*	$20
Managing Asset/Liability Portfolios, 1992 Eliot P. Williams, CFA, *Editor*	$20
Investing for the Long Term, 1992	$20
A New Method for Valuing Treasury Bond Futures Options, 1992 Ehud I. Ronn and Robert R. Bliss, Jr.	$20
Ethics in the Investment Profession: A Survey, 1992 E. Theodore Veit, CFA, and Michael R. Murphy, CFA	$20

*A full catalog of publications is available from AIMR, P.O. Box 7947, Charlottesville, Va. 22906; 804/980-3647; fax 804/977-0350.